# "POWERPLAY

—that was the name of the game. You go after what you want and you use any piece of weaponry, any piece of ammunition you can, to get it. That I happened to be the most convenient pawn around was merely coincidental. . . . I thought executives fought over strategies, business plans, the bottom line. But that was only part of the turmoil at Bendix. There were other motivations, deeper concerns, fueling this fight. And surprisingly, most of them had not very much to do with business. They had to do with jealousy and pride, ego and power—all the things that are rarely, if ever, mentioned in any Business School text."

# POWERPLAY

# WHAT REALLY HAPPENED AT BENDIX

**Mary Cunningham
with Fran Schumer**

FAWCETT GOLD MEDAL • NEW YORK

Library of Congress Catalog Card Number: 84-5407
ISBN 0-449-12829-6
This edition published by arrangement with Linden Press/Simon and
Schuster

Manufactured in the United States of America

First Ballantine Books Edition: June 1985

# ACKNOWLEDGMENTS

It would be impossible to thank everyone who has helped me with the writing of this book. However, I would like to mention my editors, Joni Evans and Michael Korda, my agent, Lynn Nesbit, and my colleague, Fran Schumer, each of whom guided and encouraged me throughout the preparation of the manuscript.

I feel especially grateful to the members of my family— Mother, Father Bill, Bombi, John, Jane, Shirl, Dick and Frank. Without their faith I doubt I would have found the strength to forgive or the reason to continue caring.

I owe special thanks to those who believed enough in me to convince me to do the same ... Phil Beekman, Cliche Chambers, Bob Dillensneider, Monsignor Egan, Barbara Figurksi, Tom Hagoort, Mert and Bob Hendren, Bobby, Frank and Andy Lynch, Bob Kasmire, Marie Leonard, Wendy Cunningham and Ivan Mader, Jack Meehan, Gerry Roche, Ellen and Peter Straus, John Walsh and Dr. Wolterbeek.

And I thank Bill for having the courage to love and the vision to guide us to a happy ending.

To Bill,
MY HUSBAND AND PARTNER—
WITH LOVE AND GRATITUDE

# PROLOGUE

*Mine is a difficult task.* I have a story to tell that still hurts, even as I tell it. It is a story of how I have come to know some precious things—the man I love and a deeper appreciation for what really matters in life—and how I have lost others—my privacy and the right to be judged simply on the basis of who I am as opposed to who people think I am.

Sometimes I ask my husband, "Do you think we'll ever be able to live a normal life, have a career, raise a family and just grow old without being the focus of public scrutiny and judging eyes?" And he says, "Yes, someday." But I think he says it as much to convince himself as to convince me.

Bill is more philosophical than I am. His attitude is that you become a Golden Boy in the public eye for only so long and then you crash. But I am still smarting. I never had the chance to be respected for my abilities. I was not allowed to be viewed as simply successful in my own right. My name was tainted in the press from Day One, and that makes me more cynical than I was ever taught it was right to be.

I write my story because no one knows, except for Bill and me, what really went on at Bendix, and even more

1

importantly, no one knows, not even Bill, what it was like to be in my position, accused of the oldest sin in business: a woman sleeping her way to the top.

There is also a part of this story that has nothing to do with sex and scandal. There's a venal part of corporate America. Personal careers get ruined and no one is spared—not friends, not secretaries, not even children. In our case, there were anonymous letters, veiled threats and attempts to bring ex-spouses and lovers into the fray. Business as usual can have a very sordid side.

And yet I've learned. More than I ever wanted to at this stage. I have learned what it's like to be a woman at the top and how susceptible that makes you to trial by media. It's one thing to be the victim of a boardroom battle; it's quite another to see it sensationalized in the public arena.

In this book quotation marks are used extensively in connection with conversations, conferences and other verbal contacts involving various persons, including Bill Agee and me. The use of quotation marks is not intended to represent or convey the exact words used, but rather to depict, fairly and in a natural way, the substance and tone of such conversations, conferences and contacts.

"Why bother?" some say when I tell them I'm writing a book. "In five or ten years, people will forget the whole incident." But this isn't a crime I want people to forget. There's a lesson—lessons—in this entire experience that ought to be made clear. Sexual accusations are serious ones. They can ruin personal lives and they can ruin careers. And with more and more women rising up the corporate ladder, the weapon of sexual accusations will be used again. Some defense is needed. And the best that I'm aware of is knowledge. Understanding.

That's why I'm writing the book. To set the record straight. To straighten out the facts. And to tell the story of what *really* happened to me at Bendix.

M.C.

# CHAPTER ONE

*I* *was a woman who* was in the right place at the right time. During the spring of my second year at Harvard Business School, I had thirty-two job offers from investment-banking firms, management-consulting firms and Fortune 500 companies. It was a time when corporations were hungry for bright-eyed, ambitious young MBAs and especially eager for women. My only major dilemma at the time, and it was an enviable one, was whether to work for the formidable, blue-blooded Morgan Stanley investment-banking firm or the more aggressive and dynamic Goldman, Sachs. I was weighing the pros and cons of these over a can of Campbell's Chunky Soup when the phone rang.

The caller, an older man, identified himself as J. Leslie Rollins, a recruiter for several of the Fortune 500 companies and a former assistant dean at the Harvard Business School. He said he had a very interesting job he wanted to discuss with me and wouldn't I like to meet him in downtown Boston to discuss the details? Actually I'd just come from an interview at the renowned Boston Consulting Group and dreaded another taxi ride into town. I had enough offers to retire on and thought I might cause a mutiny at school if I received one more (the Business

School was a pretty competitive place). My caller, however, was not to be deterred. He said my professors had described me as one of their best students. In fact, he said, one of the Harvard deans had told him, "Mary Cunningham has the best chance of being the first female graduate of the Harvard Business School to become the chairman of a non-cosmetics company." Wouldn't I just give him an hour? If only because I was curious, and because I felt I had better not refuse the invitation of a former Harvard dean, I agreed. But it would have to be a very good offer to make me turn down a $55,000-a-year starting salary in New York.

For the students at Harvard Business School, there was no higher calling than investment banking. It was the fastest and least painful route to the top. A few years at Morgan Stanley and a conscientious MBA from Harvard could become a chief financial officer by age thirty. The fast track appealed to me but I had deeper urgings as well. My strict Catholic upbringing made me take seriously my mission "to do good" and yet at the same time instilled in me a longing to carry this conviction into the real world. I thought business was the perfect answer. I could try to be a force for good in the business world. Growing up in the sixties had only reinforced this desire. At the same time I could get a taste of the action too. It was a novel approach and one that sometimes antagonized my classmates. You just couldn't be ambitious and high-minded at the same time.

The fact that I was successful didn't help much either. The day I was admitted to the Century Club, an elite organization for Harvard students considered the most promising by their professors, was the day I lost many of my friends. I remember when one of my classmates first told me the news. "Mary," he said, "do you know you've been admitted to the Century Club?" I didn't know what it was but from his voice I thought it must be some kind of disgrace. My success at job interviews further sealed my doom. I went on plenty of interviews. I liked them. I thought they were a good way to meet executives and build a "network."

Unlike most of my Harvard Business School classmates, whose parents were doctors and lawyers or successful professionals in business, I had neither connections nor firsthand knowledge of people in the corporate world. Who made up my family tree? Not bank presidents and engineers but people more concerned with saving souls than the GNP—priests, nuns, educators, perhaps a psychologist or two. Not exactly the First Family of Corporate America. Besides, these business interviews were a real learning experience. Here was a way to actually meet the characters who run corporate America. The only serious objection I heard concerning my frequent rounds of interviews was that by receiving so many job offers I was taking up someone else's place. This concerned me at the time but I figured it's a free market, isn't it? Wasn't that what this Business School education was all about? In terms of being ambitious, I was hardly alone. We were all go-getters and we all joked about one another's drive. It was a ritual at the Business School that each time someone came to class dressed in a suit, a not-so-muted groan could be heard. It was common knowledge that if you weren't wearing corduroys or jeans, you were obviously going job hunting.

People could be humorous about this matter except when it came to investment banking and consulting. These were the two most coveted fields, and in these areas my job offers engendered genuine rage. Every time an investment-banking firm sponsored a luncheon or dinner to recruit students, I was usually placed in the most desirable seat right next to the managing partner. This was primarily because I was one of the few women considered a "prime" candidate and also, I was told, because I had what people described as "wholesome" good looks. Some people called me "the Vermont Maid look-alike." (It was only later that the press made me into a "shapely veep" and a "femme fatale.") But there was another reason as well. Both in class and on the interview circuit I had a reputation for being someone who raised interesting and unorthodox questions. I skipped all the usual palaver on which way the prime rate would move or what was the latest calculation adjustment for R.O.I. (return on investment). Instead, I delved into issues like "Do you find it sufficiently creative to work in an environment as homogenous as Morgan Stanley?" or "Do you feel investment bankers spend enough time thinking about their responsibility to society at large?" The partners seemed to relish the opportunity to think about questions like these, especially after having spent hours with eager young MBAs, all of whom were trying to out-banker the bankers. This approach, plus my previous education and five years of prior job experience, gave me a significant edge. Unlike many of my colleagues, I had not come to the Business School fresh from college but had come via a New York law firm and Wall Street where I had worked in the corporate-lending and "workout" (high risk loans) departments of Chase Manhattan Bank.

If I was a "hardened, tough-minded broad" my second year of Business School, it was because I had been so thoroughly intimidated the first. It took me two and a half months to open my mouth in class the first year. The idea was to show the professors how smart you were by offering insightful solutions to the business cases. And if you could point out the errors in another student's analysis, so much the better. This was a far cry from the genteel seminar discussions at Wellesley, my alma mater, or the ponderously polite atmosphere of our dining room at home. There it was considered rude to call too much attention to yourself, and if one helped oneself to the butter without first offering it to others at the table, one was deemed a bit selfish.

I think I would have remained mute for the entire first semester had it not been for the urgings of my husband, Bo. He had graduated from the Business School five years earlier. On weekends he would often commute up to Cambridge from New York where he was a director of marketing for American Express and would ask, "Mary, have you spoken in class yet?" And I'd say no. Just thinking about it made my neck break out in hives. The longer I stayed mute, the harder it was to break the pattern until finally one night Bo said to me, "Next time someone speaks in class, just listen to what they're saying and see if it's really all that profound."

It worked. I raised my hand that day in class, ventured a fairly banal remark and, to my surprise (and relief), no one attacked it. Thanks to Bo, I was over the hurdle. I had no trouble speaking out in class after that.

During the spring of the first year I won one of the coveted nominations for the prestigious Copeland Award in Marketing and received numerous offers to work on Wall Street that summer. I was starting to gain confidence and actually enjoyed working as an intern at the blue-ribbon investment banking house Salomon Brothers, in

New York. At midpoint in my second year I received all "Excellents," and was on my way.

Now, as I watched the taxi driver negotiate his way through the rush-hour traffic on Boston's Storrow Drive, I wondered again why I was knocking myself out to meet a man I'd never heard of for some mystery job. He'd mentioned something about working as an executive assistant for a chairman or president of a Fortune 500 company. Those kinds of jobs were considered the ultimate opportunity but they didn't interest me. I'd spent a whole day interviewing at General Foods, where the recruiting officer saw me as the perfect marketing strategist for Jell-O brand gelatin. I turned down the job wondering how anyone could spend an entire day thinking about Jell-O. As a philosophy major, I had spent plenty of hours thinking about the meaning of life. But Jell-O? It was a far cry from *Cogito Ergo Sum*.

As dusk fell over the city of Boston, there I was, back on the fortieth floor of One Boston Place. It felt so strange to be there. Earlier in the day I'd been in that very same building for an interview with Braxton, an offshoot of the Boston Consulting Group, and twice in the last week I'd been there for interviews with two rival firms. Something about all this job hunting was starting to bother me. I was embarrassed for the elevator man to see me again.

Waiting for me at a table was my mystery caller, Les Rollins, a man in his early seventies who looked like a slender version of St. Nicholas. Rollins was much more open and friendly than he had sounded over the telephone, and he already seemed to know a great deal about me. He said he had been doing his homework and had spoken to my professors, who apparently thought very highly of me. He asked about my goals and I started to give him my usual speech—how I didn't want to be just another cog in a wheel ("I wanted to steer")—and how I wanted to do something more meaningful than making more money or better widgets. Midway through, he interrupted me and said, "Mary, what are you *really* interested in doing with your life?" I could tell he meant business so I told him. I told him with all the fire of a second-year Business School student and the solemn sense of mission of someone who had grown up under the influence of a priest. I was ambitious for worldly success but only as a means to influence constructive change. I must have sounded awfully taken with myself but Rollins didn't laugh. I think he felt the best people he recruited were the ones who were driven by a burning cause.

During the next two hours we wandered into other topics. I told him about being a logic and philosophy major at Wellesley and my interest in moral philosophy and ethics. Business people always seemed surprised, if not amused, by the idea that someone with my personal and academic background would be interested in commercial pursuits. The next topic, inevitably, was my marriage. "Off limits," I told him. "I don't see why it's relevant." He said he thought it was very relevant because the job he had in mind would involve a significant geographical move from New York City. Of course, under the strains of commuting, my marriage was faltering already, but I didn't want to bring that up just yet. The fact was that relocation would probably pose a problem for my marriage but I didn't want to discuss it. My thinking was to play it safe: Get the job offer first and then if it didn't seem suitable, reject it. We moved on to other issues and I overlooked his indiscretion; he really did seem interested in offering me a job, and as we talked I began to appreciate that this candor was part of his charm. Again I asked him what firm he was recruiting for and again he declined to say. He did, however, drop a few savory hints. The job he had in mind, he said, was "a most selective one," and one associated with a person "of great power and influence." My ears perked up. We shook hands and he said someone would probably be getting in touch with me shortly.

I didn't think much about our chat, but in a dull moment in class I'd occasionally wonder what the next step would be—if there was to be a next step. It didn't take me long to find out. Within a few days of meeting Rollins I received a letter from the San Francisco headquarters of Bendix Forest Products Company which said that Jack Guyol, president of the firm, would like to meet with me in person. Guyol mentioned Rollins' name and asked if my husband and I would like to fly to their San Francisco headquarters for the weekend for interviews. He said he was interested in talking to both of us. The idea of bringing Bo out for the first visit concerned me a little. I worried that he might be put on the defensive. Bo was black, and people always wanted to check him out to make sure he wasn't a Black Panther or some other militant throwback. Of course, he was a graduate of the Boston Latin School, Phillips Exeter, Harvard College and Harvard Business School and now was the director of marketing for the Gold Card at American Express, which usually reassured people, but the process was sometimes painful. Bo agreed to go. He wasn't very happy in his job and was mildly receptive to the notion of change. The chance that we might actually be able to work together after a two-year separation gave us fresh hope. A weekend in San Francisco might be just what we needed. So we packed our bags and were flown to the West Coast in the best of spirits.

We had a good weekend. It was a long-overdue reunion for us. We had both been too busy to realize how lonely we'd been. I had never been west of South Bend, Indiana, where my older brother had graduated from Notre Dame, and I fell in love with San Francisco at once. Both Bo and I liked Jack Guyol. He was a savvy man with a fatherly manner and seemed to take a special interest in us. The Forest Products Division was one of four Bendix subsidiaries and it seemed as though it might be an interesting environment in which to work. Besides, the idea of moving to San Francisco intrigued me.

Already I was starting to imagine a less hectic life. Maybe Bo and I could actually come home at five, prepare dinner, maybe even jog! It had been years since I'd lived that way. Almost from the day I graduated from Wellesley it was nonstop work. First it was late nights interviewing prospective candidates for Wellesley (I was an admissions officer there for almost a year) and then late hours at the library at Notre Dame, where I was studying for a joint degree in ethics and law. When I left law school to come to New York, it was sandwiches at midnight from the all-night deli while crunching numbers in Chase Manhattan's intensive credit-training course. And at Salomon Brothers, who ever heard of weekends? Harvard Business School was equally rigorous. There was so much to learn, and when you're paying for it, you study extra hard. I had studied too hard to think much about the quality of my personal life. There was a certain comfort in the jargon, a certain safety in the attempt to quantify and measure everything. But I was beginning to tire of the competitive rat race and thought I could quite easily adjust to California time. The only trouble was Guyol. As eager as he seemed to offer me a job, he was a little tentative. "Now, don't get too enthusiastic," he cautioned. "I'd like to hire you but someone else around here is also looking for an executive assistant and he may want to see you about the job." I told him I really wasn't interested. I was happy with Forest Products and was hoping to hear from him about his job soon.

Back in New York, Bo and I were already starting to think seriously about San Francisco, but the game wasn't over yet. About a week after our trip, Les Rollins stepped back into the picture. He said Guyol was so impressed with me that there was a possibility that even more could be in store. He said he wanted me to meet a certain individual—someone very "powerful and interesting," but it was better at this stage not to discuss any of the details.

It was clear that he thought it was an invitation I couldn't refuse but I wasn't so sure. Bo and I were already anticipating the move to the West Coast. The only thing that made me reconsider was the thought that if I didn't accept the invitation, I might jeopardize my chances for the Forest Products job. "Okay," I said. "Where do I go?"

Whomever I was meeting was in Suite 32F at the Waldorf-Astoria. I was nervous riding up the elevator of the towers at the Waldorf and wondered if I was dressed all right. I had on my black full-cut interview suit (I rotated it with my navy one) and a silk designer shirt buttoned up to the neck. My neck turned red and blotchy whenever I was nervous so I always wore high-necked shirts, even in July. This shirt had the name Lanvin on the collar. That ought to show 'em I know how to dress, I thought. The room was at the end of a corridor, which, like the hotel, had an air of faded bloom. I expected Blanche du Bois to come drifting down the hall. Perhaps that's why I wasn't prepared when a tall friendly man opened the door and said, "Hi, I'm Bill Agee."

I was a master of the interview process but I was not prepared for this one. I hadn't known much about Bill Agee before my meetings with Les Rollins, but after I'd been interviewed for the Forest Products job, I'd started to read case studies about Bendix. Every time I came across Agee's name, it was qualified by words like *Wunderkind*, "whiz kid," "boy wonder." Even before I'd received the call from Rollins, I'd had some vague notions about Agee. I'd been invited to a seminar at the Women's Student's Association to hear seven female executives talk about their work. One of the women was Karen Walker, at the time an executive in the Forest Products Division of Bendix who'd taken a few classes at the Business School several years before. She was extremely friendly and down-to-earth so when she asked me to join her and several other students for dinner, I said, "Sure." It was one of those dinners at which everything went well. I hadn't the slightest interest in working for Bendix, so naturally I was at ease and probably came across better than some of the more anxious students. I don't remember much of what Walker said about Bendix—prior to that evening I thought Bendix made washers, as in the old Bendix washing machine—but I do remember what she said about Agee. She was effusive, to say the least. She described him as if he were the Paul Newman of the corporate world.

It was 7:30 A.M. and this was supposed to be a breakfast meeting. Agee liked to start early. I, on the other hand, wouldn't have minded a few more hours to clear the frogs out of my throat. We sat across from each other at a coffee table positioned so low that it was only with the utmost dexterity that one could pick up and set down one's tea-cup. Mine kept rattling. I felt my neck turn hot and red. Agee told me to sit back and relax; for the first five minutes he'd do the talking.

This interview seemed to have four parts. Part One was "Let's calm down Mary." That was accomplished as soon as he started to talk. I concentrated on what he was saying and on intelligent questions to ask. But he helped. It was easy to relax around Agee. He was friendly and informal. He wore an open sports jacket and tipped back in his chair. This was a far cry from Morgan Stanley, where three-piece suits were de *rigueur*. I felt like an equal around Agee. He accomplished this by asking my opinion and then looking very serious, as if he were really going to think about what I'd said after I left.

Part Two was "Let's get to know Mary." I'd had plenty of practice at this. I proceeded at once with my usual speech, careful to mention Phi Beta Kappa at Wellesley, two Danforth nominations in Moral Philosophy, magna cum laude, Century Club and my long list of achieve-ments. "Oh, c'mon," he said and waved an arm as if to clear the air. "Don't tell me that stuff. Talk to me about who you really are." One has instant respect for a person who cuts short one's bluster.

I started again, this time offering the kinds of comments I had given to Les Rollins. In no time at all we were trading war stories about the Business School, from which Agee had graduated sixteen years before. It was Les Rollins, Agee said, who had brought him to Harvard. Apparently Rollins was some sort of kingmaker, whose discoveries included other moguls in business as promi-nent as Agee. That explained the Rollins connection. The mystery was becoming clear. But how did Rollins hear about me? That answer came next. Apparently Karen Walker had been so impressed with me at the earlier dinner that she had hounded Agee to get me out to Bendix as quickly as possible. Agee, who was planning some major strategic changes, was eager to find someone with a fresh perspective and lots of drive, and to start her right away.

I wasn't sure I was up for all this. I was still thinking about my possible new life in San Francisco, and I didn't see where I'd fit in. That matter was addressed in Part Three: "What Mary would do at Bendix." Here's where Agee elaborated on his pet peeve—the corporate sycophant. "The problem with being at the top of any large organization is that people around you constantly flatter you," he said. "They 'manage the news,' tell you what they think you want to hear. I want someone who'll tell me the truth." He asked me if I thought that as a result of the events of the sixties my generation was any more honest than earlier ones. "I don't know," I said. "I think we probably question authority more." "I like that," he said. "It's part of the Bendix style. We're very informal." And then, pointing to my suit with a teasing smile, "We don't wear clothes like that." So much for my Lanvin blouse and black wool suit.

Was I up for the job? That was the purpose of Part Four: "Test Mary." First came the easy stuff—facts about Bendix. Naturally I'd done my homework before the Guyol interview and had plowed through the 10K and annual reports so that I was handy with the figures: return on equity, debt capacity, cash flow. Agee smiled. He said he'd done the same thing at Business School. Then we moved on to strategy. "What is the company's chief problem?" he asked. "Lack of focus," I said, sounding very certain of something about which I wasn't entirely sure. What I did know—and this I found out from my own personal investigations around the Business School—was that few people had heard of Bendix, although everyone had heard about Agee. "People know your name but very few have any idea what Bendix does." He looked pleased but concerned. I forged on. Somewhere in the middle of all this he asked me about my husband. "I'm sure when you were being recruited for jobs, people always asked you about your wife," I said wryly. "Okay," he said. "You win that round." There was a friendly, informal nature to our banter but the friction made it move. At one point we were almost sparring, but then Agee broke into a big smile. "Even I wasn't that sharp at your age," he said. I wasn't sure that was true but I certainly was relieved. I felt terrific. I'd passed.

The tough part was over, and now it was Agee's turn. "What do I have to do to get you out to our headquarters?" he asked. I told him how appealing the San Francisco job had seemed. "Come to Detroit and you can work on forest products and every other product group as well." I told him about Bo, and that we wanted to come as a team. "No problem," he said. "We'll bring Bo out here too." The interview was just about over when he gave me a firm handshake and told me how much he'd enjoyed it. I said I'd enjoyed it too. As if on cue, a woman emerged from the next room. She wore a red dress, high heels and lots of jewelry. In contrast I felt like a hick from New Hampshire in my boxy black suit and low-heeled shoes. "I'd like you to meet my wife, Diane." She extended a cold hand. She was as placid as Agee was effervescent. I didn't envy her her position, having to play Mrs. So-

and-So, wife of Mr. Somebody, and having to vie with Bendix for Agee's attention.

En route to LaGuardia my mind raced. How could I square this with Bo? He wouldn't like the idea of Detroit. He'd think I was joking. I'd always vowed there were three cities in which I'd never live: Detroit, Buffalo and Cleveland. And here I was, about to consider a move to one of them. And Jack Guyol? Didn't I want to work for him? I was beginning to wonder about myself. Did I just keep going from interview to interview, thinking that the last one was the best? On the flight it got worse. And what about Agee? Was he for real? Maybe he was just a good talker, and maybe that was how he had gotten so far so fast. And what about that job as resident miracle worker? It sounded too good to be true. Maybe it was just a ploy to get me to Detroit. And what about Detroit? Oh, God, I hated Detroit.

I was late for class. The people sitting near me asked me where I'd been. (My suit was a dead giveaway.) When I said Bendix, no one got alarmed. I could go to Bendix with their blessings as long as I kept my hands off Morgan Stanley. Naturally, because I was late, I was called on. I muffed the answer but I didn't care.

I was starting to feel confident.

Like Agee.

It was time to get busy. I wanted to check my impressions with the authorities. My professors formed a solid bloc of praise: Agee was one of the Business School's star alumni. And everyone who met him agreed: He was an extremely likable guy. A few days after my interview, the personnel office from Bendix called. They wanted me to fly out to Detroit for a full day of interviews and bring

Bo too. I knew Bo wouldn't be thrilled. The Midwest wasn't exactly on the leading edge of racial tolerance—at least in Bo's mind. We decided he should come anyway since we still hadn't been offered the San Francisco job. That was the bait the personnel office used. "You come out to Detroit and then we'll talk about that."

Detroit was every bit as bleak as I'd remembered it from my last trip there in 1975, when, as an officer in the Workout Division of the Corporate Banking Department at Chase, I had to visit one of our then troubled clients, American Motors. Then, as now, Detroit was a city of cement and cars, its suburbs one unbroken chain of car dealers and fast-food restaurants. I counted countless numbers of Wendys, Burger Kings and McDonald's all in a twenty-mile stretch from Detroit Metro Airport to the Bendix Center.

At Bendix, Bo and I were greeted by one of Agee's secretaries and ushered into separate waiting rooms at either end of a long, glass-enclosed hall. My first meeting was with Agee and Bo's was with Charlie Donnelly, Bendix's vice chairman. I could tell from the look on Bo's face when he emerged from the encounter that it had not gone well. Charlie Donnelly was a conservative midwesterner and probably didn't know what to make of this educated black man with his lily-white Irish-American wife. My talk with Agee went well, which made me feel worse. I was dragging Bo through all this for my benefit.

Agee acted as if we were old friends. "I knew we'd get you out here," he said, as if it was inevitable I'd end up at Bendix. I liked his office. It was much more in keeping with Agee's style than the stuffy suite at the Waldorf. It was sunny and informal, decorated with a comfortable beige sectional couch and a small antique desk, not the usual mammoth block of wood that sits in most executives' offices. His dress, as usual, was casual. Shirt open at the neck, sport jacket and aviator glasses. I remember thinking the open shirt wouldn't go over too well at Morgan Stanley. On this morning's interview agenda was the Bendix senior management team except for one— Bill Panny, Agee's number two in command man, was out of town that day. Agee wanted me to meet each of them individually and he also wanted my candid impressions of them. I liked that. It made me feel trusted and also like I wasn't the only one being tested around here.

"So what do you think you're going to do here anyway?" asked Jerry Jacobson, executive vice president, and the first person I met. It didn't sound like a question so much as a threat. Jacobson appeared to be a large man, even though he was under five feet ten. He was a little heavy in the stomach and had a mustache and smoked a cigar, which made him look like *Pravda*'s version of a capitalist. He sat behind a giant desk and blew his cigarette smoke my way. "What are you interviewing for here anyway?" he probed. Apparently not everyone knew. "Agee's executive assistant," I said. Without a moment's hesitation, he said, "He doesn't need an executive assistant; I do all that." With no more delicacy, he asked about my credentials. I listed my activities at school but he brushed away my answer and said, "Let's bypass all that. What exactly are you qualified to do?"

I tried to explain what I had done at Chase and Salomon Brothers but it was a losing cause. He couldn't have cared less. In an attempt to draw him out—Pollyanna was still trying to make friends with this man—I asked him if he thought I should accept this job. "Absolutely not."

"What other offers do you have?" he asked. I reeled

off part of my impressive list. He took another puff on his cigar. I thought perhaps he might be preparing to compliment me and say, "Gee Mary with all those great offers why would you want to come to Bendix?" but he didn't. Instead, his next comment hit me like a jab in the stomach. "Perhaps you should know," he said after a pause and a fresh barrage of cigar smoke, "we had one other feisty woman around here and we took care of her." Just at that moment a secretary came to the door and asked, "Is Mrs. Gray ready for her next interview?" I could hardly wait.

I was furious. I'd never had such an insulting interview before. I wanted to cry, but God knows women can no longer cry in corporate corridors. I was so mad at being intimidated like this that I was determined to forge ahead.

If I had just encountered the big stiff who liked to scare women, I was now standing before the meek man who was terrified of them. Joe Svec, chief financial officer, was in his forties and had a short haircut. He seemed uneasy with me from the start. Agee apparently had done such a good job of building me up that Jacobson already resented me and Svec was scared of me. He hardly said a word. His eyes avoided meeting mine. The more I talked, the worse it got. I felt like a motormouth. This man obviously wasn't used to dealing with professional women, let alone aggressive ones straight out of the Harvard Business School. I kept waiting for an interruption but none came. Perhaps he had overheard through the adjoining office walls how badly my last interview had gone with Jacobson and decided not to waste his time. The secretary peered in after what seemed like an interminable amount of time. Is Mrs. Gray ready? You bet I was.

At last. A friendly face. Larry Hastie was young, handsome and personable, like Agee. He even dressed like

Agee. A lot of people at Bendix did. I'd noticed a number of Agee clones in the corridors. Hastie had just been promoted from treasurer to vice president for human resources, Bendix's euphemism for personnel, but he quickly let me know the position was only temporary. Personnel and public relations are the most common areas in which women are made corporate vice presidents and therefore don't have much prestige among most men. He said human resources experience was important for someone who wanted to be chief executive officer. He let me know he was headed that way, that he had been "mentored" by Agee. "So tell me about yourself, Mare," he said and spent the next twenty minutes telling me about himself. The only probing question he asked me was if I played a solid game of tennis. *He* played with the boss.

We spent another fifteen minutes talking about his athletic history and then I spent fifteen minutes with Bette Howe. She had been Agee's executive assistant a few years earlier and was now in a middle management job in personnel. In fifteen minutes she let me know I would not be happy working at Bendix. I couldn't understand whether she was telling me this as a confidential tip, as friend to friend, or because she didn't want me around. "You won't get anywhere in that job. You'll be a glorified 'go-for' for Agee and his cronies. Only the men he mentors get the V.P. promotions after that thankless job." The day was fast moving from bad to worse. Finally I went back into Agee's office.

"How's your day going?" Agee asked with his usual good cheer. This was not the time for a frank discussion of personalities so I stuck to the facts. I asked him all kinds of technical questions about Bendix aerospace and automotive technology and managed to swallow a few bites of my roast beef sandwich before marching into the office of Charlie Donnelly, Vice Chairman.

Donnelly, a lanky, pale-faced Irishman, sat me down in his kelly green office and said, "Nice to have a Cunningham around here." Not wasting a minute, he then asked, "How'd a nice Irish girl like you marry a black man?" Was this a bad joke or was he for real? Not detecting even the glimmer of a smile, I guessed this was his way of being cozy and frank. I returned his question. "Why would you ask such a thing?" He probably thought I didn't have much of a sense of humor.

He obviously did. Every time I tried to talk business, he deflected my question with a joke. "You've been at Bendix longer than most people," I said in my most earnest Harvard Business School voice. "What do you regard as the most significant changes that have taken place over the last few years?" "All these nice new pretty women," he said. Bravely I tried to go on. "What do you regard as the most strategically crucial issues facing Bendix today?" "Where to place the water cooler," he said. The interview continued along in this vein. He seemed to view himself as a sort of grandfather figure around Bendix and couldn't take seriously the notion that this sweet young Irish girl would want to talk business. I didn't know how we were going to fill up the next twenty minutes but he did. "Jerry Jacobson has a few more things he wants to discuss with you. Let's take you over to his office." I couldn't imagine what Jacobson could want to ask me.

Jacobson was flipping through my résumé when I came in. Looking for padding, no doubt. "Tell me, Mary," he said, "just what does it mean to be a member of the Century Club?" I told him, but he looked as though I was describing some fourth-grade nature club. "What did you *really* do at Salomon Brothers?" As I spoke, he kept peering over the résumé as though testing for inconsistencies in my oral answers to his quizzing. I thought for sure any minute he was going to jump up and shout, "Got ya!" I felt my neck start to break out. I knew I couldn't take much more of this. "To be perfectly honest, Mr. Jacobson," I said, "I'd really like to take a break now." "Fine," he said. Another weak woman. Probably needs to go powder her nose.

I wanted to leave. I was tired, I was humiliated and I was confused. I had spent the morning with one man who obviously resented me, another who was scared of me, a third who was trying to sell himself to me and a fourth who had a twisted sense of humor, to say the least. And now, in the light of these four disasters, my half-hour lunch chat with Agee didn't seem so hot either. It was two-thirty and I wasn't due back in Agee's office until four. Bo had already gone back to the hotel. I didn't know how I was going to make it. The only solution, I decided, was to leave.

Quietly, I started to walk down the hall to the phone at the front desk. I planned to call a cab and say goodbye to Bendix forever. And I would have, but the hallways at Bendix are predominantly made of glass and Agee could see me attempting a fast exit. "How are you doin'?" he asked, calling to me from his end of the corridor. He could tell from my face I wasn't doing too well. "C'mon, let's spend a few minutes in my office and talk." Why am I following this man? I thought as I walked with him back to his office. I know better than this. Everything I'd learned in my Business School course on Human Behavior in Organizations suggested I was getting all the wrong signals. And then some advice Father Bill, the priest who had taken a strong hand in my education, had told me returned to my consciousness: There must always be a *spes fructus*—a hope of victory; it was one of Saint Thomas Aquinas' three necessary conditions for a just war. This was troublesome. If I had to judge right now, clearly this condition didn't seem to be present.

We sat down in Agee's office and mercifully he did most of the talking. "I think I know what's been going on," he said. "Let's see if I've got it right. Jacobson tried to scare you, Svec didn't say a word, Hastie tried to snow you and Donnelly put you off with his warped sense of humor. Right?" I felt a little better knowing it wasn't all me. Still, I wondered how he could run a business surrounded by people like this. "Whom do you rely on?" I asked. "None of them," he said. Apparently he had inherited most of them from a previous regime. "Each of them has certain strengths but there's no one I can trust completely, no one I can depend on, no one who can function as my alter ego." I was touched. I started to understand why he wanted an executive assistant. I was beginning to figure out what the job meant. He talked about big plans for the coming years. He had been at Bendix now for seven years, the last three as chief executive officer and felt now was the time for him to make his big move. That's why he needed someone he could rely on absolutely. A first lieutenant. Someone very bright, with fresh, new ideas. The fact that I could be that person bolstered my ego and also made me feel needed. I could help Bill Agee. At the same time, the situation made sense from a practical point of view. I knew I could probably learn more working for Bill Agee than I could from anyone else, and the fact that his management team wasn't the best meant I'd probably grow stronger amid adversity.

Also, I liked the man. I thought he was a basically decent human being. I liked his style. His candor. The informality. And the confidence, too.

I felt much better now. Comforted. I had a responsibility. This person had brought me into this corporate family, shown me all its problems, and now he was asking me to help him clean them up. Already I felt involved. This wouldn't be just another job, this would be a cause, a crusade. When there's a cause with values I can identify with, I'm motivated.

In the taxi on the way back to my hotel I was already shouldering the burdens of Bendix and getting a headache because of it. By the time I walked into my hotel room at the Renaissance Plaza, I was praying that Bo would convince me to leave Detroit and forget about Bendix. Of course, when he tried to, I got upset. I found myself defending Agee. "But he needs my help," I said. "Investment-banking firms want someone with my credentials; but Agee needs *me*." "Don't worry," Bo said. "Agee can do just fine without you. He's done just fine up until now and I'm sure he'll continue to whether you're there or not." We'd been through this one before. Bo called it my missionary zeal and it was a tiresome joke between us. He could see me overextending myself already. And he knew how vulnerable I was to anyone who made me feel needed.

The next morning we met Les Rollins and his wife, Edie, for brunch. Apparently Les hadn't heard of my trials and tribulations at Bendix the previous day. He seemed as eager as ever to convince me to come to Bendix and spent most of the morning discussing various job possibilities for Bo. Agee had dropped the bomb just before I left that he didn't think he could bring both Bo and me to Bendix at the same time. Politically he couldn't afford to make two senior appointments at once. And such visible ones. As his new aide-de-camp I'd attract enough attention, and with Bo there as well . . .

"The company just isn't big enough for two senior executives of your talent," he said. He assured me, however, that he'd help Bo find a good job in the area. The two men had talked earlier in the day and seemed to respect, if not like, each other. At brunch Bo and Les ran through the possibilities. Bo had been unhappy at American Express and the talk of other jobs cheered him up. As a black executive, Bo was good "window dressing" for the company but, as with many black executives, no one in top management paid much attention to his abilities beyond that. A new job might help, but I knew it wouldn't be easy for him to move to the Motor City. And I wasn't so sure I could decide to come, knowing it would make Bo unhappy.

On the plane back to New York neither of us broached the topic. We knew it would set off more sensitive issues than either of us was prepared to deal with just yet. We spent most of the afternoon discussing things we could handle—where to eat and what movie to see once we got back to New York.

The next day was life-crisis time. I was wrestling with the two big ones—marriage and career—and both seemed to be inextricably intertwined. I could go to Bendix and avoid my problems with Bo short-term, or I could stay in New York, face my marital problems head-on and lose the ultimate career opportunity. Both seemed perilous routes. And what I knew better than to do was to use one problem to solve the other. I knew my marriage was in trouble and I had to admit it. This commuter arrangement wasn't working, despite all those pleasant banalities I'd heard about absence making the heart grow fonder, and "It's not the quantity but the quality of the time spent together." Bo and I were together fewer and fewer weekends, and when we were, we spent most of our time discussing each other's careers. It was rare that we even kissed anymore. I needed more time. I wasn't ready to write our marriage off. But I wasn't ready to turn down Bendix either.

I went to Mass alone that Sunday, as I did most Sundays, and thought about my life. Away from Bo, away from Bendix, I saw my desires pulling me in two completely different directions. I felt bereft. The minute I got home, I decided I'd make a list of all the contending job offers and all of my priorities and, in true Harvard Business School fashion, use a ten-point scale of weighted averages to come up with an objective solution. Bendix came out on top—one point ahead of the three-way tie between Goldman Sachs, McKinsey and Morgan Stanley. That didn't help much. I kept hoping Bo would say something to make up my mind but he didn't. We went out to listen to music, and over beer and pizza I agonized over my choice. I couldn't concentrate on anything else. By the time we got home, I was resolved: I was staying in New York to work for Morgan Stanley. I told Bo. He said he was relieved.

The next morning I left New York pleased to have made up my mind, but no sooner did I arrive back in Cambridge than I started to waver. I spent a miserable evening in my dormitory apartment when who should call but Agee. I told him this wasn't going to be a very long conversation. Trying to summon up my most determined voice, I said, "I think I've made my decision. I believe I should go to work for

Morgan Stanley." I could practically feel the phone line snap. But it was not like Agee to get flustered. "Forget about whether or not you come to Bendix," he said, cool and calm as always. "My concern for the moment is why you want to go into investment banking." What followed was a twenty-minute vivisection of the investment-banking industry with a couple of digs at management consulting just for good measure. "Most investment bankers are whores," he said. "They'll teach you to be a junior technician on deals and try to buy your time by cutting you in on a piece of their fat commissions. You'll never get to know either the businesses or the managements well. You'll continue on in an inbred homogenous finishing-school environment where the competition and jealousy will make the last two years at Harvard Business School look like child's play. Just think of how it'll slow down your learning curve." That was the real killer. I was a sucker for steep learning curves. "Put Bendix aside," he said. "Let's think about you. You've already done commercial banking. And you've had your stint in investment banking. You've been on the service side long enough. What you need now is to be mentored. You need someone to show you the inside, the real guts, of corporate life. Look at the case studies of every successful chief executive and in nine out of ten cases they've been mentored. That's how I got ahead. Not by sitting at some desk dotting the i's and crossing the t's on other people's deals. If you go to Morgan Stanley you'll be doing the paper work on Bendix deals. And here you have a chance to make those deals, to design them, to do the creative work."

I was losing steam. Why did I ever answer the phone? I thought. "Wouldn't it be possible to work for Morgan for two years and then come to Bendix?" I asked, sotto voce. "No," he said. "The next few years at Bendix will be the crucial ones. You'll do more deals in those two years at Bendix than you will at any investment-banking firm." This went on for almost an hour, by the end of which I was putty. I knew one thing: If Agee were on one side, I certainly wouldn't want to be on the other.

I spent the rest of the week discussing my dilemma with my closest advisers and a few professors. They were all in Agee's camp. They said investment banking was something I could do any time, but an opportunity to work for a distinguished alumnus like Bill Agee was rare. Mentorship was a favorite route to the top around Harvard, and who could be a better mentor than Bill Agee? The system's leading advocate, he was one of its youngest, most successful products as well. When he was twenty-eight, which was how old I was now, he had been mentored by Bob Hansberger at Boise-Cascade. He knew the strong and weak points of a Harvard education and was a leading advocate of the rights of women in business as well. In the eyes of my professors, no better mentor could be found. And what about the honor? Lots of people got offers from investment-banking concerns, but how many people had been offered a job by Bill Agee?

I returned to New York for another miserable weekend. Bo sensed I had changed my mind and was distressed. It didn't help when he reminded me it was unlike me to be so malleable. He said what I already knew was true: There was a deeper issue at stake. Us. He shared his concern that either way he could lose me. If he forced me to stay, I'd probably eventually leave him out of frustration. If he said, "Go now," we might never find each other again. I didn't know what to do. Meanwhile, managing partners from Morgan Stanley and Goldman Sachs were calling, urging me to make up my mind about them, too. It seemed the more reluctant I was to accept their offers the more dogged they were in their pursuit of me. (Of course it was partly my fault. Uncertain I'd have any job offers at the beginning of the year, I had avidly cultivated them all.) Now Morgan Stanley had Louis Bernard, head of corporate finance, calling me suggesting that a breakfast at the Carlyle Hotel might help my decision making. And Goldman Sachs, hoping to hit me where I was weak, assigned an inspiring ex-seminarian to recruit me, a partner who had found faith and Dow Jones compatible.

By Sunday night, I couldn't stand it anymore. I quietly walked in to the living room of our co-op and called Louis Bernard of Morgan Stanley and told him I would be joining his firm. He was thrilled. He thought I had selected Morgan Stanley over Goldman Sachs and assured me I'd made the right choice. When I sounded less than convinced he asked me if there was anything wrong. "No," I said. "I just feel badly about having to turn down another offer." "What was it?" he asked. "Executive assistant to the chairman of Bendix." "You mean Bill Agee?" he asked. "Yes," I said. "That's a pretty impressive offer," he said. Oh, no. Don't tell me that, I thought. "Well, don't worry. When you come to Morgan, we'll make sure to put you on the Bendix account. That's one of ours, you know. Besides, why would anyone want to live in Detroit?"

Next I had to call Agee. I was hoping he wouldn't be in. Before I called I looked in at Bo. He was in the bedroom engrossed in a basketball game on TV. I wondered if he had any idea of what I was about to give up in order to attempt to save our marriage. I went back to the phone and called Agee. "Hi. What can I do for you?" That boisterously friendly voice always disarmed me. I apologized for calling him at home but he said not to worry. He was only going over some reports. I told him I had something to tell him but that I didn't want to discuss it at length. "I've decided not to come to Bendix for personal reasons," I said. There was a respectful pause. "Listen," he said. "I have no problem with that decision. I understand your reasons. When I'm in New York at Morgan Stanley I'll say hello." And then his tone became very abrupt. "I guess that's all there is to it," he said and hung up.

From then on everything felt anticlimactic. I went into the bedroom where Bo was eating popcorn and watching the game. He hardly looked up. I told him what I'd done. "So, how do you feel?" he asked. "Fine," I said. I waited for him to say more but he didn't. He just went on eating his popcorn and watching the game. Here I'd given up one of the best offers anyone could ever hope to get at the Business School—and did he appreciate what I'd done? Did he really care? I wanted some reaction. Any reaction. But Bo didn't budge. He just sat there watching the damned game.

The next morning I was sitting in the living room feeling lonely, the old feeling that came up sometimes even when I was with Bo. I wondered if he really knew how I felt. After a little while he came in.

"You're unhappy with the decision, right?" he said, in his usual understated but direct way.

"Yes," I said, my eyes fixed on a stain in the middle of our living-room rug.

"You want to go to Bendix, don't you?"

"Yes," I said.

"Then you should go."

I started to cry. "Bo," I said. "I'm scared. I feel like I'm making a bigger decision than I mean to."

"You mean about our marriage?"

"Yes."

"Don't," he said, "I'll come out and join you. It may take a little time but I'll see if I can find something in Michigan." I knew he wouldn't come to Detroit. He'd promised to come to Boston the same way when I had been admitted to the Business School. I had noticed the change in visits from most weekends during the first year to hardly once a month by the end of the second year. I knew the same thing would happen again, but just now I needed to believe it wouldn't. I needed to believe it might work. Just to get me over the hurdle.

Of course I felt like a fool calling all these people back. I thought perhaps Agee wouldn't even want me now that I seemed so unable to make up my mind. First I called Mr. Bernard. He was very kind. He assured me it was better to back out now than later although he was "terribly disappointed" in me. Next I called Agee. He was out. For two hours I had to wait around the apartment feeling like a fool for giving up one job without being sure that I had the other. At noon Agee phoned back. "Mary?" he said. I prepared my speech. "I know this sounds strange but I've changed my mind. I would like to come to work for Bendix." There was a pause. "What about the reason you gave me for deciding not to come," he asked. I told him Bo had agreed to come with me. I knew I was kidding myself a little. "Good decision," he said. "I'll do everything I can to help Bo."

Classes were over the end of April and Bo and I decided to take a vacation before my graduation in June. With my decision all set, I thought I would be able to relax for a week in Hawaii, but my timing was all wrong. My mind was on starting work, not leaving school. Besides, I felt guilty and Bo was understandably disturbed.

We'd both been schooled in careerism—support each other's careers at all costs—which didn't leave us much else to say.

Three hours after we got back to New York, we received a message that Bill Agee had called. That went over great with Bo. When I called back, his secretary said, "Mr. Agee is on the Concorde returning from a board meeting in France and would like you to meet him at Kennedy Airport. He has a few projects he would like you to begin work on." I wasn't due to start work at Bendix until August 1 but I had agreed that I would do some background reading as long as I could do it in New York. "A chauffeured car will be at your home to pick you up in about an hour." I said, "Fine," and started to prepare for the meeting. I didn't want to look at Bo's face when I left.

Agee got off the plane with two or three other executives. They were all in sports jackets and khakis. I was wearing a formal navy business suit and a long-sleeved blouse buttoned up to the neck, even though it was June. I never knew when my neck would turn red. I felt awfully conspicuous, standing in line with the chauffeurs, waiting to greet him. In the car Agee shook my hand. "See you made it out here all right," he said, and immediately opened his briefcase. He handed me a list of companies to analyze, internal documents he wanted me to review and memos he wanted me to prepare for a meeting to be scheduled next week. This was my metier. I knew how to handle this kind of work. Loaded down with a bunch of papers and assignments to prepare, I was content. I couldn't wait to get back to my apartment and get right to work.

Less than a week later he called. "Hello, Mare. The work going okay?" The disarming informality. Only now he was my boss and the sound of his voice meant business. "Listen, I'm calling because I knew you'd never forgive me if I didn't give you a chance to get involved in a very critical project. If you're interested, I'd like you to prepare a confidential analysis for me. We're analyzing a potential acquisition, a major forest products concern that would round out the Bendix Forest Products Company's position. It's clear that something has to be done to strengthen that part of our business. We're having a meeting with the target company's investment bankers tomorrow afternoon in Detroit. I'd like you to be there." This wasn't part of our deal. "You can say no if you want but it's a chance to get involved at the ground level. If you decide to come, we'll have your prepaid plane tickets ready for your arrival at the airport. One of my secretaries will arrange for a car to pick you up early tomorrow morning." I wasn't really prepared to go but was even less prepared to say no. Agee had told me how he'd started work the day after graduation from Business School, and here I was balking about starting a full month later. "I'll be there," I said.

For the second time a limousine drove up to our co-op apartment on the fringe of Harlem. I was driven to LaGuardia and flown first class to Detroit. Spoiled already, I simply assumed another limo would meet me at Detroit Metro, but I was wrong. When I got off the plane, a helicopter was waiting to take me from the American Airlines terminal to the roof of Bendix!

If I'd had any doubts about my decision, I wasn't thinking about them now.

# CHAPTER TWO

*Bendix is your typical corporate* ice palace: a modern glass-and-chrome building with enough hanging plants to assure a visitor life can survive in there. Like most buildings in the suburbs of post-riot Detroit, Southfield is a safe thirty minutes from downtown. Approached from the main entrance, it's an easy walk to the chairman's office—up the front steps, through a small vestibule and down a glistening glass-enclosed corridor. I didn't go that route the first day. I came in at the top.

The helicopter dropped me on the roof of the building, where Agee's secretary and personal driver were waiting to bring me to their boss. Once inside, I could feel heads turn. Anyone sandwiched between the chairman's personal secretary and his driver was fair game for gossip, but a woman, and a young one, was fairer game still. "How're you doing?" Agee boomed when we entered his office. "You're just in time for the meeting. C'mon in." Oh, for just five minutes to catch my breath. Inside were all my old friends—Jacobson, Svec, Donnelly, and a fourth man who was introduced to me as Bill Panny, president, chief operating officer and head of the automotive group. "They're making 'em better-looking all the time," Panny said upon meeting me, and turned and winked at his guys. Muffled laughter.

The meeting was downhill from there. Every time Panny cursed, which was often, he looked my way and said, "'Scuse me, Mary," and covered his mouth with his hand. I was seated next to Agee, which flustered me because it put me in the spotlight, so I moved as far over on the couch as possible. This placed me practically in the lap of poor, shy Joe Svec, who clung for dear life to the opposite arm of the couch. I didn't speak much—I was suffering a relapse of Harvard Business Schoolitis—but when Agee did finally call on me, my comment was memorable. "If Bendix wants to be viewed as more of a diversified company and less dependent on the automotive business, perhaps it should consider moving its headquarters out of Detroit." That didn't go over too well in a roomful of entrenched Detroiters. I did summon up the courage to buttonhole Panny after the meeting. "You know, it's not the first time I've heard those words," I said. "I'd appreciate it if you wouldn't keep apologizing to me next time you feel the need to use them."

Panny nodded but my comments didn't seem to sink in. He had little further interest in me now that his pals weren't around. Agee, who'd apparently caught every word, motioned me aside. "You know I anticipated a few of these problems," he said when we were seated inside in his office. "I feel an extra sense of responsibility since I brought you out here."

"Oh I'm sure I can handle it," I hastened to reassure him, in case he was having second thoughts.

"I admire your spunk—but don't be afraid to speak up if I can help," he said.

The first order of business was finding a house. Bo

flew out for the occasion and the two of us were driven to the outskirts of Detroit by Jerry Plec, a Bendix personnel employee and our guide for the day. Plec wasn't exactly overjoyed with his task of having to help this newly hired $34,000-a-year executive assistant and her black husband find a house. "Now I've picked out five or six houses that I'd want to live in although you might not think they're good enough for you," he said. He was right. All his selections were in apartment complexes that looked as if they'd been put up overnight. In addition, most of them were in the less affluent suburbs, whose residents were not particularly eager to boast the first interracial couple on the block. "Sorry, we don't have anything," and "All sold out," were all we heard all morning. After a while, Bo offered to wait in the car while I looked, but I couldn't do that. If they didn't want us, I didn't want them. By late afternoon, as if he'd been holding out on us, Plec drove us to a nicer place called Moon Lake. I saw the first genuine smile of pleasure on Plec's face when we told him we couldn't afford it because the rent was too high.

The next day we were smart. We called Jerry Plec and told him we preferred to go out by ourselves. Bo convinced me to let him sit in the car and we found a place right away. It was a white brick colonial in a condominium development called Foxcroft. It was only ten minutes from the office and across the street from a shopping center. I liked it because the architecture reminded me a little of New England. I was relieved to find a possible new home but angry at the farce we had to go through.

Before Bo left, we were invited for dinner at the Agees with Bette Howe, the Bendix personnel director and the person who last had my job. Apparently she and Agee had had some falling out. "Had enough of his chipmunk smile yet?" she asked during one of our interview sessions.

Howe picked us up and gave us the grand tour of Bloomfield Hills, the posh lily-white suburb in which Agee and most of Detroit's new money live. "What's their house like?" I asked. "Early cliché," she said. "Wait till you see the phony columns."

Agee answered the door. "Hi, folks. Come right in," he beamed, buoyant as usual. We followed him into a large living room expensively furnished with all the usual suburban trappings—thick carpet and velvet drapes—and one unusual one—a giant indoor swimming pool. Diane was sitting at the far end of the living room.

"Hello, I think we met before. I'm Mary Cunningham Gray," I said. "This is my husband, Bo." She didn't say much. Agee came back with the drinks and told us to make ourselves at home. Their teenage daughter, Kathy, and son, Bob, came into the room and Agee introduced them. "Kath, do you know Mary graduated top of her class from both Wellesley and the Harvard Business School?" She didn't seem overly impressed. The rest of the evening moved in stages. First, Agee, Bo, and Bette and I talked business. That left Mrs. Agee silent on the sidelines. Next, Agee and Bo started telling jokes. This degenerated into the "Bill and Bo" show, in which the jokes got progressively raunchy as the evening wore on. I tried to make small talk with Mrs. Agee. "You have a lovely house," I said. "Thank you," she replied. "Did it take you long to decorate?" I asked. "I didn't do the decorating," she said. Pause. "How long have you lived in Bloomfield Hills?" I asked. "Seven years," she said. "Do you like it?" I asked. "Yes. It's quite nice."

I knew I should probably stop but that wasn't my style. I was determined to draw her out. "You know Bo and I went house hunting today," I said. "Oh. Did you?" she said. "Yes, but I'm afraid we haven't made up our minds yet." Longer pause. "I'm not used to the architecture here. It's not like New England, where I'm from. Have you ever been to New England?" "Yes," she said. "Did you like it?" I asked. "I don't know," she said. "I don't remember."

She wasn't hostile. As Bo put it, "She'd just been to one too many corporate dinner parties."

I settled into my new home as best I could. Bo promised to come out and help when the rest of my "portable home"—$250 worth of secondhand furniture I'd bought from a colleague at the Chase who was getting married—arrived from Harvard. In the meantime, I unpacked my Business School books. They fit nicely in a place the real estate agent described as "ideal" for lingerie. Otherwise, the place was pretty bare. The walls were paper-thin and I could hear the lady downstairs running her electric can opener. It wasn't much of a home but then what did I care? I knew myself well enough to know I'd be spending very little time here.

My real home would be at Bendix.

The first week I was given an office and a title. The office had no desk and the title was ambiguous. Executive Assistant. It could mean anything from a glorified secretary to a powerful aide-de-camp. Agee didn't spell it out for me either; I think he was waiting to see how I worked out.

For the first few weeks I functioned as Agee's tagalong.

He wanted me to understand every aspect of the chief executive officer's role, and I did this by accompanying him on his daily rounds. Usually this meant meetings and more meetings. The meetings were never as much fun as the "debriefing" sessions afterward. "So what did you think of what Mace said on the brakes analysis?" "The brakes analysis? I thought he was talking about the reorganization plan." "Well, he was, but he used the term only because he didn't want to disagree with Panny, who is his boss." "Oh."

This was the beginning of my crash course in corporate politics. Of course I wasn't privy to all the meetings. At 7:30 A.M. he'd call me into his office, and over orange juice he'd ask me what meetings I'd like to attend that day. I made a point of avoiding too many sessions at which a philanthropic group came to make an appeal. Not that I had anything against philanthropy; it's just that my predecessor, Bette Howe, had done lots of this and I wanted to avoid at all costs doing anything that could be construed as "merely women's stuff."

I could tell by the frequency of the meetings Agee attended which topics were important to him. Strategy and finance ranked first, but toward the end of my first month I started to notice a glut of meetings on pensions. Negotiations with the United Automobile Workers union were coming up and pensions promised to be a crucial issue. "Those idiots in finance," he fumed one day after Svec and the finance people had presented a particularly confusing report on the subject. "Why can't they ever explain anything in a way normal people can understand? I wish to hell someone would translate this to make sense."

I thought this was as good a place as any to dive in. "Would you like me to try my hand at it?" I asked. "Do you know anything about unfunded pension liability?" he asked. All I knew was that the term always appeared as a footnote at the bottom of the company balance sheets I was analyzing. "Not much but I can learn." At first he looked skeptical but then I think the idea appealed to him. "Say, wouldn't that be something. That would really put one over on them if you could make this thing intelligible. Do you have time?" "I could make time," I said. "Sure," he said, looking pleased. "Give it a try."

The month of July I lived pensions. I talked to anyone at Bendix who had anything to do with pensions. It was dull, uninspiring fare, but that was part of the challenge— to make it sing. I unearthed people in accounting who hadn't been heard from for years. One older man was so happy that someone actually wanted to listen to him that he spent two days tutoring me in the finer points of pensions. I read books and made calls. The books didn't help but the calls did. One of the people I called was George Russell, Agee's outside consultant on pensions. I arranged to fly to Seattle to interview him. When word of this got back to Joe Svec, whose department would normally handle such matters, he suddenly became more interested in what I was doing and asked if he and a few of his financial team could come to Seattle with me. Just what I needed. Two days in Seattle with Joe Svec, and his numbers men. "Sure," I said. I had no choice. It was a miserable trip. I worried that if I said too much, Svec would think I was an aggressive woman, and if I said too little, he'd think I was holding information back from him. My solution? I read a lot that trip.

The board of directors was meeting August twenty-third and Agee wanted my report written well before then. By August third I had my forty-five page single-spaced opus ready to send to the printer. Agee wanted to read it first. "Can I take it home with me tonight?" "Why not?" I said.

I knew why not. Because then he would find out I was a fraud, that I really wasn't as good as I was cracked up to be. I spent the whole night worrying and felt sick the next morning when I noticed he still hadn't come in by nine. At ten he strode into my office. "May I sit down?" he asked. "Sure," I said. I waited for him to begin. "Mary," he said, "this is the first time anyone has ever made the scope of this issue clear to me," he said. I felt my face get red.

"You like it?" I asked, meaning, tell me more. "It's fabulous," he said. "The board's going to love it. And to think you didn't know anything about pensions when you began. How long did it take you to do?" "About a month," I said. "Now why couldn't Svec put together a team and do something like this?" he said. "I'm going to discuss this with them. It should teach them a lesson."

I knew whatever lesson they learned it would be at my expense, and Agee was smart enough to know this too, but this was his blind spot. If there was one thing that Agee hated it was deadwood and when it was upper-level-staff deadwood, it irked him even more. I think that's why he was especially pleased that it was a woman, and a young person, who was showing his team up. He couldn't resist the chance.

However, I did manage to persuade him to let Svec present the report to the board. It was hardly humility that prompted my actions. I was simply being practical. I was tired of feeling disliked. Besides, it wasn't the board's approval I wanted, it was Agee's. Agee agreed, and what was even more surprising, so did Svec. I had hoped in a true burst of humility he might say, "Nah, Mary, you present it, it's your report," but no such luck. It didn't bother him in the least. It did, however, bother Agee.

The Bendix board was full of heavyweights: Malcolm Baldridge, Chairman of Scovill, Coy Eklund, President of the Equitable Life Assurance, one of the largest life insurance companies in the country, and Donald Rumsfeld, former Secretary of Defense, among others. All members sat in a large circle in the company's lavishly appointed board room. With its plush green velvet upholstered chairs and pink-and-green floral rug, it looked more like the inner sanctum of an aged dowager than a conference room in sleek and modern Bendix. A further oddity was that the conference table was missing. Agee had had it removed for better communication. Outsiders like me sat off to the side.

After Svec made his presentation, Malcolm Baldridge cleared his throat, snubbed out his cigarette, and asked for the floor. "I'd just like to say," he said, "that this is the most intelligible, most well thought out, most useful study on pensions I've ever seen. My compliments to you, Joe, and your team."

Agee waited and waited as Svec puffed out his chest. "I'd just like the board to know one thing," Agee said. "The person really responsible for this report is sitting over there," he said, and pointed to me. My neck was hot. I could feel heads turn. And almost all nodded or smiled approvingly, particularly Hugo Uyterhoeven, a fellow Harvard Business School grad, and Jewel Lafontant, the only woman on the Bendix board. This time I was the one who avoided looking at Svec.

Top management shied away from me but gradually a group of younger people, middle-level managers and recent Business School graduates, started dropping by. Usually the invitation was for lunch or drinks. I rarely had time for either, which I suppose made people think I was cold or aloof, but when I tried to attend social occasions I felt uncomfortable. My visitors seemed to come in two groups: the just plain curious and those trying to pump me for confidential information about Agee. I felt impatient with the first and uncomfortable with the second. It was clear that my choice was between being loyal to Agee and being one of the guys.

It was at an office party one night that someone came up to me and said, "It must be tough to have that job." It was the most honest thing anyone had said to me. We talked for a few minutes and I told him some of my fears. "It's not your fault; it's the problem with your job. People with titles like Executive Assistant walk around with bull's-eyes on their backs." He left me with one piece of advice: "Limit the time you play Executive Assistant."

In the wake of my pension success, Agee had a new project for me. "I'd like to make you an interesting offer," he said. "How would you like to be the person who goes through my mail?" "Your what?" I asked. "My mail. You know, sort out who gets what, a kind of chief routing officer."

I thought he was kidding.

"What's the matter? Do you think it's too much responsibility?"

"Are you serious?" I said. "I didn't go to Business School to learn to do that!"

He looked taken aback. "It's a very important job. It involves going through the mail and helping me decide who I need to find time to see and who I don't need to.

It's helping me make most efficient use of my time." I thought he was really trying to put one over on me.

"Who does it now?" I asked. "Your secretaries?"

"Of course not," he said. "I do it."

I wasn't sold on the idea but I thought perhaps I was making too much of a fuss. Besides, he told me he used to do it for his boss, chairman Bob Hansberger and other members of the top management team when he was being mentored at Boise-Cascade, and that seemed to be his model for how to mentor me.

I decided to give it a try. It turned out to be an interesting exercise. It helped me learn a lot about Bendix and more about Agee. Unfortunately it caused me some problems too. Every time I had to reroute something, I'd send it along to the appropriate department with a note, "The chairman would like your comments on the attached," scribbled on a buck pad with my initials.

Some people resented getting their messages from Agee via me. This became a more serious problem when I started to field some of his phone calls at his or his secretary's request. Certain individuals in particular resented having to run interference with me, and usually those were the ones Agee had neither the time nor the patience to deal with. One of those was the vice president in the National Affairs Office, a native Idahoan and a one-time chum of Agee's. Her interest in Agee remained high whereas his had long since been diverted to more strategic matters. Every time she called, Agee instructed his secretaries to put her through to me. "Is Bill in?" she'd say, and I'd say, "I'm sorry. He's in meetings right now. Can I help?" "I asked to speak to the chairman." "Perhaps I can help?" "If I wanted your help, I would've asked for you." And so on. Had I been more judicious, I might have politely refused to field those calls, but I was not. My job was to help the chairman, and I decided, even if it cost me a few allies, at least I was doing my duty.

Meanwhile, life on the home front was rapidly deteriorating. Twice I'd asked Bo to come out and twice he'd declined. The first was on moving day. The Thursday before I was scheduled to move, he called. "Mare, I'm sorry to do this to you but I can't be there this weekend." "Why?" I asked. Usually I tried to disguise my tone so that I wouldn't make him feel guilty, but not this time. I was too desperate to think about "the other guy." I let him know by my tone that I felt really let down. "I have a chance to really improve my situation here but it means I have to work weekends," he said. I knew how important it was for Bo to feel good about himself—we were so similar, our self-esteem rose and fell with our jobs—but inside I was panicking. I didn't want to face all those cartons alone. "Fine, Bo. I understand," I said.

Before I left work that Friday Agee asked if I was all set to move. He could tell from my voice I was not. "Bo coming out?" he asked. "I don't think so," I said. "Hey, listen, let me help you move. I'm a great helper. I'll bring son Bob and we'll both help. Really, we'd love to."

The offer flustered me. I could just imagine the chairman of the board wearing jeans and tossing cartons around in my apartment. Besides, I was embarrassed. I didn't want anyone I worked with to see all my secondhand furniture. I assured him I'd be all right but he wasn't convinced. "Listen, I have two grown-up daughters and I'd hate to see them move alone." "Thanks, but I think I can manage." "Okay," he said. "Just promise you'll call me at three to let me know everything's all right." I promised.

The moving van was already there by the time I returned home from work Friday. Boxes and cartons everywhere. It was a depressing sight. I began to unpack but the elements conspired against me. It was hot, it was humid, and the air conditioning was on the blink. After four cartons I was ready to call it quits, but I couldn't find a nightgown and the carton in which I'd packed the sheets somehow eluded me. At midnight I conked out on a mattress in my clothes. The next morning I woke up sweaty and tired. I thought of calling Bo to ask him "to come and get me out of here" but of course I had no phone. I unpacked my photos first—scenes of past peaceful summers on Cape Cod walking the beach, New Hampshire homecomings, lighting a campfire. It was more than missing Bo; I missed a way of life I never seemed to have for very long.

After five hours of unpacking, I found myself looking at the clock. I needed something to reaffirm why I was going through all of this. At a few minutes after three I went racing out of Foxcroft and down to the phone booth in front of the nearby shopping center A&P. Already uneasy about not being punctual with my call, I realized I'd forgotten to bring a dime. I raced back, grabbed some change and ran back to the phone booth. I was by now twenty minutes late. I wanted desperately to speak to a friend—but not Agee.

"Hey, how are you?" he sang. "Just fine," I lied. "I'm sorry I'm late calling but . . ." He interrupted, "Don't worry about that. I just want to hear how you're faring over there by yourself." He was so considerate. "Oh, it's all going pretty well, I guess—" but he could hear the tightening in my throat. "You're sure you wouldn't like some help? Bob and I can be right there." Everything in me wanted to say yes, I did want help—but it just wouldn't be comfortable coming from him. "No, I'll manage." "Well, let me hear you talk a little more so I can tell how you're really doing." I couldn't take it anymore. I knew if I continued to talk, I'd start to cry, and I couldn't let Agee hear me do that. "Look, I'm standing in a parking lot. I really can't stay on anymore." "Okay," he said. "If you change your mind just give us a call." And I hung up. Now I really did start to cry. I felt so foolish standing there in the huge A&P parking lot like an abandoned child trying to hide my tears. The loneliness was unbearable, and here I had just let go of my one possible life raft in that city.

At the end of my first month, there was a big party at work to celebrate the sculpture Louise Nevelson had been commissioned by Agee to design for the Bendix headquarters. I asked Bo to come out. "It'll give everyone a chance to meet you," I told him one night on the telephone. "I'm sure they can hardly wait. Good grist for gossip. Sure you even want me there?" "Are you asking if I'm embarrassed to have you here?" "Yes." "What would make you ask that?" "Oh, sooner or later that environment is going to have to rub off on you. You're living in an all-white suburb of a predominantly black city. It's not exactly Manhattan." "Bo, please. Let's not get into a racial discussion. I'm just asking you to be with me. Will you come as my husband to this party?" He said he would—but at the last minute something came up. "Sure, I understand," I said. Again.

The party was a lavish affair. The entire staff of headquarters—five hundred people—and their spouses were there. I felt awkward being there alone. It was my social debut at Bendix and I could feel people stare. There I was in my simple, unadorned gown, in that roomful of elegantly dressed women with beauty-parlor hair. I wished Bo were there. I might have attracted even more attention had there not been presences far more controversial than mine. One was Louise Nevelson, wrapped in silk scarves à la Isadora Duncan, and even more conspicuous than I among Bloomfield Hills' finest. The other was her sculpture, massive hunks of metal that the crowd viewed with a look that could only be described as bewilderment.

It was typical of Agee to tease them like that. A conservative businessman, he nevertheless liked to surprise people. During his three years as chairman, he had eliminated many executive privileges, such as specially reserved parking spots, and removed the conference table from the board of directors' room because it "inhibited the free flow of ideas." (This was typical of Agee—"one man, one vote." He had succeeded in and therefore believed in the meritocracy system.) Nothing gave him greater pleasure than presenting people with radically new ideas, particularly if he thought they could learn from them or become better people. That's what he was trying to do here. "Now some of you are going to love this and some of you won't," he said the evening of the unveiling of the Nevelson sculpture. "And many of you aren't going to understand it. But I'm going to ask each and every one of you to think about it for a few days before you make up your minds."

They thought about it but that didn't seem to change their minds. Naturally, I was made Agee's ambassador of good will for the sculpture. It was my job to enlighten the masses. Every time I heard someone complain, "Oh it's so ugly I hate looking at it," or, "I miss the water fountain," which had been there before, I'd suggest in my best Sunday school voice, "If you would only try seeing it from this angle." It didn't work. It didn't make anyone feel better about Nevelson's art—or me.

"You know that pension study you did?" Agee said one day, striding into my office. "Well, I have to give a speech in Washington before a government committee on pensions and I thought you could take a stab at it." Oh, no. I thought I was through with pensions. "I'm not sure I know what they want," I said, hoping he'd back down. "Look through these," he said and handed me some articles. "And if you could, by Tuesday?"

Monday by noon, I handed him his speech. "Can I try it out on you?" he asked after he'd had a chance to read it over. "Sure," I said and listened. "How do I sound?" he asked. My look said it all. "Okay. Tell me what's wrong," he said. At first I felt presumptuous criticizing a chairman so boldly. But he urged me on. He enjoyed receiving criticism that could help him. And mine did. I had grown up hearing the powerful sermons of Father Bill, the Monsignor who had provided a guiding hand in my upbringing, and I knew where to put the fire and brimstone. We spent three hours going over his fifteen-minute speech, but when we were done, he sounded great. I flew down to Washington to hear him. People praised the speech and they praised Agee too. That made me feel proud. He was my boss, and if he looked good in their eyes, I looked good in his.

September first was my birthday, and my family was planning a little birthday celebration for me at the Cape. Bo joined us for the occasion, but in the back of my mind disturbing thoughts began to fester. I kept wondering what life would be like without him. How would Mom feel if Bo and I officially separated? I wondered, watching the two of them stroll the beach. Or, what would my brother Frank say if his pal Bo and I were no longer together? I dismissed these thoughts as quickly as they arose. I didn't have the time or the energy to pursue them now.

In October, at the urging of the Bendix public-relations department, Bo and I were one of the lucky couples selected to appear in a Channel 7 news segment on commuter marriages. Through some extraordinary twist in logic I allowed the public-relations department to convince me that appearing on the show would be good for Bendix and might even open a few minds to racial equality. The interviews were a travesty. "Has the fact of your long-distance commuting hurt your relationship, Ms. Gray?" Staged shot of Bo and Mary holding hands. "Do you think your relationship might be deeper if you had more time to spend together?" Close-up of Mary smiling as she sees Bo arrive at the airport.

The discrepancy between what appeared and what I felt was disturbing. I knew deep in my heart that this particular long-distance commuter marriage wasn't all it was cracked up to be. I, too, had read all the articles about Mr. and Mrs. Supercouple and their Eastern Airlines shuttle married life, but the plain fact was that ours wasn't working. The reality of that fact didn't dawn on me until after the show. I put a lot less faith in talk shows after that.

I was sitting in Agee's office one autumn morning when a call came in on the squawk box: "Mr. Agee? Mr. Craig Smith of Warner and Swasey Company on the line. Can you take the call?" "Yes," Agee said. "Bill? Am I on a speaker phone?" I heard Smith ask. "Yes, Craig, you are." "Can you take me off?" "Sure."

I couldn't hear the rest of the conversation but from Agee's responses, I could pretty much figure out what was happening. It seemed that Warner and Swasey, an industrial tool and equipment company in Cleveland, was being raided by AMCA (a familiar name; irony of ironies—their headquarters were in my home town in New Hampshire).

Smith wanted to know if Agee would be the white knight and buy Warner and Swasey in order to prevent a hostile takeover. Nothing would please Agee more. Warner and Swasey was one of the companies on the Bendix target list as a perfect acquisition candidate. Agee as much as told him so, and after a few more reassuring words with Smith, he hung up. "My God. We couldn't have planned it better. Here's our chance to beef up the industrial-products group. This will make us number two in the industry."

Now there was work to do. "Find out everything you can about Warner and Swasey, everything you can on AMCA, and come in tomorrow with the number you think we should bid at," Agee said. He told Svec, Jacobson, Donnelly and Panny to do the same. The next morning everyone gathered in Agee's office with their numbers. Mine was $65 per share, not too high, not too low. The consensus of the group was to make an offer of $70. Agee conveyed our decision to Lehman Brothers, who was doing our bidding. The next day AMCA came back with $75, essentially a drop dead offer. Seventy-five had been the maximum over which we weren't prepared to go, which meant that AMCA had made a good bid. That distressed everyone. Bendix might have to drop out of the running. Again, Agee gathered us all in his office. "I want you to write down what you think we should bid, if at all," he said.

I wrote "$83" but on my slip of paper, I scribbled, "But if you're going to do it, do it now. Don't wait a minute. Don't let them think we're wavering." Agee read the notes silently and then left the room, a knowing glance to me. In a few minutes he was back. "I put in a bid for eighty-three dollars," he said, looking around the room and stopping his gaze at me. Jackpot, I thought. Now it was merely a matter of waiting. The ball was in AMCA's court.

Agee tried to keep things calm. "Now let's not get crazy about this," he said. "Let's just think about the consequences either way—win or lose." An hour and a half later, the call came in over the squawk box. AMCA had dropped out of the bidding. Warner and Swasey was ours. There were cheers and sighs of relief all around. The whole crew—Svec, Jacobson, Donnelly, even Panny—was caught up in the excitement of the moment. Craig Smith called to thank Agee for saving his company from the hostile raid. Agee ordered up champagne and everyone made toasts. It was as close a feeling of true comradeship as I'd ever had in those rooms.

"You see I take your advice seriously," Agee told me the next morning. I always got flustered when he praised me like this. It was more fun when his compliments were indirect. "So what do you have for my next assignment?" I said, cutting him short. "Oh, a little project," he said, taking a long, vertically folded sheet of paper out of his vest pocket. I could tell by his tone it was something I wasn't going to like. "Is it fluff?" I asked. Fluff was editing speeches, seeing too many representatives of charitable organizations and taking minutes—"women's work" as opposed to strategy, finance and production planning, the things in which I wanted to become proficient. My quota was about one piece of fluff for every three pieces of real work. "Okay, what is it?" I asked.

"David Maxey and PR wrote this speech for me to give tomorrow night for the sales convention of Fram automotive." Maxey was an outside consultant and another Idahoan Agee had hired to work on speeches and other press-related matters, and Fram was a Bendix automotive subsidiary. "It's not very good. Think you could take it home and fix it up tonight?" "Sure," I said. I was due for some fluff anyway. I read the speech in the bath that night, hoping it wouldn't be so bad that I would have to rewrite it. No such luck. It was terrible. A real Chamber of Commerce job. "It's because of your help, your loyalty and your devotion that Bendix is what it is today...." etc. etc. etc.

I considered leaving it alone. I could tell Agee, "It's fine. Go with it. They'll love you anyway." Which was probably true. But I couldn't. I was too much of a perfectionist and I cared how Agee looked. I didn't want to see him up there in front of all those automotive men uttering platitudes. I started working at nine and had the speech practically rewritten by 1 A.M. Just after dawn, I called Marie, one of Agee's two secretaries, and asked her if she could come in at seven to type up the new speech. She agreed, and by ten Agee had a fresh speech in his hands. Attached to the new version was a copy of the old with a note penned in: "The next time you need 'a little editing,' how about giving me a little more than 24 hours' notice?"

I wasn't particularly happy writing speeches, but I was more disturbed by Agee's next request. "You know Kathy's really having trouble doing her college applications and she thought maybe one night she could come over and you could give her a hand?" "What?" I said. This was no fair. Out of bounds. Foul play. "Look, you don't have to but I'd really appreciate it. I talk so much about how talented you are. When I mentioned that your first job out of college had been in the admissions office at Wellesley, she really perked up." What could I say? No? "No," I said but Agee looked distressed. He said he was really worried that her board scores would keep her out of the better schools and didn't want to disappoint his daughter. He told me that his friend and predecessor at Bendix, W. Michael Blumenthal, had already written her recommendations and with his pull as a trustee at Princeton she just needed a little help on the application side. All she needed was the essays. I knew it would be more dangerous to yield on this than on fluff, but I didn't want to sound mean. "Okay," I said. "Once. Just once."

I ended up spending three nights a week with Kathy for several weeks. Always on the nights when I was most tired her blue Mustang would be parked in front of my house. I tried to keep our sessions short and impersonal but that proved impossible. She wanted more than just help in writing, as discussions about the content for her essays made clear. "What disturbs you most about your life?" was the leading question in one of the essays. "My parents' relationship and the way my father treats me," Kathy suggested would be the most honest answer. "Why doesn't he pay more attention to Mom instead of his job? Why don't they talk with each other at the dinner table? Why is he so restrictive about what I want to do socially? Why can't they just work out their differences instead of always putting Sue or me in the center of it all?"

None of this surprised me. Everyone at Bendix knew that life at the Agee's was less than idyllic. I'd seen enough evidence of this back in the days of the pension analysis. Agee had invited Svec and me to join a group of others from Bendix and stop in at his mountain retreat in Idaho where he was taking his annual one-week vacation. I thought it was unusual for him to want company during his one week of summer vacation, but apparently it was common practice. According to his daughter, he always had people from Bendix come out whenever he had to be at home alone. Obviously Diane resented it. "Hope you folks can find something to eat at this gargantuan buffet," he joked, pointing to the meager luncheon fare of cold salads still in their delicatessen containers. The house hadn't been prepared for guests and the table hadn't even been set. It was as if Diane had said to Agee, "They're your friends; you clean up!" Agee was clearly embarrassed. And so were we. Still, I didn't know what to say to Kathy. Obviously, it wasn't my place to take sides. So I did what any "wise," "mature," twenty-eight-year-old woman would do—I empathized and assured her it would get better. I didn't know if it helped, but she did get into Princeton.

The only time I had real doubts about my job was on Friday nights. At five, the place emptied out. "Goodnight," the secretaries would sing out. "Goodnight," I would respond in my cheerful, businesslike voice. "Are you sure you wouldn't like to come out for a drink with us?" a few would ask. "No, thank you," I'd say. Usually, the only stragglers were Agee and me, but even he left by seven. Sometimes I worked late to avoid the prospect of going home. Where was I going? To an apartment stock-piled with Campbell's Chunky Soups and unopened cartons? It was hardly a home. It was always at these times that I'd try to call Bo. I'd phone the apartment but he never seemed to be there. The phone would just ring and ring. What am I doing with my life anyway? I'd ask myself. I didn't have an answer.

There was always Vic Tanny's. Occasionally on a Friday night I'd drag my weary body into the exercise room and there, amid gaggles of women trying to shed excess weight, I worked out until I couldn't move from sheer exhaustion. Back in my empty apartment, I'd look at the clock and wonder if it was too late to call my mom. "Hi, Mom?" "Why, hello, Mary. How are you?" "Oh, fine." It usually took her only a few minutes to root out the truth. "Mary Elizabeth, how are you, really?" "Lonely." "Well, I don't wonder you are. It's that lifestyle of yours. I think you ought to make some changes pretty soon." And I knew she was right. In the back of my mind a little idea was taking hold that after a year of valuable experience as Agee's executive assistant, I could leave. On that plan, I still had six months' duty.

Meanwhile, Agee and I were developing a more comfortable working relationship. In the beginning I was too much in awe of him to let down my guard. But as the months wore on, I felt more and more at ease. He had his foibles—and I was starting to notice them—so I didn't mind so much if he saw mine. Besides, I sensed he respected me. His phenomenal rise from the University of Idaho to Boise-Cascade to Bendix put him pretty much in a class by himself, but when he saw me with the same energy, the same diligence and the same spunk—"fire in the belly," he called it—as he had when he was my age,

I think he thought he'd met his match. This made me confident, and I was able to joke with him. "So what's your opinion on this one, Cunningham?" he'd challenge me. "Oh, I think it's full of prunes, Agee," I'd say, and we'd both crack up.

December was strategy time. And here was where my main interest lay. Even from the first talk we had ever had that day at the Waldorf, Agee had held out to me the possibility of my devoting most of my time to strategic planning and helping him reshape Bendix. All year I'd been analyzing 10Ks and poring through financial reports, looking for companies Bendix might buy into or subsidiaries from which the company might want to divest itself. The overall strategy of course wasn't mine—Agee had set down many of the parameters—but I knew my job was to pull it all together and give it shape and focus.

I knew Agee's main priorities were to get Bendix more heavily into high technology—beef up the aerospace and industrial-electronics divisions—and wean it of the over-dependence on the automobile industry. (Since automotive was the guts of Bendix, and home base for executives like Panny, this would naturally engender some resistance.) To move in this direction, Bendix had to both buy and sell. High-tech companies like Lockheed, maybe even Martin Marietta, were good potential acquisitions, and to fund those acquisitions, Bendix could sell off its natural-resource investment Asarco, and its natural resource subsidiary, the Bendix Forest Products Division. That and a few more sales would give us a war chest of about $800 million for the coming acquisitions.

I put all this on paper and added a few improvements of my own. My main additions to the plan were on the management side. I knew that if Bendix wanted to move in a technically oriented direction, it had to adjust its management style. The company's control was too centralized and burdened with a lot of bureaucratic red tape invented by paper-pushing staff executives at headquarters. Sometimes it seemed that their job security resided in creating enough forms for others to fill out so that they always appeared busy. Computer wizards and high-tech engineers wouldn't be attracted to such a stifling environment, and Agee had heard too many complaints about the tight control of one of the most notorious of the Bendix paper generators—Bill Panny. Agee knew that entrepreneurs and technologists would do much better with a more flexible style of management. And this dovetailed with Agee's inclination to cut out wasteful overhead at head office and decentralize power out to the operating units. "Decentralization" became the watchword for these organizational changes. I also felt we needed to develop a more unified business focus for the analysts and investors on Wall Street. The pieces started fitting together like a mosaic. I could hardly wait for Christmas to write it all up.

Christmas? I'd hardly thought about it. The sight of Detroit getting ready for the holiday didn't exactly conjure up visions of sugarplums in my head. All the red and green lights in the world couldn't make that city bright! Bo called to see what, if anything, we should do about celebrating Christmas but I didn't know what to say. There didn't seem much point to our getting together. Besides, I wanted to go home. And "home" now meant New Hampshire, not New York. It would be quiet at my mother's house. Plenty of time to catch up on rest and work on strategy.

The day before I left, Agee stopped in to say goodbye.

"Hey, what am I going to do without your face around the office?" he said. I responded with a joke. "Yeah, and what am I going to do with ten days of uninterrupted time? No speeches. No papers. No 'C'mon, Mare, can you do just one more thing?'"

He smiled. "Have a great holiday," he said. "And I'll be eager to hear what you have to say about strategy when you get back."

# CHAPTER THREE

*When I was five and a* half, my mother left my father. I remember running up the stairway for the last time to get my doll and thinking, This is all my fault. I felt as if somehow I had caused their separation. I vowed from that day on that I would be good, so good that it would make up for this terrible thing I'd done.

We lived in Falmouth, Maine, for those first five and a half years of my life. My father's family had developed a prosperous construction business and our name was well known locally. We were in the upper echelons of Falmouth society, about as far up as the lace-curtain Irish could go. My father had gone to one of the finest preparatory schools in New England and then to Holy Cross College, but he was less interested in books than in having a good time. One of his brothers, the family's favorite child, was killed in a car accident during college, and my father began to drink heavily after that.

My mother met him at her senior prom. She was with another, quieter man, but who could resist my father's charm? They married but it was not a good match. The country-club, cocktail-party circuit didn't suit my mother, although it was my father's lifestyle that eventually drove her away. No one mentioned his name around the house again, except that each year I received a birthday card from him. At first, they were signed just "Love, Dad," then "Love, Dad and Shirley," and then, "Love, Dad, Shirley and Jeff"—so I gathered that somehow, somewhere, he had found himself another family and, hopefully, a better life.

As for my mother, it wasn't easy for a thirty-six-year-old woman to pick up and leave. Divorce was uncommon then and unheard of in most New England small towns, but my mother felt she had no other choice. She once made the comparison to a sinking raft. "If it's going down," she said, "it is better to at least save a few than lose all." With my older brother, John, who was then fifteen, my sister, Shirley, ten, and me and my baby brother, Frank, two and a half, Mother moved to Hanover, New Hampshire, knowing that our faithful relative, Father Bill, would help us. He offered to give her a hand with the task of putting her life back together again, finding a job and raising her four children. He arranged for us to live in a small apartment in the home of a professional social worker named Fran Lyng, a tiny little woman with a huge heart, until we could move into a house of our own.

It was quite an adjustment, moving from our expansive home in Casco Bay to a tiny three-room apartment. No longer did eating out mean lovely restaurants with fancy printed menus and silver spoons. Now it was hamburgers at the nearby A & W Drive-In. The change took its toll on everyone, but it was especially hard on my mother. I remember seeing her folding our laundry, crying. I had never seen her cry before. "What've I done to all of you?" she said when she saw me there. "Life is going to be so different from now on." "Don't worry, Mom," I told her. "It's going to be all right." And then, in my five-year-old's version of Catholic theology, I told her, "Because of what you've gone through, none of us will ever have to go through it. You've taught us all a lesson that will save us from this pain." I vowed from that day on I'd always be strong. I'd never show sadness or give her reason to think she'd done the wrong thing.

After six months at Fran Lyng's we moved. My mother was able to afford a new home for us. It was a pretty house, small and cozy and typically New England with its white clapboard siding and neat green shutters. Life seemed fairly peaceful then; the past, just an unpleasant blur.

I stayed pretty close to home those first few months. I had developed a case of asthma, and rather than risk an attack romping around, I read my Childcraft books and played in the yard. My mother was busy helping John and Shirley adjust to their new life—the move was much harder on them, as they were old enough to understand its significance—which left me in charge of little Frank. I was the protective older sister and he was the tagalong little brother, but really, we were the best of friends. There was only one other person I loved being with as much, and that was Father Bill.

I never missed having a father because on all the important occasions Father Bill was there. Report cards, first communion, graduation day. He was my conscience and my teacher but he was also my friend.

Father Bill was the parish priest of Hanover, which included the college campus as well. Everyone knew him and revered him. He was close to all the families in Hanover but because of his relationship to us, he took a special interest. And, I like to think, a special interest in me.

My favorite times were in the rock garden in front of

our house. I didn't want to upset my mother, so it was Father Bill to whom I would pour out all my fears and needs. "You're not alone, Mary Elizabeth," he'd say. "Others have had this experience too. Your special task is to set an example to show others how to overcome the difficult moments." Or, "Don't get too absorbed in yourself. Think of all those suffering in this world, without enough food or clothing or shelter. Their pain is much greater because many of them do not have faith." I drank in every word. I read about the lives of saints and how they sacrificed of themselves, and this further fueled my desire to be good. While my brother Frank read about the Hardy Boys, I immersed myself in stories about Teresa of Avila and Joan of Arc.

With the lives of saints on my mind, it was a bit difficult for me ever to be "silly" or just fool around with the other kids. But this was hardly a problem at Sacred Heart School in Lebanon, New Hampshire, where I was treated as special by the nuns: Sister Geraldine, who taught me piano, Sister Carlotta, a cheerful, roly-poly nun who was my first-grade teacher, and tall, handsome Sister Veronica, who never talked down to me, but treated me as an adult. The special treatment was partly because I was a good child and partly because of Father Bill. "This is Father Bill's niece," was the way I was always introduced. And on May Day, I was the one who was chosen to place the crown on the statue of the Blessed Mother.

My attempts at sainthood didn't always win admiration. Even my older sister, Shirley, would ask impatiently, "Why do you have to be so good?" She was five years my senior and had borne the brunt of my father's indifference. She wasn't about to be close to me; I was her annoying freckle-faced little strawberry-blond-haired sister, whom everyone viewed as "so good." I wanted so badly for Shirley to love me. One night when she was out at a play rehearsal, I went into her closet and carefully picked out what I thought was a beautiful outfit for her to wear the next day. I took her favorite turquoise sweater down from the shelf and found a matching blue skirt in the back of the closet. In her bureau I found her best underwear, her cleanest socks and set everything out neatly on her bed. I climbed into bed that night happy in the anticipation of how pleased she'd be with my surprise for her. I couldn't wait for her to come home, wake me up and thank me. When she returned home and saw what I'd done, she was far from pleased. She woke me to tell me so. In my zeal to show her my love, I'd overlooked the value that older sisters place on privacy. And once again I had to learn the hard way that good intentions aren't always enough.

Most of the children at Sacred Heart lived in Lebanon and walked home from school, but I had to wait for my mother, who now worked as a secretary at the Catholic Student Center. Usually, if she was late, the nuns would invite me to wait in the convent. I loved it in there. They fed me milk and cookies and let me into the places no one else was allowed to go—the kitchen and even the nun's private chapel. It was so peaceful. I was entranced, wandering through this sacred domain. Here I was on holy ground, and yet I was standing in a room as practical as a kitchen. It was magical, this merger of the ordinary and the sublime. Even the smell reflected the mixture: a combination of Lestoil and incense.

Occasionally, if my mother was busy, Father Bill would pick me and my sister up. I loved these car rides home. Father Bill would buy us a Fudgesicle or some other treat and we would tell him about our day. He always asked questions and I was always thrilled to supply the right answers. And when I did well, he looked pleased.

In fourth grade, after three semesters of straight As, Father Bill told me that if I earned straight As the final semester, he'd take me to New York with him on business. He was working to raise money to build a Catholic student center on campus. I met his challenge and earned my first trip to New York City. We went to the Top of the Sixes for dinner that night, and the next morning to the University Club, where I was introduced to a roomful of successful businessmen interested in Father Bill's project. (He had taught me how to shake hands the night before.) Everything I saw impressed me—the dinner, the speeches, the roomful of grown-up men. But mostly I was impressed with Father Bill. Here was this good human being, a priest and a holy person, and yet how easily he mingled with all these important men. Perhaps the quiet, ethereal life of a nun had its appeal, but the real world, at least the glimpse of it I caught in New York that weekend with Father Bill, definitely seemed more exciting.

It was after dinner one night when all of us were playing our usual roles. My older brother, John, was telling jokes. Shirley was helping my mother clear the dishes. And Father Bill, who occasionally had dinner with us, was quizzing me on my catechism as my younger brother, Frank, looked on.

"What is grace?" Father Bill asked.

"Grace is a supernatural gift of God bestowed on us through the merits of Jesus Christ."

"How many kinds of grace are there?"

"There are two kinds of grace: sanctifying grace and actual grace."

"What is sanctifying grace?"

"Sanctifying grace is that grace which confers on our souls a new life. . . ."

I thought I was doing very well but Father Bill's eyes were not responding. "Mary Elizabeth," he said. "Your answers are too glib. You aren't learning to ask enough questions, to think things through."

It was decided that night that I should switch to public school. I didn't like this decision. I was happy at Sacred Heart. I felt safe and comfortable there and I liked the nuns. Besides, the public-school kids frightened me. But Father Bill and my mother held their ground. That fall I entered fifth grade at Hanover Elementary School.

The public-school system in Hanover had an interesting mix of students. There were the precocious achievement-oriented children of the Dartmouth College professors and Hanover professionals, and the less sophisticated sons and daughters of the local farmers. I got along well with both groups. I felt comfortable sitting at any table in the lunchroom, which many students did not. But when it came to picking up the phone on Saturday morning and saying to one of my classmates, "How would you like to get together?" I didn't have anyone to call.

Part of my problem was that I was fast turning into a junior Father Bill. "How would you feel if they did that to you?" I'd ask whenever one of the students picked on another. Or, in choosing sides for sports (I was considered a good athlete and usually chosen quickly), I'd say to the last student left, whom nobody wanted, "Here, you take my place." Some of my classmates thought this a bit strange. And part of it was that I was such a serious child.

My nickname "The Judge" seemed to stick because I could discuss the origins of good and evil with anyone, but when it came to fooling around, I didn't quite know how.

Not that I had had much practice. Dinner at the Cunninghams was not a frivolous affair. While other families chatted over the latest movie in town, we discussed theology and the travails of Sir Thomas More. Nor was much of a premium placed on being the belle of the ball. My mother was not a social woman. Cocktail parties and social gatherings reminded her of her unhappy days in Falmouth, and besides, she was too busy. She had a house to keep and children to raise, and her job, and these occupied most of her time. She was not a woman who suffered fools lightly.

She and Father Bill were the arbiters of my social life, and it was decided that one movie every two weeks was sufficient night life for junior high. In seventh grade, when the entire school went on a trip to Washington, D.C., I was one of two students not allowed to go. "You never know what goes on during these trips," my mother warned. "Seventh grade is too soon. High school is time enough."

Still, it pained her to think she was holding me back. I remember going to my first dance in seventh grade. The idea of going to a dance didn't alarm me so much as the prospect of making small talk. I knew from listening to other people that they didn't talk about the things we discussed at home, and yet I had no idea how to talk about anything else. The art of light social banter was unknown to me. My mother wasn't much of a raconteur and when the subject was trivia, neither was Father Bill. In my usual earnest style, I made a list. I wrote down all the topics I thought normal people talked about: the weather, the teachers at school, the neighborhood.

The morning after the party, my mother came quietly into my room. She sat at the edge of my bed and touched my hand, as she did whenever she wanted to wake me. I could tell there was something on her mind. "Did you have a good time at the party, dear?" she asked. "Yes, I really did," I said, starting to ramble on to convince her. "There was a really good band and the decorations were lovely and I saw all my friends." "Did you have enough to talk about?" she asked. "Yes, I did," I told her, wondering what all this was leading up to. "I found your list," she said, looking at me and then at the piece of paper in her hand. "Have I really made it that hard for you?" she asked.

The bane of my existence that year was that I was one of the last girls to start wearing a bra. Even flat-chested girls were wearing training bras, and although I had started to develop, I was still wearing a T-shirt at the end of seventh grade. I knew I needed to approach my mother but I couldn't fathom how to ask. I was neatening up my underwear drawer one day when my mother walked into my room. "What are you doing, Mary Elizabeth?" "Oh, I'm just straightening up my underwear and things, you know, my T-shirts and such." Mother was about to go on her way when I looked at her and said, "Mom, there's something I want..." But I couldn't finish the sentence, I was so embarrassed. I started to cry. When she finally got to the bottom of what was bothering me, she said, "I was wondering when you were going to ask. Come on. Let's go right now and get you one." But I couldn't go just then. I needed time to recover.

\* \* \*

It wasn't the same between Father Bill and me after puberty. There were no more generous hugs. He seemed to be more comfortable with Frank. I regretted the loss, and a part of me regretted being a woman as well. As for sex, my impressions of that weren't very good. The only close example of a husband-wife relationship I had had was that of my parents, and that obviously hadn't been very good. In contrast, my mother and Father Bill had a solid and happy relationship, and yet it was totally platonic. Marriage never seemed an ideal state to me, as I was reminded every time I had to check off the "divorced" box on forms I had to fill out for school.

I'd had glimmers of sexual feelings. At a party one night, I remember dancing to something soft and low by the rock band Blood, Sweat and Tears. It felt so good to dance close. I don't remember the boy I was with but I do remember that as soon as the music stopped I decided I'd better go home.

I worked very hard through junior high school. At first I studied hard to incur favor, but as I got older, it became a convenient excuse to avoid going out. I brought home As, which pleased my mother, but they never seemed enough for Father Bill. If I were to have nine As and one B, he'd say, "How do you explain that one B?" If I had all As, I imagined he would say, "Now let's see if you can do that next year."

But it wasn't only my grades that mattered to Father Bill. He would always focus on my "spiritual report card" as well. "Were you kind to your classmates?" he would ask. "Did you encourage someone who didn't do as well as you?" "Yes," I said, but I wondered why he didn't ask similar questions of Frank. "Frank needs good grades so he can get into a good college and support a family,"

Father Bill said. The implication was that I wouldn't need them. My role was to have a child who could get all the As. And besides, for me to enjoy getting As was egotistical; for Frank it was practical. As I understood the system, Frank was to be judged by the grading system here on earth. But for me, some higher authority was keeping score.

My life as a saint ended that year. I committed a sin, and the enormity of it haunted me so that I never dared try anything like it again. It was my last year in junior high school. I had just turned fifteen. Many of my friends were already dating but I only had boys as friends. Most of them were people I'd met at school or at the hockey rink, where I'd stop by to check up on my brother Frank, who was on the school hockey team. It was there that I'd see Michael, Phil and Fred—the "Irish clan"—and they'd seek my counsel on whom they should date. "Hey, Mare, who should I ask to the movies?" Phil would say, or "Mare, who should I take to the party Saturday night?" Mike might ask. But it didn't dawn on any of them to ever ask me. It wasn't just that I was shy and virtuous. Anyone who asked me out risked being interviewed by Father Bill, and that was an ordeal few adolescent boys cared to face. With only a few exceptions, the only boys who did dare ask me out were the ones who didn't know any better.

One of these boys was Mark. He'd spoken to me while waiting for the ski lift several times and several times had asked me out. I always tried to avoid the question by suggesting we go out in a group or do something "safe," like work on a project after school. Then one day, standing outside the lodge, he asked me if I'd like to see a new film called *The Pawnbroker*. My mother restricted the kind of movies I was allowed to see, and just once I wanted to see something more racy than *My Fair Lady*. Besides, I thought, who was I to think I was too good for Mark? "Okay," I said, which nearly caused Mark to fall out of his skis.

The whole affair was cloaked in secrecy and sin from the start. Since it was out of the question for me to ask my mother if I could go, I arranged to go on the sly. I told my mother I was going to a friend's sleepover party, which I was, and told Mark to pick me up there an hour later. At seven-thirty Friday night, Mom dropped me off at the party, and at eight-thirty, Mark picked me up and we went to the theater. No sooner than fifteen minutes into the film, there was a disturbing nude scene. A sign from God. I knew I should leave. I was terribly uncomfortable but not half as uncomfortable as Mark, who felt responsible for bringing me there. "I can't do this to you," he said. "Want to go?" I nodded and he took me back to the party. The next day I came home and saw Father Bill's car parked in the driveway. I knew something was wrong. He never just dropped by without a formal announcement.

I walked in the house. He was sitting in the living room, but all I could see was his profile, à la Hitchcock. I went and stood before him. "Do you have something to tell me, Mary Elizabeth?" he said, gazing at me with his steel-blue eyes. "Yes, sir," I said. "Do you want to tell me what it is?" I told him. After trimming me back for what I had done, he said, "Do you know what you've destroyed by what you've done?" I stared down at the floor. "No, Father Bill. I don't." "You've destroyed the faith I had in you. It will be difficult to believe anything you tell me again." I remained still. "Father Bill?" I said after a few minutes. "Yes?" he said. "Do you ever think I'll get your trust back again?" He looked at me long and hard, "Yes," he said. "But it will take time."

I never did anything that scandalous again, but my good behavior made me somewhat of a pariah. I was invited to parties but the tacit understanding was that I wouldn't go, or I'd show up for a few hours and then leave before the lights were dimmed. I could sense that people felt I put a damper on things.

The years between 1966 and 1969 were difficult ones in which to be going to high school. It was the end of one era and the start of another. I was old-fashioned even by fifties standards, let alone in the age of the Rolling Stones. Attitudes toward drugs and sex were changing swiftly everywhere, but in a university community like Hanover, the "revolution" hit town with even more force. The reaction on the part of people like my mother was to pull back. While everyone was going off in the direction of revolution, I was placed under even stricter controls. People were having sex and using drugs, and my idea of sin was "making out," a term that by 1968 was virtually obsolete.

When I was in high school, the relationship between my mother and me grew more strained. Our long talks and laughter became more infrequent. I started to resent the kind of life I felt she had inflicted on me. All the parents of the kids in the honors classes, which I was in, the doctors and lawyers and university professors, socialized. It was a social town. But my mother didn't participate in any of that. We weren't part of any social network. I tried to put myself in situations in which I could "help" people—volunteer work, hospital work—

any way in which I could be with people, and yet have my "service" put a distance between us. But mostly I would stay in my room and study. I felt safe up there, surrounded by my books and papers, with my readings in history and philosophy to comfort me. Even at midnight my light would still be on. But part of me resented this cloistered life.

"Why do you spend so many hours on your homework, Mary Elizabeth?" my mother would sometimes ask. "I really enjoy it," I'd tell her. And it was true. I found solace in my work. But often I was tempted to tell her what was also true: "There's such a gap between me and other kids because of what you think is 'acceptable' behavior that it's just easier to sit up here and work"; or, "Why go to a party at seven-thirty when you'll only have to be picked up at ten-thirty while everyone else stays till midnight? It makes more sense to stay home and study." I wouldn't tell her this. At all cost I wanted to avoid fighting or arguments of any kind. And yet I knew she was concerned. It pained her to see me work so hard. She wanted me to have fun, only her idea of fun was a little out-of-date. She bought me a party dress once because she thought it would help me have "fun." A party dress! In 1969!

Senior year at Hanover High School was a wasted year. Most of the girls were lost to college students and most of the boys were immersed in sports or experimenting with drugs. I steered clear of drugs, and as for college men, they were out of the question. I wasn't even allowed in any buildings on campus except for the Hopkins Center, where I took my piano lessons and gave recitals. It was my mother who made the rules, but when she needed the heavy artillery, she'd call in Father Bill. Usually I could appeal to him, but not on the issue of dating college men—he was the one who had heard the confessions of college men for twenty-five years.

"But all my friends are going to college fraternity parties," I argued. "You can't go out with college men, Mary Elizabeth, until your first year in college." With my fine analytical mind, sharpened by all those years of debate and catechism, I fought back. "What changes so magically between senior year in high school and freshman year at college that means you'll allow me then and not now?" "Then you'll be a college student, not a townie." He had a point.

The end of my senior year, an exception was finally made. The worthy suitor was a friendly red-haired football player and pre-medical student named Tom. I had met him after Mass one Sunday at the Catholic Student Center. From then on, we frequently discussed Father Bill's sermons. Occasionally we ventured onto topics of a less theological bent. "I guess a girl like you would never go out with someone like me," Tom said during the course of one of our lengthier chats. "Why not?" I asked. "Because of this," he said, pointing to a scarred lip. "I never noticed," I said, which was true. I hadn't. I was never very mindful of how people looked. Tom was so amazed at this that we started talking and had one of those wonderfully adolescent conversations in which we confessed our insecurities and reassured each other about them. Before we parted, he asked, "Would you like to go out sometime?" I felt I would but I knew I'd have to ask Father Bill first. Tom had already taken care of that. He'd asked Father Bill and Father Bill had agreed.

Our plans were to go to a party on campus given at Beta Theta Pi, the fraternity house to which Tom belonged. Beta Theta Pi was considered the jock fraternity, but I had no idea what the term implied. Besides, why worry? I trusted Tom. He got along well with my younger brother, Frank, and he was respected by Father Bill. What better credentials? He came by my house, where he greeted my mom, and then the two of us were off. It was fifteen minutes to the campus and we decided to walk since it was such a beautiful spring night. Tom looked handsome in his sports jacket and I told him so. He complimented me on the way I looked too, but I could tell something wasn't right. He said it as if he weren't quite sure. I wore a white Villager skirt, white flats and an orange-and-white-striped turtleneck—I thought orange-and-white stripes were pretty racy compared to my parochial-school plaids. Had it been 1963, I would have been dressed perfectly for the occasion, but in 1969 I looked a little out-of-date. "Prim" was the word for it.

As we approached fraternity row, I could hear the loud music. The lawns were littered with discarded plastic cups. When we arrived at the frat house, one of the brothers opened the door, and from the hallway I caught a glimpse of what was going on inside. Women were wearing bikinis and men were putting iridescent body paint on them. All this under strobe lights and neon. I was stunned. One look at my face, and Tom knew what I was thinking: How could you do this to me? You're betraying Father Bill.

Upset at my reaction, he took my arm and led me back down the street. "Would you like to go for a walk?" he asked. "Yes," I said. As soon as we were out of earshot of the house, my eyes welled up with tears. I was so overcome by what I had seen that I started to cry. I also felt confused. I knew I had failed Tom, and yet I couldn't have gone inside. It was as if I were trying to cross a bridge from the Church to fraternity row, and I just couldn't. He put his arm around me and started to comfort me. "Feel better?" "Yes," I nodded. "Would you like to go back and listen to some music?" he said after a little while. "That other stuff is probably over by now." I uttered a weak "Fine" and followed him back. There was still a little body painting going on, but we steered clear of that and went into another room where there was music and dancing. I warmed up and by the end of the evening even rolled up the sleeves of my orange-and-white top— my concession to being casual.

In April of my senior year I was blizzarded with college acceptances. I'd been admitted to Wellesley and other top schools, but Father Bill and my mother thought it best that I go to Newton College of the Sacred Heart. Shirley had gone there, and besides, I had been admitted on a full scholarship. It didn't occur to me to question their judgment, although when I arrived at Sacred Heart, I soon realized my mistake. I was at the top of my class and became class president, too, but the social life was not to my liking. It was after my first mixer—the appropriate term for the rough-and-tumble parties that passed for college dances—that I made up my mind. Wellesley, with its pastoral campus and cloistered libraries, beckoned. The irony was that had Father Bill and my mother truly understood the motivation for my decision, I'm sure they'd have approved. But I knew they wouldn't. Father Bill thought, three years at Wellesley and I might lose my soul. Without discussing my decision with either of them, I applied for a transfer to Wellesley, and the day I received word that I'd gotten in, I knew that my independence from home had begun.

# CHAPTER FOUR

*Having worked so hard at* Bendix for the first six months, I was only too happy to come home to Hanover on Christmas for a vacation. However, it was not much of a rest. I spent most of my holiday writing strategy. I also had a disturbing reunion with Bo. He drove up to surprise me December 28, the day of our fifth wedding anniversary, but we felt so uncomfortable around each other that he left the following morning. We both knew it was over, but neither of us wanted to admit it.

I devoted the rest of my vacation to Bendix strategy. I worked right up through New Year's Eve, taking only short breaks to have champagne and celebrate. I finished my report on New Year's Day. Twenty single-spaced pages. On the cover I typed: "To Bill Agee. From Mary Cunningham." It was the first time in five years I had left off the "Gray." It felt good, like finding an old friend.

Monday morning I was the first one back at Bendix. It felt so good to be back in the Bendix building. No Bo. No conflict. No emotions. My memo was on Agee's desk at 6:30 A.M. I guess he read it sometime during the day because at 5 P.M. he walked into my office and said, "Mary, that's our strategy."

January and February of 1980 were strategy time. Agee

held meetings with the executive staff round the clock. At the close of business he'd send us off with a familiar request: "Now I want you all to go home, think about what we've discussed and come back tomorrow morning with some ideas." Naturally I was the only one who took the request seriously. I would spend all night poring over documents and come in the next morning with a thirty-page memo drafted on what I thought needed to be done. "Does anyone have anything to say about what we discussed yesterday?" Silence. Then Mary would raise her hand. "I do." It was tiresome always being the good kid in class. The more I did, the more impatient Agee was with his staff. And the more impatient they became with me. "Even a twenty-eight-year-old woman can do more analysis and show more energy than you seasoned executives who've been here ten or fifteen years," he'd say. I voiced strong objection to the "even"—did he expect less of twenty-eight-year-olds or women?—but I didn't mind the praise.

Almost every week there were meetings at Lehman Brothers in New York. Bendix had switched from Morgan Stanley in the fall and was now working almost exclusively with Lehman Brothers chairman Pete Peterson and his staff. The Bendix team made these trips in Bendix's private aircraft—usually Svec, Agee and I in one and Panny and Jacobson in the other. It was considered prudent to split up the senior staff in case of a crash. I was glad I wouldn't have to spend my last hours with Panny. On board we conferred. "Airplane talk," Agee called it— the most productive kind, since no one could interrupt with phone calls or visitors. In the pre-Mary days I think it had also been the time when Agee and his executives had their heart-to-hearts, but my presence seemed to have cramped their styles. Jacobson, Svec and the rest of the crew were always formal, even guarded, when I was around. Even in the suite we periodically stayed in at the Waldorf—each of us had rooms that opened on to one large common living room that was perfect for impromptu conferences—they treated me as if I had the plague. I had the feeling they imagined I reported their every move back to the chairman. If only they could have understood how awkward I felt in these situations.

Those day-long visits were usually hectic. We were now getting into the brass tacks of strategy. It would have been nice if the Bendix crew could have presented a united front, but we didn't; people had their own not-so-hidden agendas. Panny, who'd risen from the ranks of automotive and who made no effort to adjust his informal title, "bureaucratic czar," was not likely to favor any plan that pared down automotive and decentralized control. Jacobson was beginning to make noises about wanting to scale back his job at Bendix to consulting relationship exclusively and clearly wasn't giving the strategy his all. Svec was showing his true colors as a numbers man—and a rather conservative one at that. "Show me the price-earnings ratio and I'll tell you what I think," he'd say—which was fine, except that his numbers and those of the people at Lehman Brothers didn't always quite jibe. And Svec insisted on having the last word. Several colleagues had mentioned that Svec was a frustrated investment banker and just wanted to one-up the people at Lehman Brothers. In all of this I probably appeared to Agee as a lone voice of reason. I had no ax to grind and, having been mentored by him, I spoke the same language that he did.

As we were ironing out the fine strokes of the Bendix

strategy, Agee received a handful of tickets to the Lake Placid Winter Olympics. Apparently he and Lehman Brothers chairman Pete Peterson planned to do a little business on the slopes. "Mare," he said, "why don't you plan a guest list of the people who should come, and why don't you keep a ticket for yourself too." "What?" I asked. I couldn't see myself tagging along with both those corporate chieftains and their families. "I'm not sure I can do that." "Why?" Agee asked. "There's going to be plenty of business conducted. Bendix doesn't pay for these tickets so that its executives can just have a good time." I supposed this was the winter analogy of "golf-course work." As a professional, I knew this was an excellent opportunity to get to know Peterson and be in on crucial details of the strategy talks. On the other hand, I couldn't quite see myself on vacation with two chief executives and their families. What role would I play? Executive assistant or family friend? Bright young strategist or Nanny?

My speculations weren't far off the mark. I discussed strategy with Agee and Peterson, but for almost everyone else I served as some sort of Ann Landers. Pete Peterson, recently divorced, asked me for advice on how to deal with his teenage daughter. She wasn't adjusting very well to her father's divorce and was not making life easy for Joan Cooney, the companion Peterson had brought with him to Lake Placid. Kathy Agee poured out more of her problems with her father, and even Diane took me aside and asked me for advice. I doubt that if I were a man I would have been made into a confidante like this, but as a lone woman, people naturally assumed I would have a sympathetic ear. And what could I say? It seemed hardhearted to say no, and unbusinesslike to say yes. Ultimately the whole trip made me feel uneasy but for entirely different reasons. I didn't like the glimpse I'd caught of these people's personal lives. So many high-powered businessmen didn't seem to have particularly happy personal lives.

Back in Southfield, strategy the main issue on the agenda but it wasn't the only one. As it was heating up, so were other things. Ronald Reagan was gearing up his campaign for the Presidency and Agee was high on the list of businessmen to be wooed. He was young, influential and had a liberal stand on ERA, which few others in the Reagan camp could boast. In late February and early March, the calls started coming more frequently from Jude Wanniski; by April there were calls from Congressman Jack Kemp of New York and Senator Paul Laxalt of Nevada. How did Agee react? He was torn. His head was immersed in Bendix strategy but his heart was at least in part starting to beat to a different drummer. Potomac-itis, I called it.

Naturally, I was carried along. I was becoming speech writer and press aide extraordinaire. In the spring, I found myself writing speeches with national themes—Social Security, defense spending, government waste and the technological race with Japan. I wasn't so pleased with my new role. Getting mentored by Agee on Bendix was one thing, but I didn't know how I felt about being tutored by him on the finer points of GOP politics. I had always liked Ronald Reagan—I thought he'd make a nice next-door neighbor—but I wasn't sure how I felt about him as a future President. And yet, there I was, furthering the cause of supply-side economics.

March was the month of the four-minute spot. When CBS approached Agee to join heavyweights such as Milton Friedman, Bill Simon and Congressman Henry Reuss to critique Carter's latest budget plans, he was prepared to speak out. Inevitably, Agee turned to me for assistance on the writing.

"Sure," I said when I was informed of the task. That weekend I said what I could about the Laffer curve, but my heart wasn't in it and Agee could tell. "Can't you make it a little more punchy? You know, give it some verve." He called me every two or three hours that Saturday afternoon, at twelve, at two, and at five. At 2 P.M. on Sunday, I finally came up with a version he liked. "Great," he said. But I didn't think so.

I was starting to grow weary of my job. I knew it would be over in June, but I didn't know where I would go from there. As far back as January and February Agee had started talking to me about my next move. "How would you like to be a corporate officer?" he casually mentioned one day. He knew I would. This was not without precedent. Bernard Winograd, who was twenty-five when he worked for Mike Blumenthal as executive assistant, was promoted shortly thereafter to director of public relations, and then, at the age of twenty-eight, was named corporate treasurer. There was considerable protest because of Winograd's age, but this was quickly quashed in a special meeting called by Agee to defend Winograd's capabilities. This was, after all, Agee's style; he believed in the merit system and championed the talent of younger people. Bette Howe, because she concentrated on what was generally regarded as fluff—philanthropic appeals, Bendix public image, and social events—went only as far as director of corporate personnel—not an executive-level job. But Agee had let me know that I'd done my job better than either Winograd or Howe and so I expected an executive-level job. "I've been talking to several members of the board of directors and they're delighted with the idea. They think you deserve it." "Thanks," I said. "And I think the best place to put you is in human resources or public relations," he added.

That was the part I didn't like. I kept trying to move away from the direction of personnel and PR, and I certainly didn't like the idea of following in the footsteps of Bette Howe, who by now had moved from public relations to personnel. "That's not quite the direction I had in mind," I said, but it was hard to argue with Agee. He said he needed someone "really good" to reorganize and motivate the department. Fair enough. After all, the department had struggled through five different heads in five years. But each one had been forced out one way or another— not a big selling point for the job. "Can't I reorganize it without taking the title?" I asked. "Well, let's wait and see."

Partly on the strength of the four-minute spot, the Reagan aides had another request. They asked that Agee accept the honor of providing the five-minute introduction of Reagan at the Detroit Economic Club luncheon scheduled for May. Too many business leaders still viewed Reagan as an ex-actor, and a strong endorsement from someone as respected as Agee might bring them around. This was heady stuff. Reagan's appearance was considered crucial, coming one month before the Michigan primary and two months before the GOP convention, which was to be held in Detroit that summer. Pete Hanaford, a close Reagan adviser, also asked Agee to put in writing his thoughts about what Reagan should say in his talk. Naturally Agee turned to me to work on the project. I thought Hanaford was just going to use the ideas as suggestions but when

I sat down to hear Reagan's speech at the luncheon on May 15, there they were—my words coming out of Reagan's mouth. A good portion of his speech was my statement, in some parts word for word. Agee called me up afterward and introduced me to Reagan.

If this was a thrill to me, it was a greater one to the folks back home. Practically every week I'd call my mother with reports of some new person I'd met. "Hey, Mom, guess whose hand I shook today? Ronald Reagan's. And Jack Kemp and Paul Laxalt stopped by to talk." She always enjoyed these phone calls. Here was a chance to see the faces behind the names she was seeing in the local *Valley News*.

On the other hand, it was also a little disconcerting. It was one thing to hear the chairman of a corporation speaking one's words; it was another to hear them coming from the lips of a possible future President of the United States. It didn't make me feel very secure about the country.

If I functioned as speech writer and press aide at these affairs, I was also asked to provide something people thought of as "the female touch." When Agee wanted someone with him to ease a conversation or welcome a new face, he'd summon me up to the dais. Diane always hung back; she had made her displeasure at having to be at such functions clear. This was particularly glaring at a thousand-dollar-a-plate dinner sponsored by the Reagan people the night before the Economic Club luncheon speech. Agee and Diane sat at one of the head tables. I sat at a table with other Bendix executives and their spouses. While Agee talked animatedly with Reagan, Diane stared off into space. Even when they were side by side they inhabited separate worlds, which was painfully obvious to everyone.

I was becoming increasingly indispensable to Agee, but at my own expense. And I started to resent it. I was too busy to live. My entire life was devoted to Agee. I got messages from my mother warning me I wasn't living a balanced life, and she was right. But I found it difficult to extricate myself either from Bendix or from Agee. The demands of the job were insatiable. I'd try to round out my life, to make plans to see someone for dinner, and then Agee would say, "Mare, I really need you for this one, could you please just cancel that?" That was the flip side of mentorship they never told you about at Business School. Once you were mentored, how did you get un-mentored?

My hope was that come June 1, I'd have my own job, separate from Agee. Then I wouldn't be so dependent on him. But I had other worries concerning my future. The atmosphere at Bendix was starting to grow tense. The automobile industry wasn't in the best of shape, and people at Bendix, as well as all over Detroit, were starting to worry about their jobs. And with Agee rumored to be pondering major changes in the corporation, no one felt safe. Tension among Agee's executive staff was mounting. Jerry Jacobson was making noises about going over to Burroughs, where his old friend Mike Blumenthal was now in charge. Panny no longer even bothered to hide his disdain for Agee and his new strategic plan. Svec didn't know whose side to take and Charlie Donnelly, who had announced his early retirement in September of 1979, was on his way out. Agee had virtually no executive team. My sense was that Agee was going to have several minor wars on his hands over the summer, and, as his loyal executive assistant, I could get caught in the crossfire. I wondered if this might not be a convenient time to leave the front lines.

On the other hand—and there were always "on the other hands"—what about my loyalty to Agee? What about my commitment to my job? And what about the satisfaction I was feeling from a job well done, not to mention all that I had learned?

On June 1, Agee formally offered me the job as vice president for corporate and public affairs. "If I can't appeal to you on the basis that I truly need you here (he knew he always could), let me appeal to you as your mentor," he said. "You'll be a corporate vice president. This will launch you in your career." The title did have a certain panache. And with the Republican Convention coming to town in a month, it would be an important one. "And you can still do all you want in strategy because I intend to keep you on as my executive assistant," Agee said, anticipating my every doubt. "Furthermore, I'm advised by personnel that this promotion entitles you to a raise," he said, sipping his iced tea. "Yes, I should think so," I said, "since apparently I'll be doing six jobs at once." I was getting bold. "Let's see. Your salary is thirty-four thousand now. Why don't we raise it to thirty-nine thousand?"

I didn't want to sound ungrateful, but I had hoped for considerably more. I'd turned down $55K right out of Business School.

"Well, it's more than a ten percent increase," he said, noting my dismay.

"Yes, but inflation is going to be over fourteen percent this year," I said. "I think I'm training you a little too well," he said with a playful smile. "Seriously, I think a five-thousand-dollar raise would be easier for the organization to swallow." I'd heard that line before. "And besides," he said, "Larry Hastie says that five thousand sounds about right for the first raise."

Larry Hastie. My pal! "Look, I don't care about the money so much as what I'm going to do. I don't intend to become some PR flack. I want to do strategy," I said.

"I want you to do strategy," Agee said. "But first you need to be credentialed." This seemed reasonable enough. Besides, corporate vice president in whatever field was no title to sneer at. Perhaps in the midst of all those late-night work sessions, I'd lost sight of what it meant.

On the 26th of June, Agee's secretary peeked into my office. "Mary? Ready?" I wasn't sure for what. "It's the board of directors meeting and they want to see you." "Me?" What've I done? I thought, thinking of Sister Veronica summoning me up to her desk. "Oh, I'm so excited for you," she said, noting my concern. As soon as we entered the board room, I saw a circle of smiling faces. "Directors of Bendix, I'd like to introduce you all to our new Vice President of Corporate and Public Affairs, Mary Cunningham." There was a generous round of applause. "Now let me introduce you individually to each of our directors," Agee said and led me around the room. One by one, I shook their hands. Malcolm ("Mac") Baldridge, Chairman and Chief Executive Officer of Scovill, Inc., Coy Eklund, President and Chief Executive Officer of the Equitable Life Assurance, Donald H. Rumsfeld, President and Chief Executive Officer of G. D. Searle & Co., and former Secretary of Defense. Paul Mirabito, Chairman of The Burroughs Corporation, Alan Schwartz, Detroit attorney and Director of The Burroughs Corporation, Harry B. Cunningham, Director and Honorary Chairman, K Mart Corporation. Hugo E. R. Uyterhoeven, Timken

Professor of Business Administration, Harvard Business School. Jewel S. Lafontant, Partner, Lafontant, Wilkins & Butler, law firm. And so on, until I'd been introduced to them all. Coy Eklund, a leader on equal rights issues, took my hand in both of his and expressed his confidence in me. Lafontant, the only woman and the only black on the board, was especially warm. "It's with special pride that I welcome you, Mary," she said.

There were other lovely sentiments expressed, and, as I sipped my wine at a lunch with members of the board, I thought how far I'd come. At twenty-nine I was the youngest female corporate vice president of a Fortune 500 company in America, and whatever my doubts about my first year at Bendix, I felt only the greatest hopes for my future right now.

# CHAPTER FIVE

*Certainly it wasn't a career* in business I had in mind for myself when I made my first step out into the real world, which, in 1969, meant the perfectly manicured green lawns of a collegiate environment. Business was the farthest thing from my mind during the first of my formative college years.

It was quite a switch, moving from Sacred Heart to Wellesley. There I was with my one suitcase and battered trunk, watching as another student's chauffeur unloaded a trunkload of Gucci luggage. The fact that I was at the lower end of the Wellesley social stratum was made painfully clear to me in my first introductory economics class. The instructor had everyone write on a slip of paper her family's income, which she then proceeded to graph on a bell-shaped curve. There, way over to the left on the curve, was my number, the only figure in the less-than-$5,000 category.

I was happiest sitting in my room, decorated in sunny yellows to offset my melancholy Irish temperament, reading Aristotle, Plato and the Greek philosophers. But what they said about balance really hit home. I was well aware that I had too little balance in my life. I knew intuitively that my upbringing had been a little extreme. At Wellesley,

I could already see people's eyes glaze over when I started to talk about theology or ethics. "Did you actually let him up to your room?" someone would say, divulging the details of her latest exploit, and I'd contribute an observation about human nature gleaned from Aquinas.

My first dilemma was what to major in. I felt at home with philosophy, but something about the notion of majoring in it disturbed me. "Isn't that just what you'd expect of Mary Cunningham?" my alter ego said. "Twelve years of theology and now a major in philosophy. How predictable." And I agreed. Destiny seemed to be pushing me in the direction I'd been going all my life—philosophy, religion, ethics—and yet I was desperate to leaven my "otherworldliness" with studies that might be of more direct use in this world.

I poured out my frustrations to Ingrid Stadler, my idol and chairman of the philosophy department. A short, dark woman with deep-set eyes and clothes that looked "artistic" to me, Stadler listened quietly as I told her about my conflict. "You don't see many ads in *The Wall Street Journal* for philosophy majors," I said. Her response after one of our lengthy conversations was to direct me to Robert Heilbroner's book called *The Worldly Philosophers*. It was about Adam Smith, John Maynard Keynes and other economists and how they made practical use of their abstract ideas. I saw how philosophy could be grounded in "the real world," a phrase still potent in the early seventies. With Stadler's help, I came up with the perfect solution: a combined major of logic and philosophy was both practical and theoretical, disciplined and creative, quantitative and qualitative. There it was. My major. My passkey into a more well-rounded life.

My social life, of course, lagged behind. I was dating

two men—Tom, from my high-school days and Alec, a
Harvard student of the Darien, Connecticut mold. Alec
was a tall, lanky rugby player, and his arrival at my dorm
always elicited a chorus of "What a hunk" and "Mary,
where'd you find him?" And yet I was fairly oblivious to
his charms. He and all the other tall, handsome prep-
school men I met left me unimpressed. I suppose, in some
vague way, they reminded me of the yacht-club set from
which I imagined my father had hailed. Good Catholic
boys like Tom, on the other hand, seemed less like romantic prospects and more like pals. I felt sisterly toward
them although as my sophomore year progressed, I felt
more and more annoyed by Tom and his restrictive comments.

While I was trying to grow, to expand, to soak in new
ideas, Tom was trying to anchor me back to the old. This
bothered me and yet I seemed to need the security of
being with someone as reliable as Tom. My feelings toward Tom and my life in general confused me. Who was
I? I wondered. Was I really this studious and devout young
woman at whom people smiled approvingly on Hanover's
Main Street and referred to respectfully as "the Monsignor's niece" or was there someone else lurking inside
me, yearning to come out? I didn't know, but like gen-
erations before me, I decided to go abroad and find out.
Only, instead of searching in the cafés of Paris or in the
ashrams of India—my rebellions were always more conventional—I decided to take a year in Ireland, where
perhaps I'd discover my "roots."

In order to supplement my scholarship for this Irish
sojourn, I spent the summer working on Cape Cod. My
mother and grandmother owned a small cottage in Chatham
and my family always spent the summer there. I had two

jobs. From 5 A.M. until 8 A.M., I played short-order cook, serving up bacon and eggs to the fishermen who came for breakfast at Larry's PX. Then, at 8:15 A.M., I'd quickly step out of my white polyester waitress's uniform and thick-soled shoes and slip into my bank teller's uniform: a Talbot's skirt and a round-collared blouse. My experience as a teller did not bode well for a career in commercial banking. I was slow to balance out my accounts, and I was always accidentally tripping off the alarm. I never remembered that if you pulled out the last fifty-dollar bill in the till without disengaging an electronic device, it would automatically cause the alarm to go off.

It was interesting to observe the different ways people treated you in such contrasting jobs. With the fishermen I was "Mare," their buddy, someone they could joke around with. With the customers at the bank, it was all business. Money changed hands through a Plexiglas window and in a plethora of polite "Hello Miss Cunningham's." In all honesty, I had much more fun slinging hash.

With sufficient funds for room and board, I set sail for Ireland that September on the *Queen Elizabeth II*. My shipmates included a lively contingent of Rhodes Scholars on their way to Oxford. The voyage was a perfect excuse for a mid-Atlantic romance—or so some of my shipmates tried to persuade me. "Just think of what a beautiful experience it could be, here at sea, far from the troubles of home." I heard many variations on that theme. But I was immune to such entreaties. I still wasn't ready for much more than a handshake or a brotherly game of Ping-Pong and quickly reverted to my old role of being everyone's "friend." After five days, we docked first at Le Havre and then at Southampton.

It was somewhere in the mid-Atlantic that I started to

feel homesick. There was no turning back now. Perhaps this year abroad wasn't such a good idea after all, I thought. But as we pulled into port, a little band on the dock started playing what sounded like "My Country 'Tis of Thee." Oh, isn't that nice, I thought. They're playing an American hymn to greet us. Except when I listened more closely, I found it was "God Save the Queen." The Rhodes Scholar standing beside me had made the same mistake. With the British national anthem blaring, the sun setting over Southampton and my stomach still a little queasy from my week at sea, I had a sudden urge to cry. "It's going to be a long year," my companion said with a knowing smile, and I agreed.

In Dun Laoughaire, I was met by my "adoptive" Irish family, the Collinses. Mrs. Collins had made only one request to the college authorities: "Don't send me any female American students." American women were well known for their "emancipated" ways and Mrs. Collins didn't want any of that in her house. It didn't take her long to learn I had not yet been "emancipated." "Mary, why don't you go out a bit more?" she coaxed, watching me study for hours at a time in my room. I was not entirely comfortable at the Collinses. My room was literally the size of a closet, and I was charged twenty-five pence per shower and twenty-five more to use the heat after 10 P.M.

As usual, I was rescued by my studies. My major was P.P. & E.—Oxfordese for Philosophy, Politics and Economics, which I supplemented with several courses in law, since at that point, I planned to become a lawyer. I was tremendously excited by my courses and yet I was homesick as well. Perhaps it was my loneliness that caused me to see Tom in a much more favorable light. At my urging, he decided to visit me early in December. At first I was glad to see him, an emissary from back home. But toward the end of his stay our relations grew strained. Tom had definite ideas about our future that I didn't share. He wanted to become engaged. I told him marriage wasn't the plan I had in mind—at least I wasn't sure just now. "Fine," he said. "But when you come back, I don't want you to call me unless you're prepared to marry me." And on that ultimatum we parted, uneasy friends.

I had some very difficult times that year. One of the worst was a few weeks after Tom's departure, on Christmas Day. My scholarship didn't provide for a flight home for the holiday so I arranged by mail to call home on Christmas Eve. It was 4 A.M. in Dublin and 11 P.M. in Hanover. One by one, I spoke to my whole family, Mom, my grandmother Bombi, Father Bill, Frank, John and Shirl, their voices faint over the transatlantic line. How lonely I felt when I heard the silence and then the dial tone after they'd hung up the line. In isolated splendor I sat on my bed and opened each of their cards and carefully wrapped presents. They'd mailed them in a suitcase to me the week before. I read and reread their notes and looked at my gifts but it only made me miss them more.

My spirits improved after January. Breaks between sessions are seven weeks long in the English school system, and for foreign students, those seven weeks can be pretty lonely if one doesn't have any plans. I made plans and kept busy. I was recruited onto the Trinity College ski team to represent them for two weeks of races in Austria. Skiing was fun. I even met two students I knew from Dartmouth. At first I was sure they were a mirage, so lonely was I for a familiar face from home.

The rest of the academic year I devoted myself to my

studies and I received excellent grades. Somewhere during the course of the year it occurred to me, however, that my life wasn't all that different from what it had been like at home. I studied, attended Mass and wondered about my soul. So where was the change? I wondered. What had become of my identity crisis?

After my adventures abroad, senior year at Wellesley seemed a bit dull. My identity crisis wasn't solved, but for now was in its dormant state. That other mysterious woman I thought might lurk inside me apparently wasn't planning to emerge. And I no longer had Tom to pester me. Not long after I returned from Dublin, I called him. We'd been friends for three years now and it seemed a bit extreme not to call simply because I wasn't ready to marry him. He was insistent. "I told you not to call unless you were ready to become engaged. Now think about it for another day and then let me know your answer. But if it's no, Mary, then it's over between us."

I felt miserable. I didn't want to marry Tom but I didn't want to lose a friend, either. I walked the beach all night and only with the greatest difficulty summoned the courage the next day to tell him my decision. "I'm not ready to get married so I guess this is it," I said. At which point Tom said, "Well, I didn't really mean what I said. We can still go out. What are you doing this weekend?" I was furious. Here he'd put me through twenty-four hours of agony and, in the end, didn't even have the backbone to stick to his decision. That was the end of Tom and me.

It was back to basics—books and classes. As usual, I didn't have much of a social life. Occasionally I saw Alec or went to a dance. It was at one of these dances that I met Marc, a snappy, wisecracking character from Harvard and West Point who didn't interest me in the least. After a couple of dances, he gave me the usual line. "Would you like to come back to my apartment for a drink?" By now I was adept at saying no. It was precisely because I had so little interest in Marc that one of the women he was dating asked me to stand in for her. She was sick and couldn't attend a Harvard Business School party with him, and she asked me, as a favor, to take her place. I really didn't want to go—Business School parties bored me—but I consented. After all, Marc seemed like a nice enough person, at least, and the evening might provide an interesting break from studying, I thought. Marc came by, picked me up in his green Corvette Sting Ray and tried to impress me from Wellesley to Cambridge with tales of his beloved sports car. How am I ever going to suffer through a whole evening of this? I wondered.

My first thought when we got to the party was to look for someone sober enough to drive me home. I saw a candidate as soon as I walked in the room. He was a tall, distinguished-looking black man who looked like a professor with his short-cropped beard. He noticed me, too, and in a short time we were talking. "Do you want to dance?" he asked. "No, not really," I said. "Good. Neither do I. Let's talk."

We made our way into a room where the music wasn't quite so loud and started to talk. He sat on a chair and I sat on a couch. At some point during the next seven hours the party must have ended because by the time we stopped talking the host had gone to bed and everyone had left. It was light outside. Marc had gone without even checking up on me, I thought, but I hadn't noticed. I wasn't aware of anything except the incredible sincerity and honesty of this man to whom I spoke. He told me about his family, how his father had been one of the first blacks to graduate from Boston University Law School. We talked about school busing, and Bo—"Howard is my name but everyone calls me Bo," he said—joked about being the first student bused between prep schools. He'd gone from Boston Latin "where they taught me to memorize things" to Exeter "where they taught me to think," and then on to Harvard College and Harvard Business School, where he was studying now. I liked the way he put things. His language was informed but down-to-earth. No polite Wellesleyisms. And how different he was from his Business School peers. So many of the ones I'd met were pompous and boastful. But not Bo. He seemed wiser, more mature. There was something of the philosopher about him. And something of the cynic too. He made fun of everything Harvard Business School stood for and yet was humble enough to say he needed it.

"Really, a cynic is just a sensitive person underneath who's been badly hurt," I said. "How would you know?" he asked. I wasn't sure how I did, except I did. No two people could have held more divergent views and yet, rather than separate us, they seemed to draw us together. Something of the idealist in me appealed to the cynic in him and something of the cynic in him was drawn to the missionary in me.

It was sometime after 6 A.M. when we got up to go. Bo drove me home. Once back at the dormitory, there were none of the usual cat-and-mouse games about saying goodbye. Bo simply extended his hand and in his quiet and dignified way said, "That was one of the most moving conversations I've ever had—and I don't get moved easily."

When I got back to my room, only one thought raced

through my mind. "I've just met the most incredible person." I sat as if in a daze. I knew that something very important had just happened. On impulse I picked up the phone and called my mother.

"Mom, I've just met someone very special."

"That's nice, dear. At seven-thirty in the morning?"

"No. At a party last night. We sat up all night talking. He's so interesting, Mom. He went to Exeter and Harvard and now Harvard Business School, but he's not like your usual Business School type."

"Well, that's wonderful, dear. I was hoping you would finally meet someone like that. Now why don't you go to sleep and get some rest."

It didn't even occur to me to tell her he was black. I was too absorbed in all that had happened the night before. Besides, I'd grown up hearing countless Sunday sermons about the Brotherhood of Man and the Fatherhood of God and I took them all very seriously. I felt, for the moment, oblivious to everything except the incredible experience I'd just had.

I saw Bo three or four times in the next few weeks. Once he took me to sit in one of his classes at the Harvard Business School. From his seat on the uppermost bench in the back of the room, we peered down on everyone. Students and professors alike called him "the professor," perhaps because of his dignified air, enhanced by his beard with its two white streaks. He was extremely well liked, and popular with all the students in his section.

After class we wandered about Cambridge. Bo introduced me to his puppy, Morgan, an Old English sheepdog, and the three of us romped around on the banks of the Charles. "If your God exists," Bo would say, "he created

two creatures on this earth who are truly colorblind—
you and Morgan."

Word got around that I was seeing Bo. "You don't
know what you're getting into," other suitors told me.
Twice in the next week I refused Bo for dates but only
because I had other plans.

"Someone has gotten to you, haven't they?" he said
one night over the phone. "No," I said. "Really, I'm just
busy."

"Don't you know how to tell me no?" he said, obviously hurt. "Don't worry. You can say it. It wouldn't
be the first time." His words stung. I had no intention of
stopping our friendship and I told him so. "Are you busy
on Saturday?" he asked. "I am," I told him. "How about
Sunday?" "That's when I go to Mass," I said. I knew he
would take it as a rebuff so I asked if he'd like to meet
me afterward at St. Paul's, the church I attended in Harvard Square. There was a long pause. "Do you know how
long it's been since I've been inside a church?" he asked.
"Well, you could meet me out front, or you could come
inside when it's over," I said. "No, no," he said. "I'll meet
you out front, on the steps." But in the middle of Mass,
he came into the church and knelt down beside me. I had
a new feeling about Bo after that.

We were happy together. Bo was my friend and con-
fidant and I felt utterly at ease with him. He must have
felt that way too because his appearance changed. His
face brightened. He looked happier. We made a wonderful
*ménage à trois*, the three of us—Bo, Morgan and I.

It was springtime and the weather was getting nicer. I
thought it would be a perfect time to drive with Bo to
Hanover, which was so pretty this time of year. I called
my mother and told her I was going to bring my new

friend home. "Great," she said. "I've been eager to meet this young man."

"Are you sure your mother is prepared for this?" Bo asked when I told him. "Sure," I said. "I mean have you told her about me?" "Of course," I said. "About my skin color?" "Well, I didn't tell her that. My mother is very open-minded. I don't think you understand." "I don't think you do, Mary. I think you should have a talk with her before I come."

Still I argued. I told him my family had no prejudice and that my mother had often welcomed black students at Hanover High School into our home. Bo groaned. My naiveté irked him and pleased him at the same time. "Look, do me a favor, Mary," he said. "Give your mother a call. And promise me you'll talk to her when the two of you are alone."

I called home that Sunday. "Mother," I said, after we had talked for a bit, "there's something else I want to tell you." "What is it, dear?" "My friend, Bo Gray. He's from Roxbury, you know." "Yes?" she said, and paused. She didn't know what to make of this. "Mary? Is there something else you want to tell me?" "Well, yes, Mom, but it's not that important." "What is it, Mary?" "Bo is black," I said. There was complete silence. "That's not a problem to you, is it?" I added quickly. "Well, no," she said. "Good, because I'm looking forward to his meeting you," I said. "Yes, dear," she said, her voice trailing off.

We did not leave for Hanover in the best of spirits. And no sooner did we pull up in front of my mother's house than Morgan leaped out of the car and started tearing after Murphy, our half-Labrador, half-Irish Setter. Murphy was less than gracious. He barked and growled at his guest. We walked into the house but no one was home. Mother must have run out to the grocer's, I thought. Suddenly I smelled something burning. A pot of burned spaghetti sauce was smoking on the stove. I started to remove the pot but was interrupted by the sound of Morgan's plaintive howl. The dogs were fighting again. Bo grabbed Morgan. I grabbed Murphy. Like two boxers squaring off before a fight, we faced each other in the kitchen, dogs in arms. "Off to a great start," Bo said, and both of us started to laugh.

It was much better after that. My mother came home, and just seeing Bo dispelled whatever disturbing image she might have had of him. I think she genuinely felt warmly toward him. And so did I. The deep voice. The soft-spokenness. The firm handshake. I looked at him during dinner and felt proud of this strong, gentle man. Toward the end of the meal, Father Bill came in from one of the Saturday night courses he taught on ethics. He was pleasant but very formal. He talked to Bo about Bo's background and his plans to work for the Chase Manhattan Bank that fall. I didn't say very much, which was unusual for me. I was too busy sensing everyone's reactions.

After dinner, Father Bill and Bo adjourned to the living room. They must have been doing all right, I thought, because I could hear both men laughing over each other's jokes. Mother and I, however, had some serious talking to do.

"Just what is this relationship, dear?" she asked as we started in on the dishes. "It's a very special friendship I have with a very special human being," I said. She looked at me long and hard. "I think you're falling in love with him, Mary," she said. "You may be right," I said. "But so what? If it's going to happen, it'll happen." I was starting to feel defensive. "I'd like you to come up next weekend, so we can talk about this—alone," she said. I was beginning to feel uneasy. I was afraid she would try to convince me not to see him. "Mom, don't let me down on this," I said. "Don't be like other people and say what I think you're going to say." "Mary Elizabeth," she said, "I haven't said anything yet. I just want to see you alone."

I drove up the next weekend and faced a full-court press. There were long and difficult sessions with both my mother and Father Bill. I spoke with my mother first. "I knew someday I was going to have to have a conversation like this with you," she said as we sat down on the living room couch. "Now, what I'm going to say is going to upset you, but try to listen," she said. "I've worried about you for a long time. Of all the four children, you've always been the most idealistic. You've always been the one who's taken Father Bill's sermons to heart. But there's a world out there and the people in it don't always act the way they ought to. You're not wrong for having your beliefs. It's just that you don't understand how cruel the world can be."

"I know what you're going to say and I don't want to hear you say it," I said. "I don't want to hear those words coming from your lips. You're going to tell me, 'It's not a question of spirituality or right or wrong.' Right? 'It's just a question of practicality.' Right?" "It isn't what I believe, Mary. It's what the world believes that will make it so hard." "That's a cop-out," I said. "I just worry for your happiness, dear," she said. "Think of the hardships and sadness something like this could bring into the world." "Think of the love and beauty it could bring," I replied. She paused for a minute and refolded her hands in her lap. "I think I've done a terrible injustice to you. I've been too protective."

Father Bill came over later that afternoon. I walked up to him as he strode across the lawn but for the first time, I didn't kiss him. I held out my hand instead. He ignored the hand and hugged me, hard. My eyes filled with tears. "I know what you're going to say," I said. "But I don't want to hear you say it. Please." He led me inside. "We just don't want you to be hurt, Mary Elizabeth. That's all." I was angry. "How come you say one thing to your parishioners and another thing to me? Isn't there one God? Aren't we all His children?" "That's true, Mary Elizabeth. And before God there are no racial differences. But in the world you must live in, there are. You're my niece and I'm concerned for your happiness. Don't you understand?" I understood only too well. He wasn't acting like a priest. He was acting like a father. And not "Father" with a capital F.

A few weeks before classes ended, Bo asked if I were going to invite him to graduation. "I think I'd better keep that a family day," I said. I had already given the matter some thought and decided not to do anything that would upset my family. I felt I owed them that much. Bo, however, took it as a rebuff. He interpreted it as my way of saying "It's been a nice interlude. So long." We parted with only the most tepid of goodbyes.

Both Bo and I had our separate plans for the fall. Bo was moving to New York to start work at Chase Manhattan Bank, and I was going to work at Wellesley as a recruiter for the Admissions Board. Wellesley had been generous with my scholarships and I felt I owed the college a year of my time. And besides, a year's hiatus between college and law school seemed like a good idea.

As for the summer, I'd also been offered a summer position teaching Intellectual History at St. Paul's, a private prep school in Concord, New Hampshire. It seemed like a pleasant respite. Diploma in hand, I set out for the "real world," one of thousands of women entering the work force in an age considered ripe for bright young women.

I spent my weeks busily keeping up with my intellectually precocious wards at St. Paul's and my weekends talking quietly with my mother at home. Bo was not a topic. I think Mother was hoping it had gone away. I thought perhaps it had too. A beautiful relationship that had no place in time—that's how I viewed it in my better moments. In my worse moments I assumed Bo was besieged by starlets in glamorous New York and had forgotten about his quaint, old-fashioned, religious friend from New England.

But in August I suddenly heard from Bo. The return address on Fifth Avenue confirmed my suspicions. I imagined him writing in between feasting on caviar and champagne. But his letter quickly dispelled any such notions. He gave me a simple account of his rather humdrum life. His tone was strictly business. At the bottom of the letter he wrote: "P.S. Is this 'distant' enough for you?" I then understood why he hadn't written. He thought I had meant to break things off. I wrote back to him that afternoon. In a few weeks we started to see each other again.

If I had imagined Bo living in the lap of luxury, one glance at his apartment straightened me out. His co-op was indeed on Fifth Avenue, and also right on the fringe of Harlem. His dwelling was bare except for a refrigerator, a large couch, a bed and an abundance of dog hairs. Not only couldn't I imagine any starlets here; I wasn't sure I wanted to spend any time here myself. But Morgan made me feel welcome, and in no time at all, Bo and I were back on one of our talking jags. I decided to play decorator and help make the house look more like a home.

In the fall I began my recruiting job at Wellesley. It was interesting and brought me frequently to New York, where I recruited students from inner-city schools. I spent a lot of time with Bo. Slowly our relationship deepened. There was no dramatic moment of passion in which we suddenly fell helplessly and hopelessly in love. It was more gradual than that. I remember listening to soft blues music in Harlem one night and knowing that this man with whom I was dancing was no longer just a friend, but something more.

The closer I grew to Bo the more distant I felt toward my family. No more weekly long-distance calls home and no more weekends with my mother. Relations between us cooled. Her disapproval, although it was no longer expressed, caused me to push home out of my mind. I missed Mom and Father Bill but I tried not to think about it.

It was Father Bill who broke the ice. He called just after I'd returned from Mass on Easter Sunday. "I've prayed very hard on this issue, Mary Elizabeth," he said. "I've tried to play devil's advocate but perhaps I've played the role harder than I should have. I just want you to know that I believe in you. And I will always support you in whatever you do as long as it's right before God. If there's love between you and Bo, it must be God's will, and I support you both." Then he put my mother on the phone. "We've missed you terribly dear," she began. "If there is any time that you need our support and backing, it's now. It isn't that we don't think Bo is a wonderful man—I'm sure he is—it's just that we have been so worried about what's ahead for you two. That's all." Easter had never meant more.

That summer was a fairly enjoyable one although there were so many unanswered questions in my mind. I decided to take paralegal courses at a small university on Long Island before leaving for law school at the end of August. When I wasn't studying, Bo and I explored New York, enjoyed concerts in Central Park and street fairs in Little Italy.

It wasn't easy being an interracial couple, even in New York. Wherever we went we were observed. People either stared disdainfully or came up to us and gushed about what a wonderful and beautiful thing they thought we were doing. Occasionally Bo and I could even joke about it. Certainly the image people had of us and the reality of our lives were two vastly different things. Here was Bo, this big, tall, handsome black man "—and you know how good black men are," we'd joke—and here was I, this blond innocent. In actuality, I was probably New York's only twenty-two-year-old virgin with the one man who was patient and kind enough to tolerate my so-called "old-fashioned" schoolgirl ways.

During the winter, I'd been admitted to Notre Dame Law School, where I was planning to study for a joint degree in ethics and law beginning in the fall. Bo knew of my plans and didn't question them. We were a "modern" couple, and for both of us there was no question that work came first, even if it meant we'd be separated for a while. Besides, neither of us knew where our relationship was going. We'd never talked about any sort of "commitment." In September I packed my belongings in my little yellow Opel, which I'd bought with the savings

I'd made from all the summers I spent waitressing on Cape Cod, and headed west, to South Bend, Indiana.

The sight of Notre Dame's gold dome with the statue of the Blessed Mother on top told me, "Here's where you belong." But that was no longer completely true. Parietals, that ancient rite that had long since been weeded out at East Coast schools, were still in force in South Bend, Indiana. But only in the women's dorms. And just in case anyone had any intention of breaking the rules in that gray and gloomy all-women graduate dormitory, nuns resided in several rooms as a reminder that any breach would not go unnoticed. Legend had it that two previous occupants of my dorm had been suspended for having a man in their room after ten.

I readapted myself to the academic life easily enough, but I missed Bo. And I also felt pangs of guilt. True, he hadn't asked me to stay, but it wasn't like Bo to make those requests. Our plans were not to see each other until Christmas, but in late October I received an unusual midnight call from Bo. His best friend from Roxbury, Johnny Coates, had drowned. I never heard Bo sound so down. "Are you okay?" I asked. "I'm not sure," he said. "Would you like to come out here and see me?" I asked. "I don't think I can afford to right now." "Look, why don't you come? We'll figure out some way to pay for it."

It was a mistake. South Bend, Indiana, was not yet ready for an interracial couple, and instead of making Bo feel better, the visit made us both feel worse. Obviously Bo couldn't stay with me in the dormitory, so we checked into a nearby hotel. The manager took one look at us and sized up the situation at once. Of course he didn't take me seriously when I asked for adjoining rooms. Bo gave him his credit card but the manager wouldn't accept his

ID. He assumed any black man carrying a card that said "Second Vice President, Chase Manhattan Bank" must have stolen it. "Let me see yours, Missy," he snapped, and I gave him my student ID. He took the card and then threw the keys at us.

Our rooms were at the end of a long dark hall, as far from the main wing of the hotel as possible. The bed was unmade. The ashtrays were full. And there were cigarette burns in the lampshades. I looked at Bo. He looked so sad, embarrassed that he had to put me through all this. And here it was he who was in need of comfort. I thought of all I was doing to this man, hurting him by bringing him out here like this. I couldn't bear it any longer.

It was that night I decided to marry Bo. "Would you like it if I came back East with you?" I said, the sight of the hotel manager's smirk still fresh in my mind. Bo looked at me. Never in all our two years of friendship had he ever said anything as definite as "Stay. I want you. I need you," as other men might. But he did that night. "Mary," he said to me, "if you come back with me it would be the most important gift anyone's ever given to me."

"Then help me pack my bags," I said.

Early the next morning I called to tell my mother of my decision. "Well, dear, if that's what you really want," she said.

I felt good about my decision. Everybody in the dormitory helped me pack up. And Bo and I took off in my Opel the next day.

Once again, back in New York, I immediately began the search for a job. We were to be married in eight weeks. Our lives were grounded in a conventional working couple's routine. Work, work, work. Within the first two weeks I found myself a job as a paralegal with a New

York law firm, Kass, Goodkind, Wechsler and Gerstein—just the place for a nice Irish girl—and was too busy working to pay attention to much else. My mother took care of the wedding details.

We were married in December. The wedding was small but beautiful. After the ceremony, we spent one night at a Hilton hotel in Northampton, Massachusetts, on our way back to New York, and then returned to the city the following day. Any more of a honeymoon was out of the question. Both of us had work to do. Bo was busy at Chase and I was already making a name for myself at Kass, Goodkind, Wechsler and Gerstein, where, as the firm's first female nonsecretary, I was distinguishing myself as a paralegal. My job was to call Seventh Avenue garment-center firms and warn them that unless they paid their bills, my firm was prepared to initiate bankruptcy litigation against them. No one in the firm actually expected any settlements to result from these last-ditch calls. The delinquent accounts had already been unsuccessfully contacted for collection by one of New York's largest factoring concerns, but I felt it was my special mission to help these people figure out a way to avoid bankruptcy. I produced creative settlement plans and collected overdue bills from a record number of cases. I also learned how to sound tough. And I often wondered whether people would have settled their accounts so quickly if they could have seen the face behind that stern voice over the phone.

Working as a paralegal was a job, not a career, and I had bigger goals in mind. I had planned to continue law school at Columbia in the fall, but now I was having second thoughts. The partners at the firm kept telling me I was a born negotiator and should go into business. And

Bo seconded the idea. He was doing well at Chase and encouraged me to apply to their corporate credit-training program. I interviewed for the program in May and was accepted in June. At the time, I didn't even know a good definition for the term GNP.

The eighteen-month training program was nonstop work. The goal was to take "high potential" college-graduate neophytes and make corporate lending officers out of them. The killer was the graduate-level accounting course, which a full one-quarter of the class flunked. Before it started, a couple of wise-guy undergraduate business majors went around the room trying to predict who wouldn't pass. Naturally they started with the women. "How many years of accounting have you had, Mrs. Gray?" they asked. "None," I said. That marked me for certain doom. Fear inspired me to work extra hard and the hard work paid off. I had the highest marks of anyone in my class and was ready to move on with renewed confidence.

The other courses in the program were equally intense. It wasn't like college where, if you failed, you received an F. Here if you failed you were fired. And with my husband working in the bank, I felt that would be doubly embarrassing. I worked so hard that I finished the training course in record time. But not without some loss to my personal life. I saw less and less of Bo even though we worked in the same bank. "How's your work going?" "Great, great," I'd say, calling him between classes. "How about yours?" "Oh, I'm hanging in there." "Good. Just keep it up." We were more like mutual cheerleaders than husband and wife.

I chose as my next stop the workout area—also known as the "criticized loan" department—so I could deal directly with upper-level management on high-risk loans. I figured that this job would give me the opportunity to have a bigger impact sooner on the bank's bottom line. As a corporate lending officer, one of my first accounts was the American Motors Corporation, which was in serious financial difficulty. (I remember my first trip to corporate headquarters. They were in an awful industrial suburb of Detroit called Southfield. Who'd ever want to live here? I wondered.) Including the extensive loans to AMC dealers, the bank stood to lose in aggregate more than $80 million from the AMC account. It was these and similar problems that occupied most of my time during the next year as Bo and I each gave more time to the bank than we did to our marriage.

We had different styles, as was made even more clear by the differences between our jobs at work. Bo was a second vice president in the organizational-behavior department, which was on the staff side. I was in corporate lending, a job on the line side of the bank, with responsibilities for P&L (profit and loss). It was on the line side that people moved more quickly to the top, as my superiors were forever reminding me. Our jobs suited our temperaments. I approached work with more determination. Bo was more pensive, more "laid back." Our differences complemented each other but they sometimes created a distance between us as well. I often wondered whether my hard work was creating a distance or whether the distance itself was what caused me to immerse myself in work. I wasn't sure. My response to this, as to many of my personal problems, was to work that much harder.

I was quickly promoted to Assistant Treasurer. My grandmother Bombi couldn't get over it. "Imagine our Mary Elizabeth—the Assistant Treasurer of Chase Manhattan Bank." I had to explain to her that there were several thousand assistant treasurers at Chase. She and my mother were still very proud. But the promotion only encouraged me to work harder. Already I was starting to develop a drive to manage more than loans. "Why work as a lending officer when you could become a Chief Executive Officer yourself?" my clients would prod me. The route from assistant treasurer to the top of the bank was long and slow. Second vice president. Vice president. Senior vice president. Executive vice president—the pyramid seemed so steep and time-consuming. There were faster ways to travel, and one of them, I noted, was to have an MBA. All around me I saw Harvard MBAs whizzing right by me. It made me stop and think. I discussed the situation with Bo and both of us decided it was time I took the plunge. We had had a similar talk months before when Bo was growing restless with his job at Chase. At that time I did my share of cheerleading and urged him to take a new job at American Express, which he did. With his encouragement now, I applied to Harvard Business School, was admitted and started packing for Boston in the fall.

My first year at Harvard Business School was anything but easy. I remember looking at the clock my first night at the books and realizing I'd only done two out of three assigned cases—and already it was 2 A.M. I didn't think the way many of my classmates did, and I saw this was going to be a problem. I'd be wondering what motivated the Chairman of the Board while my classmates would be talking in terms of variable costs and cost overruns. I had to retrain my mind, which was a difficult process. Like resetting a bone.

Of course I missed Bo, again more than I had expected. He and I had been married for almost three years now. We had convinced ourselves that the Harvard experience wouldn't cause much of a change in lifestyle as long as Bo could find a job in Boston the summer before classes began. He wasn't very happy at American Express anyway and saw little chance for advancement beyond the director level. But the job situation in Boston in 1979 was grim. Days of job hunting left Bo frustrated and drained. It was three days before classes were to begin, and Bo had just come from his final interview. I could tell from the look of discouragement on his face what an exasperating experience it had been. "Nothing at Arthur D. Little?" I asked. "That's what they said," he replied. He took off his jacket and I could see the sweat stains under his arms. I couldn't bear to see him go through any more of this.

"Why don't we just commute, at least in the beginning?" I said, trying to sound cheerful. He seemed relieved. I wondered for a moment, Does he really want to be with me or is he just as happy to stay in New York? The question haunted me.

Here at Harvard Business School, at the citadel of American capitalism, not much of the collective spirit—all for one and one for all—prevailed. Instead, everything was a brutal zero-sum game. This was especially apparent in some of the study groups. These were small units of students who met nightly allegedly to help each other review the day's work. Of all the study groups at the Business School, mine was considered to be the most cutthroat. Someone would discuss a case and then try to put a lock on his idea. "You can't use that idea in class tomorrow; it's mine," one of my classmates would say. This "ownership of ideas" made conversation unpleasant, to say the least. My reaction was not to speak up in class. But I knew I couldn't survive amid this atmosphere for long. I discussed the problem with Bo, and seeing me so upset, he urged me to change study groups. I did and situated myself quite happily in a much more civilized group.

The competitive environment was distressing me but I had other problems as well. Financially I was under great strain. I had already taken out a $20,000 loan for Business School, only after having convinced myself that it was the best investment I could possibly make in my future. But I could hardly afford to hop on a plane or pick up the phone any time I felt like speaking to Bo. I had left our car in New York with Bo, and as a result, most weekends he drove up. But by the time he arrived, he was too tired to do much else but nap. On our meager budget (commuting ate up all our reserves) we could rarely go out for dinner, so I'd try to prepare at least a reasonably attractive meal. Our rule was not to discuss business over the weekend. But in such a competitive atmosphere this left me anxious. I'd bump into a classmate during the weekend who'd say, "I feel so much better. I had the whole weekend to figure out all those things I didn't understand in class." That always caused me to feel doubly scared. By Sunday afternoon, with tons of work to do and my best friend on his way back to New York, I'd feel on the verge of panic.

My response was to try to make myself numb. Whenever I felt lonely, I'd block it out. Whenever I felt frightened, I'd block it out. People encouraged me to socialize more at the Business School but being married made that awkward. Weekends were reserved for Bo, and, as Mrs. Gray, I didn't exactly feel free to wander off with my classmates to the pub. Throughout most of that first year, my life was work, fear and loneliness.

By second year things picked up. I grew accustomed to the environment and learned to adapt. I grew used to living without Bo, perhaps too much so. He grew weary of his weekend drives north, and we started seeing each other less and less. By winter our visits were down to about one a month. This might have troubled me more except that at the time my thoughts were diverted. Having won several awards and with straight Excellents in my half-year grades, I was gaining confidence in my abilities now. I was also taking a certain amount of pleasure in them. I saw I could go far if I wanted to, and this acted like a drug on my work-weary mind. In the middle of the second year my thoughts were on the future. The bright side was the many job offers I had. The negative side was, what would become of Bo and me? I decided to leave the answers to both of these questions up to fate. It was then that I received the call from a man I'd never heard of before, a man who identified himself as Les Rollins.

It was the call that brought me to Bendix.

# CHAPTER SIX

*If during my first year* at Bendix I was exposed to the nitty-gritty of corporate management, during my second year I was thrust headlong into far more racy fare: corporate gamesmanship, or, how to play political hardball. It was a lesson I wasn't entirely ready to learn, although no sooner did I begin my job as vice president for corporate and public affairs than I saw I'd have to.

Bendix was a very different place in June of 1980 than it was a year before when I first arrived. Agee's executive team, no solid block of support my first year, had by now disintegrated into a shadow of its former unglorious self. Charlie Donnelly had announced his early retirement, Jerry Jacobson was going through what at first seemed like a midlife career crisis, and Bill Panny started to act in strange and mysterious ways. "Whatever you say, boss," he'd smirk, which left everyone nervously on edge. It was exactly as Agee had predicted: He had no one at the top he could rely upon and so became increasingly dependent on me. Everything he'd told me during our breakfast at the Waldorf was true. Only then it seemed like a challenge; now it filled me with something akin to dread.

But it wasn't just in the inner sanctums at Bendix that

something was wrong. There was trouble on the outside as well. The Detroit of 1980 was hot, depressed and unemployed. The automobile industry was taking a beating, and even the upper-level executives were feeling the pinch. All over Bloomfield Hills, country clubs were rife with talk about debunked executives and serious cuts in pay. From Dearborn to Grosse Point, people sat on edge. All kept their fingers crossed in the hopes that riots, if there were to be any, would wait until after the GOP convention, which was scheduled for mid-July.

In the midst of this torpid summer, I began my tenure as Bendix's youngest corporate vice president. I had a lot to learn, but my biggest lesson was one they never taught us at Harvard Business School. It was called Corporate Politics, or who played ball with whom.

As the new vice president for corporate and public affairs, one of my first tasks was to reorganize the department. The two directors under me seemed to be engaged in a series of turf wars. David Taylor, smooth, in the midst of a divorce and in his forties, was always complaining that Bill Haney, his sidekick, "never got any work done." Haney, the meeker of the two, complained that Taylor had "an exalted image of himself" and "wasted time hanging around with media types." I put Taylor in charge of external affairs and Haney in charge of internal affairs, which caused both of them to fight less with each other but more with me. Taylor seethed underneath that I'd been promoted over him. Who is this twenty-nine-year-old upstart telling us what to do? he wondered. Haney did too. It was the only issue on which the two saw eye to eye.

But the Haney-Taylor turf wars were minor compared to the next obstacle I faced. Her name was Nancy Reynolds, and she came with the title Vice President of National Affairs. Her role was to run the Washington Office, which meant wining and dining Senators, Congressmen and other important denizens of Capitol Hill. What Reynolds may have lacked in terms of hard-core management experience for the job, she made up for in her connections. Her father, D. Worth Clark, had been Senator from Idaho, and she had worked as an administrative assistant to Nancy Reagan in California, a job that involved everything from letter writing to baby-sitting for the Reagans.

A lot of people balked when Agee first made Reynolds a vice president. He'd known her at Boise-Cascade, where she had been a lobbyist reporting to a middle manager involved in public relations. When Agee came to Bendix, she'd lobbied hard for the job. And once on board, she didn't waste any time making her presence felt. This didn't win her a lot of friends. At a time of severe budget cutbacks elsewhere in the company, she was known for the lavish dinner parties she gave in Washington and the fancy new office she'd had the company buy. "I never could manage her anyway; how can you expect Mary to now handle someone like that?" Charlie Donnelly asked Agee the day he assigned Reynolds to report to me in my new job.

Shortly after my promotion at Bendix, I called to make an appointment to visit her office so we might get better acquainted and get things off to a good start. When we finally did meet, relations between us were strained. Technically she was my subordinate, but at fifty-three, Reynolds wasn't about to let any junior woman with an MBA push her around. (I had been told by more than one colleague that she'd also had trouble dealing with the other senior woman at Bendix, board member Jewel Lafontant.) She hurried me through the office and then asked if I wouldn't prefer to talk over a glass of wine in the privacy of her new home. That was friendly, I thought, and readily agreed. We didn't discuss business; instead, she let me know how close she was to certain key individuals in the Washington press corps. "If I were you," she said in an attempt to give me a piece of motherly advice, "I wouldn't spend too much time being seen with Agee. Those things have a funny way of landing in the press." Her tone was about as motherly as Don Corleone's.

On the plane on the way home, I tried to figure things out. I had no idea what the past relationship between Reynolds and Agee might have been, or why she seemed so intent on distancing me from him. I wondered why Reynolds was warning me about appearances when she herself was comfortable about being seen dining out with him. But rather than engage in speculation, I pushed thoughts of my Washington trip out of my mind.

There was a downside to being a youthful success, as I was fast beginning to learn. A certain kind of watercooler gossip was drifting my way. I was in the ladies room one day when I heard one secretary say to the other, "Well, you would be a vice president too if you had long blond hair and wore a size six." But I dismissed such comments as sour grapes. I decided a certain amount of mudslinging was inevitable.

My department wasn't the only one I needed to reorganize. Major changes were brewing in the Strategic Planning Department. As early as February, Strategic Planning executive vice president Jerry Jacobson had been making noises about leaving Bendix. He talked vaguely about plans of opening his own consulting business and perhaps doing some work for Bendix on the side. At the time, Agee wasn't certain if Jacobson was serious. "Do you think he really means it or is this his way of telling me he wants a little more attention?" Agee asked me at one point. "I don't know," I told him. I knew Jacobson was still smarting from recent criticism from several of his colleagues that he made a practice of using their ideas and not according them proper credit. "Why don't you sit down with him and have a heart-to-heart?"

They had several heart-to-hearts but nothing definitive came of them. At the same time, changes were being made in another part of Southfield that were having their effects on Bendix. W. Michael Blumenthal, Agee's former mentor and his predecessor as Bendix chairman, had been made chairman of Burroughs. It was Blumenthal who had originally brought Jacobson to Bendix; friendship between the two men went as far back as the sixties, when both of them worked for Undersecretary of State George Ball. Occasionally Jacobson had dropped hints that what he'd really like to do was consult to both Bendix and Burroughs. "Foul play," Agee said. He was mystified at how Jacobson could even consider it. With Burroughs and other direct competitors of Burroughs on the list of companies Bendix was considering as potential acquisitions, it was obviously a gross conflict of interest. "You can't play both sides of the fence, Jerry," Agee told Jacobson at the time.

No longer certain where Jacobson's loyalties really lay, Agee slowly started to leave him out of the key strategy sessions. This was difficult since Strategic Planning was Jacobson's domain. And who would naturally fill the void? Mary. The all-purpose vice president. In May Jacobson came clean with what he apparently had been planning all along. He told Agee he was moving across the street to Burroughs, to work for his old boss and pal, Mike Blumenthal. He gave Agee one last golden opportunity to match his friend Blumenthal's offer—a salary substantially in excess of what he was making at Bendix—and the title of Vice Chairman. Agee let the golden opportunity pass. It was agreed that Jacobson would officially resign in August, but in effect he became a lame duck in May.

This left Agee with a major hole in his executive cabinet. He turned to me to fill it. But first the planning department had to be reorganized, at least to keep things going smoothly until August, when Agee could officially make a move to fill Jacobson's slot. The reorganization didn't take much time. I changed around a few titles and lines of command and had things running smoothly by July. It was the sort of thing an outside consultant would charge $50,000 to do, take six months to complete and convey his recommendations in a six-volume report. My staff and I managed to do it in a few days, at no extra cost, and we gave Agee the recommendations in a one-page memo.

My major new project that summer was the Bendix brake study. If this was the year of my political education, the brakes study was my baptism by fire. For a long time Agee had suspected that the company was losing its market share to foreign competition and even some U.S. companies in the manufacture of brakes. He suspected the automotive division needed a major restructuring—not expansion—in order to become healthy again. He made it known that it was not too soon to begin examining alternatives that involved moving production facilities to lower-cost regions and cutting back on unprofitable product lines.

Partly at Agee's behest, Panny went out to investigate the matter. Panny's solution was to buy from Chrysler their entire brake-manufacturing facilities. When Agee heard the proffered solution, he was more than slightly disturbed. For one thing, merely increasing volume would only compound the cash-flow drain. But for another, Panny's so-called recommendation was already in the midst of full-scale negotiations. Panny had negotiated with Chrysler behind the scenes without Agee's authorization.

This maneuver did not enhance Agee's confidence in Panny. And so, in June, Agee decided to launch a more objective all-out investigation of the brakes division. He wanted to know if the operations were, in fact, inefficient, and if they were, to begin immediately to enforce necessary cost controls to slow down the losses. Communication of these changes to the rest of the organization would smooth the way for public acceptance of the new strategy, in which the automotive division would play a less dominant part. My mission, should I accept it (and when did I not?), was to prove or disprove the thesis that Bendix was no longer competitive in the production of its commodity brake parts. I had eight weeks in which to analyze the entire product line, its economics and the competitive dynamics for the forseeable future. I selected seven internal assistants to help me with the study. To insure objectivity, the task force had three people with solid experience in automotive, who would, if anything, have a vested interest in saving their jobs, and four people from outside automotive.

It was not an easy task. Up until recently, brakes had been the heart of Bendix's manufacturing business. It was for inventing the first reliable four-wheel brake system that company founder Vincent Bendix had made his name. To recommend massive cutbacks in this area was tantamount to committing sacrilege.

Each week my comrades and I, clipboard and pencils in hand, flew down to South Bend, Indiana, to round up our statistics. People knew our visit did not bode well. It was widely known that Agee was not a big champion of the commodity side of the automotive brake business. He had grown impatient with the monthly excuses for the ever widening discrepancies between budgeted costs and actual costs. The losses were mounting. Rumor had it that major segments of the division would either have to be pared down or joint-ventured out.

Here was Bendix, the largest employer in South Bend, conducting a full-scale investigation to see how profitable its brake business was at a time when the unemployment rate around Detroit was twice the national average and the Big Three auto companies were laying off people left and right. And here was Mary Cunningham, the chairman's most visible ally, being sent in to do the sharpshooting. We weren't exactly greeted with open arms.

But these obstacles were minor compared to the major one we faced. And his name was Panny. Panny was furious when Agee put me in charge of the new task force. He had suggested two of his own men to conduct the probe. Agee bypassed them because of their obvious pro-automotive stance. He wanted a more objective leader for the study and assumed that I, as an automotive outsider, would fit the bill. And just to insure objectivity, he put two Panny-endorsed candidates on the task force as well.

But that didn't make Panny any less angry with Agee.

For a long time now, relations between the two men had been tense. It was clear that Panny was not going to endorse a strategy that pared down his domain; and rather than adapt himself to the new policy, as a more farsighted executive might have done, Panny fought back. He chafed at everything Agee said; he hoisted the flag for what was clearly a losing cause. At the Lehman Brothers meetings in New York he was so disruptive that Agee was reluctant to bring him along.

All of this was extremely unpleasant for Agee. He'd had high hopes for Panny back in the fall of 1977, when he'd first hired him from Rockwell. At the time, both men had discussed the possibility of Panny's being Agee's eventual successor. But that was before Panny's rebellion. After months of confidential advice from people at various levels of the company that Panny was bad-mouthing Agee behind his back, Agee, in February, finally had a frank talk with him. He told Panny he could no longer consider him as his possible successor. For Agee to tell this to Panny was his way of being honest, but unfortunately it backfired. From that meeting on, it was out-and-out war. Panny started casting around for villains and reasons other than his own actions to blame. The brakes study was just one of his many targets. He told Agee my team and I were disrupting operations at the plants. He tried to limit our access to information. Whenever I would try to meet with him to learn more about his assessment of the business, he was always "too busy." But his automotive colleagues were not. And the more help they gave us, the more Panny tried to stand in our way. Several of the automotive members of the task force began to fear for their jobs. Word was out that Panny disapproved of their cooperation with the project. He let it be known that talking to any member of the brakes study task force was tantamount to committing treason. "What does *she* know about brakes? Ms. Harvard Business School. When has she or Agee ever gotten car grease on their hands?" And as his final act of warfare, he immortalized the task force by referring to it with a new name: "Snow White and Her Seven Dwarfs."

As far as such a thing was possible, the task force tried to stay above it all. We went about our business coolly and briskly, determined to get the job done. As a team, we got along exceptionally well. Hard work and long hours turned strangers quickly into friends. Often members of the group would get together after long work sessions for pizza on weekends, for non-automotive talk and beer.

Not that the brakes study was the only thing I had on my mind. The Republican Convention was only weeks away, and as head of corporate and public affairs, with national affairs reporting to me, I was put in charge. With Agee so close to the Reagan camp and one of the foremost businessmen in Detroit, naturally Bendix was going to have to host a fair number of parties. "Take care of that, will you, Mare?" he said. "Take care of what?" I asked. "You know—the parties, lunches, dinners—the usual stuff." He couldn't have made a worse choice. The Cunninghams of Hanover weren't exactly known for their party-giving abilities. "What's there to figure out?" I asked. "Oh, you know. Who to invite. Where to seat them. What to serve. Where to have it. When. What time. You'll figure it out." I wasn't so sure I would. "Use that entrepreneurial spirit of yours," he said, looking up at me with a wink.

What my entrepreneurial spirit told me was to stay out of areas that I knew nothing about, so I did what any bright young executive would do—I delegated responsibility. I enlisted the aid of everyone from Chester, the Bendix chef, to Nancy Reynolds, who, because of the significance of the occasion, agreed to pitch in.

Those were whirlwind weeks. There were parties day and night. As many Vice Presidential hopefuls as there were—and there were lots that summer—that's how many parties Bendix gave. There were luncheons for George Bush, Gerald Ford, and John Connally, and dinners for Howard Baker and Paul Laxalt.

I might have had my hands full regardless, but an event in Agee's personal life doubled my work that month. Diane had abruptly left for the summer with the intention of not returning until her divorce was final. She had told Agee, in no uncertain terms, that she didn't intend to come back to Detroit that summer and play hostess for a lot of visiting GOPs. Which is probably why Agee came into my office one day and said, "I need help. Do you know how I can hire a top-notch cleaning woman?" Up to my head in hydrovacs and master cylinders for my brake study, the last thing I wanted to do was advise Agee on finding a cleaning woman. "What do you need a cleaning woman for?" I asked. "Ronald Reagan may be staying over at the house and it needs a good cleaning." I was tempted to say no, but I didn't. I found Agee a cleaning woman and then tried to extricate myself from the business of his domestic chores. But I wasn't always successful.

Agee was planning a dinner for Senator Paul Laxalt and his wife at his house the Friday night before convention week, and asked if I would like to help out, along with Nancy Reynolds. Once inside Agee's kitchen, Nancy Reynolds took charge. She divided up the menu, with

Carol Laxalt doing the salad and Agee cooking the steaks on the grill. I was assigned the artichokes. Unfortunately, anything other than Campbell's Chunky Soup was beyond my ken. I bravely put the artichokes in the microwave, set the timer, and closed the door. Unfortunately my debut as microwave chef was not entirely successful. The outsides were cooked but the centers were as hard as rocks. By the time I got around to boiling them, it was time for dessert.

On that Sunday Agee threw a party for his friend Jack Kemp's forty-fifth birthday. William Safire, Jude Wanniski and Steve Forbes of *Forbes* magazine were there. In the middle of the party, Wanniski strode up to Agee and said, "You'd better come rescue your executive assistant or you won't have her for much longer." At the other end of the room, I was rapt in conversation with none other than Thomas Pownall, president of Martin Marietta. Pownall was trying to encourage me to consider a job at Martin Marietta. "There's more to life than brakes," he said. Like missiles? I thought. "I'd like to learn more about your business. Maybe one day I'll visit your operation," I said.

Last to leave the party was a young whiz kid named David Stockman. By way of complimenting his host, he said to Agee on his way out, "You'd be a perfect candidate for OMB [Office of Management and Budget]." But Agee had the last and, in retrospect, the definitive word. "David, with your photographic mind and the way you handled the Chrysler issue—I can't think of anyone better for the job than you."

I learned a lot during convention week, talking to Senators, Congressmen and important CEOs, and had a good time as well. No one questioned my presence—all the top Bendix executives were there—but the fact that Diane Agee was not gave some people a chance to talk. During one of the parties, Senator Laxalt and Mrs. Laxalt challenged Agee to a game of mixed doubles. "Who's my partner?" Agee asked. "I know who my preference would be," Laxalt said, smiling at me. It never occurred to me that the Bloomfield Hills crowd might see me playing tennis with Agee and get the wrong idea. My only concern was whether my game was good enough. After all, I didn't want to embarrass myself in front of a U.S. Senator and my boss. It turned out that Agee was assigned Pete Hannaford, Mike Deaver's public-relations partner, to play out a singles match in the next court. I was paired with Senator Laxalt to play against the ultracompetitive Pete Peterson and his new wife, Joan. I probably played the best game of my life. Laxalt was so good, he scared me into whacking 'em. The score, Laxalt-Cunningham, 6; the Petersons, 2.

It wasn't until the night of the convention that I allowed myself to feel a little in awe of the company I'd been keeping. These nice folks I'd been joking with all week at the various luncheons, dinners and tennis sets were future Vice Presidents and Cabinet officers. I felt a little like a kid in a candy shop. The streamers, the balloons—I was swept up by the pageantry of it all. I sat next to Agee and the rest of the Bendix crew. Frank Sinatra sat behind me and I met Barbara Walters and Kay Graham for the first time. On my left were Betty and Gerald Ford. What moved me most wasn't Reagan's acceptance speech but the fact that throughout the entire convention Betty and Gerald Ford held hands.

* * *

The brake study brought me quickly back down to earth. It was due a few weeks after the convention. The action of racing to meet a deadline kept my adrenaline level high, but something else kept me on full tilt, and that was fear. I sensed this was going to be the showdown with Panny.

The night before the presentation, the task force met to put the finishing touches in place. All the complex esoterica of brakes, we'd managed to master. It was the little things that got us. The binders we had bought were far too small for the studies, and someone had to run out at the last minute to find bigger ones. It wasn't until 2 A.M. that we finished. The result was a several-hundred-page study that filled three volumes, in aggregate five inches thick.

We presented our controversial findings at one-thirty the next day. The conference room on the main floor wasn't big enough to seat the top executives. We met in Conference Room C in the basement, just down the hall from the cafeteria. The combination of nerves and the nearby kitchen odors made me ill. As leader of the group, it was up to me to begin. I looked around the room. The atmosphere was decidedly tense. I remember thinking, If only I could come up with a good joke, it would put everyone at ease. But I couldn't. Instead I just sat quietly reviewing my notes. Agee waved his right arm as a signal to begin. I cleared my throat. I made a few brief introductory remarks and then let each member of the task force present his report. This was the first time many of the men on the task force had ever spoken before Agee, and many of them were obviously scared. I noticed how their hands shook as they pointed to the various charts. It struck me how much confidence I'd gained. It meant nothing to me now to speak before the chairman and his henchmen. Even Panny couldn't shatter my cool. I had watched the processes of power too closely now to be intimidated by them. The chairman of the board was just the chairman of the board, and his henchmen just men, and not all particularly capable ones at that.

Things would have moved ahead smoothly were it not for the constant interruptions, most of which came from one source. "Pardon me," a red-faced Panny blurted only minutes after we'd begun, "but you've got page twelve put in upside down." Or "Did you notice the typo on page seven," or "How is it that such a brilliant group can't even spell the word "brake"? And, "You mean it took you guys eight weeks to come up with those recommendations? There's no news here."

No one else seemed to agree with him. For, with the exception of Panny's outburst, the top management sat and listened intently for over two hours. And when it was over a round of applause was interrupted only by Agee offering congratulations on "the finest internal consulting job performed at Bendix."

Except for Panny, no one disputed our conclusions, which by now were obvious: The commodity-production part of the brakes division was no longer a profitable operation for Bendix. It was losing the company millions of dollars. Unless it could be drastically reconfigured, major parts of it had to go. Even Svec nodded as we presented the figures, except when Panny's eye caught his gaze. Then he quickly cast his eyes down. Panny could see the handwriting on the wall. Even his own line men agreed.

It was after the brake study that he attempted to launch a full-scale mutiny. When Agee called a meeting, Panny would call one afterward, arguing against the things Agee had said. He started bad-mouthing Agee at every turn. But his techniques backfired. Even Panny's allies grew weary of his tactics. It was his closest subordinate, Lee Henry, who eventually reported Panny's maneuverings in detail to Agee. Such tactics were clearly suicidal on Panny's part, but it was Panny's fervent hope that Agee wouldn't be around much longer. He was counting on the fact that come November Agee would be off to Washington, leaving the company to him.

Throughout all of July and August there was press speculation that Agee would be considered for a Cabinet job. Secretary of Commerce or Office of Management and Budget were the two most frequently named. And then, in August, Agee received a call from the Reagan people asking him to be the national business chairman for Reagan-Bush. The post had previously been held by such Republican business leaders as Don Kendall, chairman of Pepsico, under President Nixon. It was generally considered a pre-Cabinet appointment. Agee discussed the offer with me. It was tempting; Agee had thoughts of someday implementing his economic theories on a wider scale. And moving from business to politics was not without precedent among people he knew. His father had left business and run for the State Legislature when he was about Agee's age, and Agee's predecessor, W. Michael Blumenthal, had left his term as Bendix chairman midway through to join the Carter Administration as Secretary of the Treasury.

But Agee had greater concerns at home. Here he was in the midst of implementing the new strategy, which he'd labored over for the past two years, and his executive team was pulling apart at the seams. He couldn't just pick up and leave. After considerable soul-searching, he reached his decision. He accepted the position but made his priorities clear to the Reagan camp. Under no circumstances would he even consider an appointment in November. It didn't take much arm twisting to convince Mac Baldridge, a politically ambitious member of the Bendix board, to serve as vice chairman of the committee.

Panny, however, continued to fan rumors that Agee was planning to leave. But by mid-August he had better fodder for his campaign. The mystery of Diane's summer absence was slowly seeping out. She and Agee had been talking about a divorce for some time now and apparently had decided now was the time. Idaho state law mandates a six-week residence requirement before permitting divorce in that state, which explained her uninterrupted stay there. Agee mentioned his pending divorce to me and asked me if I might know of a convenient place where he might store his books and other belongings until he could find a new home. I knew there was a vacant apartment at Foxcroft, which I arranged for him to use as a storage place on a short-term lease. Agee had told only a few of the other executives on his staff about the divorce, but the word spread quickly. Not that anyone was surprised. It had been rumored for years that the Agees would be getting a divorce—the only question was when. The timing was just ripe for Panny. He had a heyday with this. His favorite joke was that Agee was going through his midlife crisis. I had even started hearing rumors about Agee and me but I didn't take them seriously.

Panny's rumor mill was only one source of aggravation. Agee had a problem of even greater magnitude, and it concerned someone who up until now was for me merely a name from Agee's past: W. Michael Blumenthal.

Call it a love relationship gone sour, or a father-son liaison in which something went awry. Whatever it was, it was clear that what went wrong in the relationship between Bill Agee and his former mentor, W. Michael Blumenthal, was more than either of them knew. The wounds were too deep for it to merely be a matter of business.

They first met at a job interview in February 1972. Blumenthal, then president of Bendix, was on his way to becoming chairman and was looking for a chief financial officer, someone to fill the number two spot. Agee, then senior vice president and chief financial officer of Boise-Cascade at age thirty-four, had already achieved a reputation as something of a *Wunderkind* and was looking to test his mettle in more challenging circumstances. The executive headhunter Russ Reynolds had put the two of them in touch. Their meeting took place at a hotel just outside of Detroit Metropolitan Airport. Agee had flown in for the day.

Immediately they hit it off. Agee found Blumenthal fascinating. He had never met anyone like him. Blumenthal and his family had fled from Germany during World War II and ended up in Shanghai in the Chinese version of a displaced persons camp. He came to the United States just after the war, in 1946, and went to Berkeley and then on to earn a Ph.D. at Princeton. From there, his career was a series of jobs in government and politics. He served as Deputy Assistant Secretary of State under George Ball, first in the Kennedy Administration in 1962 and then, in 1963, under Johnson. After a few more years in government, he returned to Princeton, where he taught government. To Agee, all this bespoke a world he'd only recently grown aware of. Up until now, most of his associates were conventional Idaho family men, to whom even Harvard sounded a little exotic. And here was Blumenthal, hardly your conventional businessman. He was sharp and spoke with impressive familiarity about both academia and politics, two worlds Agee wanted to learn more about. At age forty-six, Blumenthal had been in business for only about five years, whereas Agee, who was only thirty-four, had been in it all his life. Suddenly that life seemed so narrow.

Blumenthal was likewise smitten with Agee. The younger man's raw intelligence and instinctual grasp of business impressed him. He marveled at Agee's candor and charm. "The way Blumenthal describes Agee, you'd think the guy walks on water," Tom Murphy, former CEO of General Motors, once said. There was a second intensive meeting, and shortly after that, Blumenthal offered Agee the job.

They worked beautifully together. A blending of opposites. Where Agee was strong, Blumenthal was weak, and where Agee faltered, Blumenthal could guide the way. Blumenthal considered himself an intellectual. He was a pro on politics, particularly on the international scene, and fluent in several languages. Agee knew one. But where Blumenthal was gruff with people and ill at ease in crowds, Agee was a natural. He liked people. He was outgoing and friendly and had an easy way with them. He was also a numbers man, whereas Blumenthal was not. They divided up the duties and each took control of separate spheres. Agee rolled up his sleeves and busied himself in mastering the facts. Blumenthal took control of the external affairs. He liked to have his information digested for him so that he could weave his analyses around it. Agee was a genius at numbers and facts. It was an exceptional team. The wordly European and the bright young American *Wunderkind.*

Socially they were friends as well. Both men had marriages that were unraveling and were just as content to play tennis and talk business with each other as to sit around their unhappy homes. Also, like most men in business, neither of them had cultivated many close friends outside business. Agee worked too hard to have many friends and Blumenthal did not have the personality. Other than Agee, two of his closest friends were George Ball, his former mentor, and Jerry Jacobson, whom he brought to Bendix. During Christmas of 1974 and 1975, Agee and Blumenthal took their families to the same resort community in Florida. Blumenthal's wife was too strong to appeal to the more passive Diane, so the women went their separate ways while the men played tennis and talked business.

In the fall of 1975 and the spring of 1976, Blumenthal's ambitions started to widen. The automotive business was floundering and Detroit was becoming too small for a man of Blumenthal's drives. He spoke to Agee about trying to get a Cabinet level job or perhaps running for the Senate. Slowly, as his attention turned more to Washington politics, he turned more and more of the company over to Agee's hands. In the summer of 1976, he started feeling Agee out on the move. "If I went to Washington—and I'm not saying I will—what would you do about this?" Or, "Well, if I'm in Washington next year, you could always do this." But he was never definite. It was always hypothetical. Even as late as October and November of 1976, he said he wasn't going to Washington—but if he did, he made sure Agee knew that he had great plans for him. In November it was official. He promoted Agee to president, effective December first. Three days later he started wooing Carter.

On January 22, 1977, Blumenthal was officially sworn in as Secretary of the Treasury in Washington, while Agee was officially made chairman of Bendix in Detroit. To the reporters who covered it, Agee was so young, and Blumenthal so visible, that some assumed Agee was merely keeping the chairman's seat warm for Blumenthal. Blumenthal decided to set things straight. Before he left, he and Agee had a final chat. "I always look ahead," he told Agee. "I don't know what I'll do after my four years are up, but the idea of my coming back to Bendix is not even something we should ever have to discuss. I worked at Bendix when my former chairman [A. P. Fontaine] was still on the board and it strongly handicapped me. I don't want to do the same to you. As chairman, you should be under no obligation at all to take me back. It's now your company; take it where you believe it should go."

And Agee did, although at times it meant reversing certain practices Blumenthal had initiated. One of these was to divest a part of DBA, a French subsidiary named Ducelier, that had been Blumenthal's baby. Agee managed first to turn the operation around and then sold a part of it, at a $13 million profit for Bendix—something he later found out irked Blumenthal. And Agee's cancellation of Blumenthal's order for an even larger corporate jet as well as his corporate suite at the Waldorf didn't win his predecessor's approval. He also made some changes in personnel. Some of the cronies Blumenthal had brought with him from the government and seeded at Bendix didn't turn out to be as good in business as they might have been in politics. Agee leveled with them about their future at Bendix and let several of them go.

If this bothered Blumenthal, he didn't say so at the time. Busy in their separate spheres, the two men had hardly kept in touch. Once a month, or less, Blumenthal would call Agee just to have somebody to talk to. In 1978 they spoke maybe once every couple of months and in 1979, only two or three times. Agee and Blumenthal got together in Florida during Easter vacation in 1978. At the time, Blumenthal expressed some discontent with his job—he wasn't getting along too well with Carter—but he re-iterated what he had told Agee two years ago: "There's no need to keep the seat warm for me."

Relations between Carter and Blumenthal were mer-curial, to say the least. One day Blumenthal hated Carter, was ready to quit and tell the world what an ignoramus Carter was; the next day Carter was being nice to him and Blumenthal was happy again. In February he'd talk to Agee about whether he should leave government and write a book, and in November he'd declare he had no intention of leaving. Agee assumed it must be politics that made people so volatile. But in the end, Blumenthal's lows outnumbered his highs.

In the spring of 1979 Blumenthal acknowledged what everyone else in Washington had known for some time—that he and Carter just couldn't see eye to eye. The press widely reported that Carter had lost respect for, and trust in, Blumenthal and that Robert Strauss and others in the inner sanctums of power wanted Blumenthal out. Part of the problem was Bert Lance, Blumenthal's unlikely nem-esis. From the start, Blumenthal assumed that as Secre-tary of the Treasury he'd be profiled as the financial genius, the numbers wizard, Carter's economic guru. He was wrong. From the day he came to Washington, Lance cut a huge swath in social and political circles and in no time was more powerful than Blumenthal. On Inauguration Day, it was his old friend Bert Lance whom Carter took into his arms, appointing him director of the Office of Management and Budget. The wordly professor had to step aside and watch this good ol' boy from Georgia get Carter's ear on economic matters.

But it wasn't just Blumenthal's disdain for the rural contingent that won him the enmity of Hamilton Jordan, Jody Powell and finally, Carter. It was also his tactics. He talked against people and reportedly operated behind their backs. His thirst for power appeared to be insatiable to some of his colleagues. On the cocktail-party circuit he was outspoken in his criticism of the Carter Administration and attempted to tear down certain policies and people to make himself look good. Increasingly he was pushed from the inner circles of power until finally in the summer of 1979, just when I was finding my way around Bendix, Blumenthal found that he had gone too far. Carter had requested the resignations of Blumenthal and two or three other Carter appointees. The newspapers called it a purge. At that point, Blumenthal called Agee for advice on what to do. A job at Bendix never even came up. What Blumenthal said he wanted to know was, Should he write a book? Go back to teaching? Perhaps get involved at another company?

Depressed and uncertain about what to do, Blumenthal took off for Hawaii. He went without his family. Several weeks later, he came back. He'd grown a beard and, according to Pete Peterson, who knew Blumenthal through their mutual friend, George Ball, looked like an unhappy, unkempt, fifty-three-year-old hippie. During his vacation, his hatred for Carter had grown into an obsession. He told Agee gleefully about several of his presumptuous schemes, one of which was to personally go to Carter and ask him not to run for reelection and to let Ted Kennedy run for the Presidency for the benefit of the country.

In September 1979, Agee invited Blumenthal to attend the U.S. Tennis Open at Forest Hills in New York. The two of them were walking down the street after the match when Blumenthal said, "You know Coy Eklund asked me to come back and sit on the Equitable board. I assume that was your doing?" Agee said he and Coy had discussed the idea and that Agee had said he thought it was a good one. And then, out of the blue, Blumenthal said, "How come you haven't asked me to come back on the Bendix board?" Agee was stunned. "I thought you disapproved of what a former chairman's role had done to you. I took you at your word that you wouldn't want to meddle on the board as a former chairman. Why are you even bringing this up?" Blumenthal turned on his heel and walked away.

On June 17, 1979, Agee and Harry Cunningham, a member of both the Bendix and the Burroughs boards, first discussed the idea of merging the two companies. Both men agreed that potentially the two companies were a great fit. Bendix's strategy was beginning to take shape, but its broader mission, to move into more high-tech fields, was yet to be fulfilled. Burroughs, which made computer parts, was widely recognized as the industry's laggard stepchild. It wasn't in the same league with IBM, Honeywell and Texas Instruments. Its P/E (price/earnings) ratio was low and the company had been relatively stingy on R&D (research and development) expenditures. Harry Cunningham suggested that Agee's management talent was exactly what Burroughs sorely needed. The idea had definite business appeal for Bendix as well—Burroughs was the kind of high-tech company for which Bendix was looking. In two separate conversations Cunningham offered encouragement to Agee that the possible merger was worth pursuing.

But the relationship of the two boards bothered Agee. "Put your ethicist hat on, Mary," he said to me at the time. "When does a business opportunity become a conflict of interest?" he wanted to know. I wasn't precisely sure, but the whole idea of having boards of directors so closely related disturbed me. Agee sensed an additional problem. How would Paul Mirabito, then chairman of Burroughs and also a member of Bendix's board, feel about Agee as his successor? In late August, Cunningham and Schwartz offered to check it out. "He thinks it's a hell of an idea," Cunningham reported. "You know Paul thinks of you as a son and says he couldn't think of anyone he'd rather have replace him. He's just not comfortable with the automotive segment of Bendix's business yet." But the idea, having been hatched, heated up interest at Burroughs in finding a successor to Mirabito.

In the meantime, who should decide to return to Michigan? None other than the vanquished Michael Blumenthal. His on-again-off-again marriage appeared now to be on again, and he was back in Ann Arbor with his wife. Casting about for something to do in the wake of his inglorious exit from government, he started talking to the people on the Bendix board, friends of his from the days when he was chairman of Bendix. The fact that Mirabito at Burroughs was now looking for a successor soon came to Blumenthal's attention. He went to talk to Paul about the job. From what he was hearing, it seemed to Agee that Blumenthal's once casual interest in Burroughs had now intensified into a no-holds-barred campaign for the chairmanship. It had become a job he had to have. Members of the Bendix board were now becoming noticeably politicized. Blumenthal's return to Southfield was forcing them to choose sides. Board meetings at Bendix were becoming more strained than they had been. Blumenthal's candidacy for the Burroughs chairmanship had politicized the ranks. Mirabito abruptly decided that the Bendix-Burroughs merger was a bad idea and that he should keep Burroughs a separate company with its own identity and its own chairman. Blumenthal made it known that he would be only too happy to step into that position when Mirabito was ready. Thus began not only Blumenthal's reign at Burroughs but his war against Bendix.

No sooner had Blumenthal returned to town than Agee began to hear reports from several key personnel that he was trying to raid the Bendix ranks. Apparently he started calling employees from his old bailiwick and tried to lure them over to Burroughs across the street. When Agee got wind of this, he picked up the phone and confronted Blumenthal on it.

"I don't know why you're doing this, Michael, but calling my people and trying to get them to work for you is unfair," Agee said. "I didn't call anyone at Bendix," Blumenthal answered. "I can't help it if your people approach me. It's not my fault they're unhappy at Bendix." Agee had been told by more than one of the Blumenthal targets that this wasn't true, but he decided to let the matter rest.

But the real fireworks came during the summer. Just at the time when Agee was up to his neck in strategy, and at the same time having his hands full with both Panny and Jacobson, Blumenthal chose to raise a previously resolved pension issue.

"What's going on?" I asked, seeing Agee frown while I was waiting to see him about a strategy matter. "I can't believe what Blumenthal's done," he said. "I don't understand it." "Understand what?" I asked. It was late in the afternoon and Agee seemed to want to talk. "How can he justify going behind my back and maneuvering to get thirty thousand dollars a year from Bendix when he's contractually not entitled to it?" he began. "What do you mean?" I asked. And then Agee told me the tale of Blumenthal and his terminated supplemental pension.

Apparently Blumenthal had made a deal with Bendix before he left that he would receive approximately $30,000 a year as a sort of "supplemental payment" over and above the terms of his already substantial pension. Before he took the job in Washington, he convinced the company to pay him a lump sum of $120,000 in recognition of the fact that he couldn't accept such a pension while working a full four-year term in the government. But when he decided to go to work for Burroughs, Paul Mirabito, then chairman of Burroughs, made it a condition of employment that Blumenthal forfeit any further supplemental pension payments. The consulting required to earn the payments was considered by Mirabito to be a conflict of interest. Blumenthal agreed. But in June, once Mirabito had safely retired, Blumenthal launched a full-fledged campaign to get his supplemental pension back. And instead of going directly to Agee and asking for it, he went behind Agee's back and tried to persuade Hal Barron, Bendix general counsel, to write out the checks.

The Bendix board addressed the issue in early August. It was a particularly touchy affair because of the incestuous relationship between the two boards. All the members of the Bendix board who were also members of theBurroughs board—Paul Mirabito, Coy Eklund and Alan Schwartz, plus Harry Cunningham who, until recently had been on the Burroughs board—urged Agee and the other members of the board to give Blumenthal his pension. "Let Mike have it," they said. "What difference does it make?" Agee and the non-Burroughs members objected. "It's not right," one director said. "What does he do for Bendix to deserve this kind of payment?" another asked. Agee agreed that it was unwarranted, since a contract had been signed by Blumenthal waiving his right to it. Besides, at almost every annual meeting, a shareholder would ask why Blumenthal had gotten the first $120,000 lump sum he'd negotiated for himself in the first place. The board and outside counsel finally convinced the Burroughs contingent that the request represented not only a breach of contract but also a significant conflict of interest. Blumenthal was told he shouldn't have tried to maneuver behind Agee's back and that he couldn't change the terms of a binding contract. The matter was finally resolved. I was relieved. In the midst of everything else he had on his mind, Agee didn't need to be playing cowboys and Indians with Blumenthal.

I had met Blumenthal only once. I was visiting Bendix's Washington office when I had first come on board. It was the first time I'd been to Washington, D.C., since seventh grade, when my family took a trip to "our nation's capital." Agee wanted to introduce me to Nancy Reynolds and a few people on Capitol Hill. At the time, Michael Blumenthal was using one of the offices in the house that represented the National Affairs Office. Apparently he had just left the Carter Administration, in what, I gathered, wasn't the friendliest of partings. As the chairman of Bendix, Agee felt it was only proper that he offer Blumenthal, a former chairman, the use of a Bendix office and secretary, as well as a chauffeur and company car, until he could get settled. At the time, Blumenthal was doing what everyone in Washington who gets kicked out of office does—he was writing a book. The idea of having someone who was "out" in Washington power circles share her office offended Reynolds. She also didn't want anyone looking over her shoulder or criticizing the money she spent cultivating political contacts, now a hot topic at Bendix. But Agee prevailed upon her. He felt it was the least he could do.

He was about to introduce me to Blumenthal when Reynolds interrupted. "I need to speak to you, Bill," she said, taking Agee by the arm. "Just go in and introduce yourself, Mary," Agee said. "I'll be right in." I went up to Blumenthal's temporary office and was about to knock on the door when a gray-haired man, a little older than Agee, came out. "Mr. Blumenthal?" He stared at me out of cold blue eyes with deep circles under them. "I'd like to introduce myself to you. I'm Bill Agee's new executive assistant." He looked somewhat taken aback. I felt rather uneasy all of a sudden. "Oh, really," Blumenthal said with a cynical smile. "And what is it that you do for Mr. Agee?" I still wasn't quite sure how to describe the job so I gave him my usual Harvard Business School speech. "Well, it's a flexible job, where I work on whatever projects the chairman needs help with. I'm there to assist him with whatever projects he needs me for." Blumenthal looked at me for longer than I care to recall. He looked at me from head to foot. His expression was clearly accusatory. It made me wonder what he knew or had known about such jobs that I didn't. I found out sooner than I would have liked to.

from head to foot. His expression was clearly arrogant, it made me wonder what he knew or had known about nice jobs that I didn't. I found out sooner than I would

# CHAPTER SEVEN

*A*ugust *crept by. The days* got hotter. And the atmosphere deteriorated at Bendix. Layoffs were piling up and Bendix was not immune. But it was one thing to hear about people being laid off in South Bend or at any of the other Bendix plant sites; it was quite another to start talking about cutbacks at home headquarters, and that's what was starting to happen. Partly because of the recession and partly because of the strategy that aimed at decentralizing and streamlining the bureaucratic overhead of the company, Bendix now had to pare back its corporate staff. That meant people at Southfield would have to go. People's reaction, quite naturally, was, "Does that mean me?" Slowly, throughout the summer, little slips started circulating telling each department head how many people they should let go. Secretaries kept their eyes open for these little pink slips. In my department I was told by Haney and Taylor that we could afford to drop two from the roles. I asked them who were the employees they needed most. There were only two employees not named by either, a woman and a black. It was ironic, but I felt less defensive about this than a man might have because these were truly the people who were least essential. It was in this atmosphere, with layoffs, unemployment and cutbacks all around, that August drew to an end. The air was steamy. Prime time for a scandal.

Negotiations on the sale of Bendix Forest Products Company had been going on throughout the summer, and it was finally determined that the company would be sold. The divestiture would allow Bendix to accumulate the necessary cash to invest in more high-technology acquisitions. Agee struck a very favorable deal with Kolberg, Kravis and Roberts, a leverage buyout team, which had agreed to buy BFPC for $435 million. This would be the healthy start of the war chest from which Bendix could make its future acquisitions. The decision was top secret. It would decrease the value of the sale if everyone knew it was on the block. Only certain board members and I knew for sure. Agee was committed enough to make plans to go to San Francisco to discuss the sale with Jack Guyol.

Agee asked Steve Schwarzman of Lehman Brothers and me to accompany him on the trip. He believed that it might be reassuring to Guyol to have me there because of the friendship we had developed during my tenure at Bendix.

Agee was also bringing his ten-year-old son, Bob, out and wanted me, as he often did, to talk to him. Agee was concerned about how Bob was reacting to his parents' divorce and wanted me to help him understand the need for them to have a father-to-son talk. "Talk to him, Mare," he said. "You were only five when you had to understand why your parents were separating. See if you can help him open up." If Agee had been less caught up with the strategy, I might have balked, but under the circumstances, I didn't want to see any ten-year-old sitting alone wondering what it all would mean for him. I wanted so much to help Bob.

We arrived in San Francisco on a Friday night. Agee and Guyol went off to have a first meeting alone. I had drinks with someone from my not so distant past, Karen Walker, the woman who'd met me at Harvard Business School and urged Agee to fly me out to Bendix for an interview. We walked from her office at Bendix Forest Products into a nearby bar for a drink. I'd hardly had a chance to broach the subject of the Bendix Forest Products sale when Walker said, "So tell me. Have you fallen in love with Bill Agee yet?" I nearly fell off my bar stool. "Oh come on," she said. "Everyone falls in love with Bill Agee." Somehow, it was hard for me to think of Agee in that light. I'd seen him tired. I'd seen him vulnerable. I'd caught more than a glimpse of his personal life and found it almost repellant. I wanted no part of it. If it were ever possible for me to have fallen in love with him it would have been at the beginning, way back, when I first started working for him, when he seemed so powerful, so charming, so invincible. But my brief phase of hero worship had long since ended. As the months wore on, he seemed less a knight in shining armor and more a needful man, and now a particularly weary man—nothing more, nothing less.

The next day Agee's younger sister decided to fly down to San Francisco to see him. She had heard the news of Agee's recent divorce and wanted to "celebrate" what she considered a long-overdue resolution. Celebration wasn't exactly the mood Agee was in over either his divorce or the imminent BFPC divestiture. But he had neither the time nor the patience to spend pointing out the insensitivity of her cavalier attitude. He delegated the task to me. I gathered she didn't appreciate my reluctance to listen to old war stories.

In an effort to change the subject I asked her how her work had been going. She was off again, this time on a tirade about the crisis she was facing at her newspaper job in Oregon. I was struck by her vehemence in trying to convince me that her problems in her job were because of discrimination. She asked what I thought about bringing a lawsuit against the paper or "exposing it to the world" in the way she said she knew so well as a member of the press. My efforts to dissuade her from any retaliatory action she might later regret didn't go over too well. She was ready to do battle.

I didn't see Agee much during the next few days; I gathered from his calendar that he was spending a lot of time with his board. It wasn't until a few days after we'd been back in Detroit that he came in to see me. "Mary, we need to talk," he said. Such abrupt interruptions were not Agee's style, but as things had been tense around Bendix lately, what with Panny's antics and Blumenthal's subversive attacks, not to mention the prospective layoffs of two hundred people from corporate headquarters, I assumed Agee was coming in with more of the same. I was wrong. It was even more serious than that.

"I've been getting some troubling calls recently from Harry Cunningham and a few of the other members of the board. They want to know if there's something going on between you and me." "What?" I said. I couldn't believe what I'd heard. "Now it's not that they think there is anything," he said, before I could feel the full weight of the accusation sink in. "In fact, they've each reassured me that they don't believe there's anything really wrong. It's just that they've been getting a few anonymous letters...." "What letters?" I interrupted, my neck turning red. "Letters urging them to investigate the relationship between you and me." "From whom?" I asked, scarcely able to catch my breath. "I don't know. They've been anonymous. But it's someone who doesn't like me. Or you."

I sat back in my chair. I had the terrible feeling that there was more to come. "Who else has been getting them?" I asked. "Harry Cunningham, Mac Baldrige, Coy Eklund, Don Rumsfeld," Agee said, naming members of the all-powerful Organization and Compensation Committee of the board, which controlled salaries and promotions, and basically had control even over the tenure of the chairman. "They told me because they wanted to give me a chance to respond, and I did. I told them we had a close business relationship and that I considered you a trusted friend, but that that was it. There wasn't anything more. And I asked them if the rumors were widespread among the board," he said. "What did they say?" "Cunningham said he thought most of the others had gotten a few calls suggesting the same sort of thing. But after I spoke to them they were very apologetic. Eklund said not to worry. He said he was angry that anyone would dare to pry into an executive's personal life, that it was nobody's business. He said that any responsible member of the board wouldn't take it seriously. He was sure that they just wanted to inform me that this was going on and see if I had anything to say about it."

This was outrageous. A certain amount of jealousy and gossip was inevitable. But this was character assassination. "How dare they," I said, my voice rising, the anger welling up inside me. "I can understand some idle chit-chat, some rumors here and there, but anonymous letters and phone calls to the board? That's foul play," I said.

"What kind of people would make this stuff up?" "I don't know," Agee said. "I know a few directors confided that Blumenthal had spoken to them. But they seem to see through his motives. He apparently tried to lay all the credibility wrappings on, you know. He said, 'as a former chairman' he was concerned, that he'd gotten 'reports' and that people were disturbed by your 'proximity and access' to me." "So what's wrong with that? How am I supposed to do my job? By telephone?"

I could take a lot of things. I could take too much work. I could take being scorned by Panny and his boys. But I couldn't take this. Any other rumor but this. With my background, this was the worst thing anyone could say about me, and I didn't react to it as coolly as someone else in my position might have. All I could do was think of my mother. Of all she had gone through before her divorce. And what would Father Bill say if he ever heard this gossip? I started to cry. I think Agee was shocked at how upset I was. He wasn't sure how to react. "Is there something I can do? Would you like me to leave? Maybe you'd like to take a little time off." "I don't know. I don't know what to do," I said. On top of everything else, I felt humiliated. It was embarrassing to have to talk to Agee about this. I suddenly felt stripped of my business armor. I asked him to excuse me and left.

I got in my car and like an automaton drove home. I took note of all the familiar signs and billboards as if that would keep me calm. "American Airlines," "The Real Thing." "Wendy's—4 Miles Ahead." My head was killing me by the time I got home. Without even waiting for it to get dark, I went to bed. When I next opened my eyes, it was 4 A.M. I had a terrible pain in my chest; my left side felt numb. I tried to get out of bed but couldn't move. I waited for daylight and then I called my mother on Cape Cod.

"Mother?" I said. She was surprised to hear my voice. "I don't feel so well," I told her. "I think maybe I'd like to come home for a few days." "Mary? Are you all right, dear?" she asked. "Yes, I'm all right," I told her. "I just think I could use a few days' rest. And I'd like to see you and spend some time on the Cape." "Of course, dear. I was hoping you'd be home around your birthday. Your brother Frank is looking forward to seeing you. Why don't you come home for a few days and just take it easy?"

I called the office and told Agee I needed to take some time off. "Look, Mary, I'm sorry," he said. He didn't seem to know what else to say. "Take as much time as you need. And try to remember, these things have a way of settling down. Call if there's anything I can do," he said.

I took the first flight I could get out of Detroit. When I landed in Hyannis, my mother was there with the car. I told her about my chest pains and, without even stopping off at the house, she drove me to the doctor's office. The diagnosis was tension and extreme fatigue. I was given a prescription for little pink pills—muscle relaxers—took one and, when we got back to the cottage, went to bed. I slept for close to forty-eight hours. When I awoke, two whole days had gone by. It was eerie losing two days out of my life like that. My mother fed me, soothed me and then, when she felt I was ready, led me out onto the porch. "Mary," she said, "I think it's time for one of our little talks."

I couldn't talk without crying. I told her about the letters and about the board. "It's part of business, Mary," she said. "Your Mr. Agee is a very successful man and people are always jealous of people like that." "But how am I going to do my job?" I asked. "Maybe you can't," she said. "I'm not sure it's so good for you to be working there anyway. You don't seem to have any kind of normal life. When was the last time you saw a movie?" she asked. It had been months. "Have you made any friends?" "Not too many," I said. "I think you've sacrificed yourself enough for this job and this chairman. He'll just have to find someone else."

The next day I took a long walk on the beach with Father Bill. It was the same shoreline we'd walked along when I was a child. And I felt like a child again, so needful and unsure. "It's not that I believe I'm that important," I told Father Bill after explaining everything to him. "It's just that I feel he needs me to help him. He's under attack—but I sense that I'm being set up. I think I'm being used to make Agee look bad. I'm really scared. Part of me wants to run away as fast as I can from that whole group of people. But another part feels like I'd be letting my boss down. It's at a time like this you always said to show loyalty." With his years of experience in understanding human nature, Father Bill grasped the issue. "Just remember one of Thomas Aquinas' conditions for waging a just war—'*spes fructus*'—there has to be some 'hope of victory' in order to wage a just battle."

I looked at the ocean. What if I never went back? Why have to deal with all this? But then, why give in to it? It would be foolish to leave now after all the work I'd put in—and just when it was finally going to pay off.

I stayed through my birthday. My mother baked a cake and the five of us—Mother, Bombi, Father Bill, Frank and I—sat around the table and had a little celebration. It was such a lovely moment—the people I was closest to in the world, the little white-iced cake, with its forest of flickering candles. Twenty-nine of them.

If I had hoped it might all go away, that it had all been just a brief episode, some dirty tactics, and that would be the end, I was wrong. Events seemed more and more to take on the appearance of a mystery novel. There was a second, a third and a fourth anonymous letter to the board. All four were given to the Bendix security department. They all bore the same postmark—Royal Oaks, Michigan—and according to security, they had all been typed on the same machine. Questions were being raised more frequently by board members and people were starting to talk. "What's going on at Bendix?" people at the Bloomfield Hills Country Club would say. "You know the Agees are divorced. I saw poor Diane at the grocery store and you should hear what she thinks about Agee's assistant." And on. And on. *Ad nauseam.*

By Labor Day, news of Agee's divorce had spread throughout the company. The level of water-cooler gossip had reached a fevered pitch. What could be more titillating than the notion that this *Wunderkind* was having an affair with his blond executive assistant? And what an opportunity for anyone who had any ax to grind against Agee. Not to mention what a story this would be for the press. It had power, sex, divorce, money, everything that sells papers.

A few days after I returned, I went in to speak with Agee. My throat felt tight. It was no longer like talking to a friend. As if by instinct, the two of us were suddenly more formal with each other. He sat upright, instead of the way he usually sat, with his legs on the coffee table, and I sat as far away from him as possible.

Now I did most of the talking. "I'm not trying to downgrade the importance of my learning curve," I said. "It's just that there are some things that are more important. Like my health and my reputation. This whole experience has made me realize there's something wrong with the way I've been living. There's no balance in my life. I haven't been eating well. I haven't gotten enough sleep. I hardly even find time to go to daily Mass." Agee started to interrupt but for once I didn't let him. I wanted to finish my speech. He sat back and I continued. "You've taught me a lot and I don't begrudge what you've taught me on a professional level, but you've also taught me something else. I've watched the personal side of your life and I see what all this achievement has cost you." This was a low blow, I knew. He was still reeling from the emotional and financial effects of his divorce. "And as far as the letters to the board, I don't know about you, but I can feel an awful lot of pressure building up in this organization and I think something's going to have to give. People are looking around for a convenient scapegoat for their problems. I'm just afraid that scapegoat might be me. I'm beginning to feel more like a lightning rod than a shield for you. Anyone who wants to strike you down can use me."

Agee looked at me. "I know what you mean. But you've got to know I never intended for you to give up everything else for the sake of the job," he said. "I'd like nothing more than to see you start to do other things in your life." His tone was somber. I think he felt guilty. "As far as the atmosphere in this company is concerned, I know things are tense, but with all the changes happening here, you have to expect a certain amount of restlessness among the natives. I think it's not quite as serious as you think. Blumenthal is making a little mischief but I can handle that. And Panny—" He looked weary here. He hated to admit a failure of any kind, and Panny qualified as one in his own mind. "I can handle the situation. He's been a huge disappointment but I want to deal with him as fairly as possible. I think the cauldron will stop boiling as soon as I have a chance to handle both problems. As far as the letters go, I don't really see why you're so upset. It's all kind of silly. If it weren't hurting you so much, I'd find it almost humorous. Who's going to believe a thing like that? It's so foolish." "If it's so foolish," I said, "why did the board confront you on it?" "They didn't confront me. They just wanted to let me know what was going on. They were doing me a favor."

A favor? Don Quixote to the end. "I can take a lot of things," I said. "I can take late nights in the office. I can take the nasty comments from Panny and his boys. But I can't take an accusation like this. I can't take it. Do you understand? I can't take it."

My face felt hot. My chest pains were back. Agee looked at me. "What are you trying to say? Do you want to leave? Do you want to resign?" I tossed the question back to Agee. "You're my mentor. What do you think I should do?"

He paused. "Look, Mary. I'm not going to debate with you. If you want to resign, I'm not going to stand in your way. But I can hardly agree that your time here has been a total loss. If anyone asked me for the three things I've done here that I'm proudest of, one of them would be hiring you. And as far as your professional development goes, I disagree with you. You are much better off now than when you came. You're credentialed now. If you go back to New York, there's not a firm that wouldn't grab you up quickly with your experience. You've had ten years of experience telescoped in one. And I won't stand in your way."

He was being so gracious, I felt like a real child. Maybe I had overreacted. I thought about just what I'd do if I did leave Bendix. Where would I go? Certainly I didn't want to just go back to New York and become another investment banker. I'd spoken to Steve Friedman at Goldman, Sachs in June and he had told me, "Mare, when you're ready, give us a call." But the thought of leaving Bendix upset me. How would it feel tidying up other people's deals after having designed my own with Agee? And the strategy—why should I leave now just when everything was beginning to fall into place? Why should I allow rumors and gossip to dictate my career? This whole thing would probably blow over. The board of directors believed in Bill. They knew the miracles he'd worked at a time when every company in Detroit was losing its shirt. Bendix was reporting record earnings at the same time Burroughs and other companies were reporting record declines. The board wouldn't want to see him fail. They couldn't afford to lose him.

I thought again about what Agee had said. That I was one of the three things he'd done at Bendix that he was most proud of. That moved me. "I hope you know I really don't want to leave," I said. "But I need to live a more normal life. We need new rules." "New rules," he said and we shook on it.

If rumors were what chiefly occupied my mind, strategy occupied Agee's. The plans had been hatched; the confidentiality stage was over. Now it was time to build a consensus within the company. A meeting was scheduled the week after Labor Day at the Detroit Plaza Hotel. On the agenda was the sale of Bendix Forest Products, as well as the final plans for decentralization. Just before the meeting, Agee was approached by Lee Henry, Panny's underling and the number two man in the automotive division. He wanted to share a piece of confidential information with Bill. "Have you been hearing what I've been hearing?" Henry asked. "What's that?" Agee said. "Panny's planning to leave Bendix. I've been told that he's interviewing with an automotive-parts company for another job. I think TRW was mentioned." "What?" "Do you know anything about it?" Agee asked. Henry said he didn't and both men went in to start the meeting.

All the key executives, both line and staff, were gathered. And of course Panny was there. Agee opened the meeting, starting off first with the Forest Products sale. No complaints there. Next he covered the acquisition strategy and the move toward high-technology products. Still no problem at all. Then he started talking about decentralization.

At this point, one of the secretaries came in with a call for Mr. Panny. Since all the key executives from Bendix were in the meeting, it seemed a little odd for Panny to be receiving calls unless they were from outside Bendix. Henry looked over at Agee. Agee ignored the interruption although he looked a bit dismayed. He outlined the strategy, carefully explaining the new high-technology direction in which the company intended to move and the decentralized management changes that would take place. Suddenly Joe Svec passed a note to Agee. The note confirmed that a South Bend radio station had just carried a report that Panny was resigning from Bendix to work for a competitor.

Agee paused and then continued. The more he explained the plan, the more enthusiastic the audience became. In part, this may have been because Agee was a persuasive speaker, but it was also because people genuinely agreed with the overall strategy, particularly the part about decentralization. It offered subordinates more control over their work and promised to free them of much of the senseless paper work that had crept in during the Panny regime. The people who worked directly under Panny were happiest about this new move. More than a few people at Bendix chafed at his autocratic style, and no one liked his constant demand for written reports and memos. As the meeting progressed, it became more and more clear to Panny that even his own people were enthusiastic about Agee's ideas. The greater their enthusiasm, the more disruptive Panny became.

After several votes, he tried to reopen for discussion what had already been laid to rest. "You sure you folks know what you're doing?" Or, "I don't know about these fancy new ideas. Now I know you went to Harvard Business School, Bill, but I'm not sure you people up there understand anything about cars. I mean, how can you run an automotive business with clean hands?" he said, looking for a laugh from his men. But no one was laughing. Even Agee now saw what people had been telling him all along. Panny had to go.

After the meeting, he asked Panny to step aside. "Bill, I think I've been more than patient with you. I've supported you and backed you even when my own board suggested I do otherwise. But I think now I've seen enough. You're being extremely divisive. And if you're interviewing for other jobs, the least you could do is tell me you are. I don't like it when I have to learn first from others what you have on your mind."

Panny countered, "I bet what's really bothering you is

my attitude toward Cunningham. You know I'm not impressed."

"Frankly, Bill, you're entitled to your own opinion. But that's not the issue here. The issue is work. And I'm not sure it's good for either of us to go on this way. I think perhaps it's in both our interests to end this relationship now," Agee said. "Bill, I'm going to have to ask for your resignation. Think about it tonight and then come see me in my office first thing tomorrow."

Before he left that night, Agee stopped by my office. He looked wan. "It's so strange the way things work. I've never felt more elated about any business accomplishment than about this strategy, and the response I saw people have to it this afternoon—and yet, at the same time, I've never felt more upset about what went on between Panny and me today."

"I understand, but you've had to let senior executives go before, haven't you?" I asked, trying to grasp what was really bothering him. After all, my training and experience had taught me—and I knew Agee agreed—that if people were not doing the job, it was to everyone's advantage to let them go. The bottom line was the bottom line. And usually if they weren't making the mark, it was better for their careers in the long run to let them make a new start elsewhere. But Agee had another concern. "It's not that," he said. "It's just that I've never been involved in a firing that had so much potential to blow up in my face."

The next morning, when I came in the secretaries were already there. According to my "new rules," I was coming to work at 8 A.M. now instead of 6:30 A.M. "Panny's in there," Agee's secretary Marie told me, nodding toward Agee's office. "Been in there since seven." She gave me a knowing look. Agee confirmed it later that day. Bill Panny was out.

A few days after the firing, Agee made it official. A "blue memo"—signifying it was from the chairman—went out to all department heads. The memo was brief and to the point. "After two years of exemplary service, William P. Panny has decided to resign." It included a full list of Panny's accomplishments with the company. Of course Panny hadn't resigned—he had been fired—but Agee allowed him a graceful exit. It wasn't Agee's style to be petty or mean.

Other than a perfunctory notice in the *Detroit Free Press*, not much was made of Panny's dismissal. Around the office the news was received with a remarkable degree of calm. People knew what a disruptive agent Panny had been and seemed relieved to see him go. The organization appeared to heal quickly now that he was gone.

Meetings of the chairman's council were much more peaceful now with Panny gone. Svec no longer had to straddle the fence between Agee and Panny, and people were visibly relieved not to have to witness what had become an unpleasant boxing match. Now there were just a few of us left on the staff side—Agee, Joe Svec, Larry Hastie, Hal Barron, and me. It was clear that some new blood had to be brought in. Agee decided to add the key operating or line executives to his advisory council—Mace Reynolds, Lee Henry, Paul Hartz, Craig Smith and Bill Purple. He also formally added a few staff executives— John Weil, Senior VP of Technology, Larry Hastie and Hal Barron. Bendix was operating now without a vice chairman (Charlie Donnelly had retired in September), an executive vice president of strategic planning (Jacobson had joined Burroughs full time in August), and a president. That left a gaping vacuum in the executive council. It was decided to fill the two senior positions—vice chairman and president—with people from outside, for which Bendix engaged the executive-headhunting agency Russell Reynolds Associates of New York, but to fill the strategic-planning position from inside. "I stand ready to serve," Larry Hastie told Agee at one of the executive council meetings, "and by the way I think your aide-de-camp would make a terrific vice president of human resources." But Agee didn't respond. He was put off by Hastie's back-slapping style and had other plans in mind. "We'll have to think about this, Larry."

The rumor mill seemed to have slowed down now with Panny gone, but every now and then snippets of gossip or unkind words would make their way back to me. Every time I received one of these, it felt to me like a kick in the gut. It was awful knowing that there was still someone out there trying to get me, and I let Agee know of my concern. "It still upsets you, doesn't it?" he said. "Of course it does. Why shouldn't it?" I said. "Look, Mary," he said. "There isn't a person here questioning your competence," he said.

"Competence? Of course they aren't questioning my competence. They can't. There's nothing they could say. They're questioning my ethics. I'd rather they questioned my competence. I could defend that. But how can I defend my ethics? What should I do? March into the board and tell them I'm a really good person and I don't sleep around with people?"

The accusations had its most perceptible effects on the relationship between Agee and me. Whereas before we felt totally comfortable with each other, now we felt awkward. It cost us our ability simply to be friends. Now we were under a strain. No longer did he feel comfortable dropping off a study on his way home from work at my house. And the idea of asking him for a ride to work, as I had done in the past when my car was on the blink—he was the only one at Bendix who went to work as early as I did—was now out of the question. "Getting a lift with the boss?" Hastie once said to me after seeing me hopping into Agee's car one day on the way home from work. Flustered, I didn't answer him at the time. But now it made me angry. Didn't Hastie often catch a ride home with the boss and vice versa? And weren't the two men steady tennis partners? My sudden need to watch myself around Agee made me feel self-conscious and angry and made our former good working relationship upsetting now.

Still the anonymous letters kept coming. By now there had been about a dozen of them. Agee found out that toward the end of the summer Blumenthal had actually paid a visit to one of the key Bendix board members, Harry Cunningham, to ask him about this alleged "affair." "Say, what's Agee got going there? Is he having some kind of midlife crisis or has he just lost all judgment? It's one thing if he wanted to have a fling on the side, but to make her Vice President for Corporate and Public Affairs and now to let her effectively run Strategic Planning? This is beyond the realm of appropriate corporate behavior," Blumenthal had said. Or so a former director had told Agee.

Whether the board believed Blumenthal or not, clearly several of its members were concerned. They started to comment on, and offer advice on, the most sensitive details of corporate etiquette. "It doesn't look so good—

with your office next to hers," a few of them told him. "The cosmetics of these things are important, Bill." "And people are wondering what she does. She's been your executive assistant, a vice president for public affairs and she does strategy as well?" Agee had explained my role to the board earlier when they promoted me, and they had accepted the explanation then. But now the seeds of doubt had been planted. Even the most innocent comments now evoked concern.

On September 15, Agee chose to raise the matter again to the board. This was contrary to his usual way of proceeding, which was not to bother the board with petty politics and infighting at headquarters. But the tension was growing worse, and Agee could see how upset I was. Pete Peterson and other advisors had encouraged him to discuss the matter openly with his board. It was Agee's hope that he could put the matter to rest once and for all.

The all-powerful Organization and Compensation Committee met at the Equitable Life Insurance Company building at 1265 Avenue of the Americas in New York. Several board members were there—Harry Cunningham, Mac Baldrige, Coy Eklund and Jonathan L. Scott, former chairman and chief executive officer of A&P. I waited outside. After an hour—the relationship between Agee and me wasn't the only issue discussed—Agee called me in. "Mary, I've told the board what I have to say on this issue and I thought perhaps you would want to say something to them." At which point Agee left the room. I didn't know where to begin. Harry Cunningham, sensing my discomfort, smiled paternalistically and broke the ice. "Look, this is very awkward for you, I'm sure. No one here is accusing you of anything yet, and we're sorry you have to be put through all of this. But perhaps there's something you'd like to express to us." I started to speak although I felt too strong a sense of anger and humiliation even to know where to begin. "If what you are asking is, do I have anything other than a professional relationship with Bill Agee, the answer is no. Absolutely not. I'm angry I even have to say it."

There was an awkward silence all around the room. I looked every man straight in the eye and watched as each cast his eyes down. Except one. Harry Cunningham didn't want to miss a moment of this inquisition. Maybe he thought if he stared hard enough I'd collapse under interrogation and admit, "I did it! I'm guilty." I sensed this and was starting to feel a modicum of pleasure in just staring right back. "I don't see that we need to waste any more time on this," Coy Eklund said, and I got up and left the room.

One of the issues raised by the meeting was the confusion over my role, since although my title was Vice President for Corporate and Public Affairs, I had been functioning for almost a year as vice president of strategic planning. "If she's performing these responsibilities, then why don't you give her the title and perhaps that will end the confusion once and for all," Coy Eklund suggested, and Hugo Uyterhoeven agreed. Agee said it was what he had planned to do and most of the board enthusiastically agreed. "Are you sure corporate America is ready for a female who looks like Mary to be in that role?" Donald Rumsfeld said. But his comment was taken as a joke, and the board and Agee agreed he should officially move me into Jacobson's old office.

"I have some good news," Agee said—something I certainly hadn't had much of these days. "I've polled the board and we're all in agreement. We'd like you to be the new vice president of strategic planning." A few months ago I would have been ecstatic to receive this piece of news. But now advancements in my career left me feeling unmoved. "I think you're ready, and I think it's time to do it," Agee said. "Besides, the board feels there's a certain amount of confusion about what you really do, and this ought to help straighten that out." If the board was behind it, that meant they couldn't take Blumenthal's or Panny's insinuations that seriously. I felt as if it were new vote of confidence and, in that light, was happy to accept the job. It was, after all, what I most wanted. "I'm glad to do it," I said, and without much change in my daily activities, I switched over into my new job.

My promotion seemed like small news compared to all the new changes that were being made. There was a new strategy to put in motion and, with only four of the original members still on the chairman's council, that meant more work for each of us to do. Hastie, however, was obviously smarting over my promotion. "Well, I'm sorry they didn't promote the best man for the job," Hastie said. "I'm sure you would have made a fine vice president of strategic planning, Larry," I said. "Well, good luck, anyway," he said. The reaction was more unusual from my former colleague, Nancy Reynolds. "How will I ever function without you?" she said. My pal.

I had made Agee promise when the issue had first come up that he would keep me informed about every new development concerning the rumors about our relationship, so I knew by now, when he walked into my office with a certain look on his face, that there was more bad news. The external director of public affairs, David Taylor, had come to him with the grim news that both major newspapers in town, the *Detroit Free Press* and the *De-*

*troit News*, had recently received anonymous letters similar to the ones that had been sent previously to the board. "We've got a real PR problem brewing," Taylor had told Agee. "Some of my guys (Taylor always referred to the media as "his guys") want to know more about this attractive young woman who's just been promoted," he said. "And I think you've got to be straight with them." David Taylor, over whom I'd been promoted on my way to becoming Vice President for Corporate and Public Affairs, was none too good a friend of mine. "You're good with the press. Why don't you talk to them. Have it out once and for all."

Agee wasn't sure this was particularly good advice and wanted more time to determine what he wanted to do. "Can't you handle it?" he said to Taylor. "I don't want to make it seem any more important than it's already been made to be."

"Sure. Look, I've already told them that just because you've gotten a divorce recently and Cunningham's separated from her husband doesn't mean you're running around with your blond executive assistant, but they don't seem to believe me."

Agee was clearly annoyed. It irked him that at a time when he was in the midst of launching his strategy, and with the recent vacancies created by Panny and Jacobson on his mind, he had to deal with what he viewed as foolish gossip.

But the rumors weren't going away. If anything, they were getting worse. By now, everyone at the Bloomfield Hills Country Club had heard about Panny's departure. "I got between Agee and his girlfriend," was the way he liked to explain it. And a few Panny loyalists still at Bendix echoed the same line in the Bendix corridors. People in the business community were curious too. Panny and Jacobson, gone during the same month? A coincidence? Or was there a coup going on at Bendix? And it was not just Detroit that had its eyes on Bendix. Word about the new strategy had already sparked considerable interest in the business community at large and *Fortune* magazine had decided to send not just one, but two, of its reporters to find out more. They had asked Agee if they could have the exclusive story on the strategy. They expected to be allowed to sit in on any meetings during the week they would be investigating the story. Their timing was impeccable. Agee was preparing for the company's annual employees' meeting. With Taylor's strong encouragement, Agee agreed to allow *Fortune* in to do its story.

Each year, Agee held a meeting for all six hundred employees at the Southfield headquarters. This year's meeting was scheduled for Wednesday, September 24. It was part of Agee's "participatory" or "democratic" style to answer any and all questions the people at Bendix might have on their minds. Agee's long-standing popularity at Bendix was in good measure based on his candor and open style. Since few employees dared to stand up and ask what they really wanted to know, a few days before the meeting each year Agee had a few of his executives poll the organization collecting questions from the rank and file. This year, the pollsters were Hastie, me, Svec, David Taylor and Bette Howe from personnel. A few days before the meeting, the five of us gathered to go through our lists of questions.

"Let's get to work on what to say," Agee said, a few days before the meeting. The five of us gathered in his office with our questions from "the people." First and foremost in the minds of the people were the rumored layoffs. "How many people are going to lose their jobs?" "Will they be retrained? Relocated?" Then there were dozens on the Panny-Jacobson purge. "Was Bill Panny fired or did he really quit?" "What about Jacobson? Why did he leave?" "Who will take his place?" Many wanted to know if there was any truth in the rumors that Agee would be going to Washington, as the former chairman, Blumenthal, had done. "Are you really going to Washington?" "Will you go if Reagan wins?" And then of course there were the questions about me. "Why did you and the board select such a young woman to be a corporate vice president?" "How close is your relationship with Mary Cunningham?" These were worded in various ways but they all wanted to know the same thing. "Exactly what is your relationship with Ms. Cunningham?"

Quickly we went through the questions, but whenever one came up about me there was an awkward pause. "Sorry I have to bring this up, but I did get one about you, Mare," Hastie said, genuinely apologetic. David Taylor was less apologetic. "A good twenty percent of the people I spoke to wanted to know about what's going on with you and Mary, Bill," he said, not even looking at me. Joining right in, Bette Howe offered, "Well, I got even more of the same stuff." Only Svec and I hadn't encountered any. Svec was probably too embarrassed to say, and certainly the people I interviewed wouldn't dare raise the issue with me. In all, about one-fourth of the questions had to do either directly or indirectly with me; it was clearly an issue. But in Agee's mind, it was still not a relevant one.

The other issue that came up was whether to invite the press to the meeting. Agee had scheduled an interview with a reporter from the *Detroit Free Press* about a week before, but at the last minute canceled it because of the exclusive offered to *Fortune*. Taylor urged him to change his mind. "You've got to have the local press there. If you don't invite them, they'll find out what went on anyway and write whatever they want." But Agee was reluctant. This was his annual meeting with his employees, and he bristled at the idea of being forced to open it up to outsiders, let alone the press. "This is my meeting with my employees, not some show for the press," he said. "I don't want to have to worry about what I say or how I say it. Besides, we've never invited the press to an employees' meeting in the past. Why should we start now?"

Taylor leaped to his feet. "Look, more is going on this year. The strategy. Panny. Jacobson. And those letters. You've got to discuss this issue of the relationship with Mary," he said. Agee was irritable now. He was tired of having the issue constantly brought up. "Look, David," Agee said. "If it has to be dealt with, I will. But let's get on to more important issues right now. I have six hundred employees to face and a major new strategy to explain."

Taylor, Svec, Hastie and Howe left, and I stayed back with Agee to help him with the speech. We spent most of our time discussing the strategy. Agee wanted to be sure we explained it in a way everyone could understand. We also worked out a way to explain what had happened with Panny and Jacobson without acknowledging the bad blood that had gone on. "And of course I'll announce your promotion and the others," he said just as we were finishing, leaving me to believe he might not address the troublesome "relationship" issue at all.

It wasn't the first time Agee had been faced with an issue like this. A year and a half ago he had promoted

Bernard Winograd, his assistant at the time, to treasurer of the company, and Larry Hastie, his former executive assistant, into the role of vice president for human resources. Winograd was only twenty-eight and Hastie thirty-six. The promotions of two men so young caused such a commotion that Agee had to call a special meeting of the employees to explain those promotions. "We promote on ability around here, not seniority, not age, not anything else," he said. His statement put an end to that crisis. But this one was more troublesome, more awkward to discuss. There were clearly no examples out there of what to do. And it fell in the category of issues he'd rather not face, when important ones like the strategy were on his mind.

On Monday, September 22, Agee, Svec and I flew to Boston for an analysts' meeting. We considered it a dry run. A few hours before the financial analysts' meeting, which was scheduled for that afternoon, Agee stopped in to see Hugo Uyterhoeven, a professor at the Harvard Business School, and one of the members of the Bendix board Agee respected most. What Agee wanted to know was just how seriously he ought to take the escalating campaign to smear his name. Hugo had always had an air of philosophical calm, and this was surely a time when both Agee and I could benefit from some of that. The two men spent what Agee later described as a "soul-searching" hour or two, at the end of which I was asked to join them. "I think it's most unfortunate that you've been made to feel that you must defend your private lives or answer charges like that to me or anyone else," Uyterhoeven said. "As long as Mary continues to do the outstanding job that she has been doing, you have nothing to be concerned about. What you do or don't do in your personal lives is nobody's business. I'm sorry it ever came up." We both couldn't have agreed more.

The analysts' meeting that afternoon was a smashing success. Agee discussed the Bendix Forest Products sale as well as the possible sale of Asarco. Bendix Forest Products' book value was currently $120 million; Agee had negotiated a selling price of $425 million. That would mean a $305 million profit to Bendix from that alone. And Asarco, which he'd bought at slightly under $20 a share, he was now planning to sell for $55 a share. With six million shares, that would mean an additional $210 million profit for Bendix. The analysts were noticeably impressed. The figures *were* impressive. Then he went on to outline the strategy. He explained the divestiture plan, the decentralization plan and the acquisition and growth plans in high-tech. Everything moved along right on course, but best of all, the speech received excellent coverage in the Boston press. Articles in the Boston newspapers hailed Agee's bold new move and laid out the strategy in crystal-clear terms. Exhilarated and riding high on the wings of the new strategy, Agee, I and even Svec felt encouraged on the flight back to Southfield, although anxious for the more important employees' meeting that was next.

Before he left, Svec asked Agee if he could speak with him. "Alone," he said, nodding over at me. And then, in a lower voice, "It's about Mary." "Well," Agee said, looking surprised, "anything you have to say that concerns Mary you can say right here. Mary? Don't leave." Svec looked at me. "I really think the situation with the rumors has gone too far," he said. "It could destroy your career, Bill, and it could destroy your reputation," he said, nodding toward me. "I'm not sure she's useful to you anymore."

I couldn't take it any longer. I practically threw my glass at him. "I'm tired of all those pigs," I sputtered. "Of the slime. Of everyone with their heads in the gutter. I should be spending every ounce of my energy trying to do my job, and instead I have to spend every ounce defending my integrity. I can't do it. I won't do it. I might as well resign." "Mary, come on. Don't react so fast," Agee said. Svec looked at Agee. "She's right, you know, Bill. She should resign." I couldn't listen to another word of this. I left the room. I didn't want to hear any more.

A half hour later, Agee called me at home. "Look, I know how upset you are. But hang in there. It's going to blow over. Not everyone feels like Joe Svec. You've got lots of friends there. Trust me. I'll see to it. What more do you need than the chairman of the board on your side?"

At seven-thirty the next morning, Agee gathered his troops around him. It was the final dress rehearsal before the meeting, which was scheduled for four o'clock. We were midway through reviewing the speech when a call came in over the squawk box. "Mr. Agee?" It was Marie. "There's a call for you from the *Detroit Free Press*. I told them you were in a meeting but they said it was urgent." "All right," Agee said. "Put it through."

We all listened to the voice that came over the squawk box. "Mr. Agee? This is Lou Heldman at the *Free Press*. I hear you fellows are having an employees' meeting over there this morning and I was just wondering if you wanted to invite some of us from the press." "Lou, it's not an open meeting although I'll be happy to speak to you afterwards. Talk to Marie or Barb. Maybe they can set up an interview for you." "Well, we hear there are some important things that are going to be discussed at this meeting and we'd like to be in on them." "I'll be glad to discuss those with you—but afterwards."

"Mr. Agee. Perhaps I should remind you that whether you invite us or not, we're able to infiltrate that meeting. You've got a fairly serious leakage problem within your top ranks, in case you hadn't noticed."

Agee put his hand over the mouthpiece. "What do you think I should do?" he asked Taylor. "You have to invite them," Taylor said. Agee looked at the rest of us. I shrugged. I didn't know whether he should invite them or not. Hastie looked blank. "Besides," Taylor pushed on, "those guys from *Fortune* are going to be there. You might as well let the local paper in." "All right," Agee said. "Mr. Heldman, we'll extend an invitation to you to attend the employees' meeting. My secretary Marie will give you the details." After he hung up, he said to Taylor, "I suppose if we let the *Free Press* in, we have to invite that reporter from the *News*." "Might as well," Taylor said. "Okay, Dave," Agee said. "You take care of that. Now let's get on with this speech. We only have a few hours to go."

The air around Bendix was festive that morning. For most employees, this was like a day off from school. Most days, not much out of the ordinary goes on inside the Bendix building, and an "event" such as this, particularly when the MC was someone as charismatic and interesting to everyone as Agee, was the subject of a certain amount of not unexpected fanfare. Except that this time there was tension in the atmosphere as well. People knew a certain number of layoffs were going to be announced. But fear over this issue was offset by interest in the other issues they hoped Agee would discuss, the inside stories about what happened to Panny and Jacobson, whether Agee would be leaving to go to Washington, and what, if anything, he was going to say about me.

The meeting took place in the Civic Center Auditorium, just across the road from Bendix headquarters. Most employees just walked through the parking lot. There wasn't any need for me to take a car. I walked over to the Civic Center by myself. I was tired from going over the issues with Agee and from the recent one-day trip to Boston. Besides, I also felt somewhat on edge. I knew one of the reasons everyone was so excited about this meeting was because of me. I felt so odd being the person in so many people's thoughts, and yet it felt so lonely walking over to the Civic Center. There were what looked like thousands of faces already inside. Agee was standing up front talking with some of his staff. I slipped into a row in the middle of the auditorium. I thought I'd be less conspicuous there. At a few minutes after four, the meeting began.

Agee stood behind the podium. "I know that there are a lot of burning questions out there. What I was thinking about doing perhaps was to just deliver a brief message to you and then leave. [Laughter] People relaxed. Even I relaxed. Agee could do that. He had a hypnotic ability at times, and it was part of why people at Bendix loved him so much. "But I obviously can't and I won't," he continued, "because why I am here today is to bring you up-to-date on where the company is, where it's going and why we have done some of the things we've done. And at the end, I hope you'll feel as strong and confident about the Bendix Corporation as the board, top management and I feel about this company today.

"We have had a difficult and interesting and paradoxical year," he began. He was perfect at this, the captain of a storm-battered vessel assuring his crew that everything was under control. "We have had a year in which our automotive business has not done well, and our aerospace division has had an outstanding performance." He went on to outline the various viscissitudes in the company. On the upside, he talked about strategy, about what he was doing and why he was doing it. The audience seemed genuinely enthusiastic. On the downside he talked about the layoffs. "Now I know we are talking about two hundred people whose lives are affected by what I have just said, and all I can do is to assure you that we will be as humane as we know how. . . ." He proceeded to outline all the ways in which the company would assist those relocated or laid off.

"Now, many of you have asked questions about issues on your mind, and I'm going to try to answer those questions. The question I hear a lot on is, 'If Governor Reagan is elected President, will Agee go off to Washington?' Anyone hear that question before?" [Laughter from the audience.] "OK. Let me tell you the answer, and I'm not going to give you a political answer. Politicians always tell you 'I have no current intentions' or 'no present plans' or whatever. But I'll tell you exactly what I've told the board. I promise you that if Governor Reagan were elected, or if Jimmy Carter were elected, and if either picked up the phone and asked me to come to Washington, I would not, repeat, would not and cannot go. There are many reasons for it but the principal reason is that I feel so strongly about helping to transform this company from where we are today to real greatness. The timing would be very poor even if I could be so presumptuous as to speculate that somebody might want me to come to Washington. So I promise you, unequivocally, that I am not going to Washington if asked this fall or in the foreseeable future."

Next he addressed the matter of his executive staff. "One of the questions that I've heard from many different quarters is 'Why was Bill Panny fired?' Bill Panny was not fired. Bill Panny is an outstanding executive. He's a good man. He made many valuable contributions to Bendix. But the management style that we are going to have in this company in the years ahead [will be different]—and the fact that my principal job is to make sure that whoever is in that number two position has the capacity to take my place is the reason surrounding the decision that Bill made to leave the company.

"Now on to Jacobson. Jerry Jacobson was not fired," Agee said. "Jerry Jacobson had an opportunity that he couldn't refuse. It's a financial package, a title and a position that I was unwilling to meet. . . . I wish him all the best."

He continued with the next executive move. "I've been told by many people, and I know that it is buzzing around, that Mary Cunningham's rise in this company is very unusual and that it has something to do with a personal relationship that we have." Someone coughed. A curtain fluttered. The room grew very still. I wondered what Agee was going to say. A part of me wanted him to get up there and really give it to those people who'd been ruining my life with their gossip and smear campaign. But another part of me wanted him to ignore it. Not to say anything at all. Ignore it and maybe it would go away. I had no idea what Agee would do next.

"Sure, it's unusual. Her rise in this company is unusual because she's a very unusual and a very talented individual. But her rapid promotions are totally justified.

Throughout my career, I have felt so strongly about this topic that I wanted to share a little bit with you because I've been the beneficiary of people who have allowed me a chance, perhaps ahead of my time. And that has to do with grounds for this promotion. It is based solely upon excellent performance. Those are the standards that I've always set for myself, and those are the standards that I have set for those who work closely around me. And I can tell you, the contribution that Mary has made has been outstanding, and if you had the opportunity to measure it to the degree I have, you too would see the job she has done is without peer in this company. At the same time, I tell you it is true that we are very, very close friends, and she's a very close friend of my family. But that has absolutely nothing to do with the way that I and others in this company and on the board evaluate her performance. Excellent performance is what really counts in this world. This is an axiom that I have always followed and that I am always going to follow. Next question."

That was less than two minutes of speech that lasted over an hour. I was desperate to know people's reactions but I dared not look. I kept my eyes riveted on Bill Agee. The rest of it was devoted to strategy. I was too overcome to concentrate, but I could sense Agee was doing a wonderful job. The audience was really with him and he seemed to be rallying the troops to his side. When it was finally over, I got up to leave. I was grateful to put that issue behind me.

But no sooner did I start to go than I noticed a short, pudgy man from the other side of the room making a beeline for me. "So, how long have you been sleeping with the boss?" he said. "What?" I said. I couldn't believe what I'd heard. "I'm not going to dignify that question with an answer," I said. "Then you're not going to deny it?" he asked. I wasn't well versed at the time in reporters' games. "Let me ask you in another way," he said. "Isn't it unusual for a woman like you to be in so high a position?" I felt the anger welling up inside me. "It's unusual, I suppose, but not that impossible," I said. "Don't you think it's odd for someone with your background to be in that job?" he persisted. I was so out of it I thought he meant wasn't it odd that a philosophy and ethics major like me would be in business. "Look," I said. "I don't have to carry this conversation any further." "It doesn't matter whether you do or not. I've got my story," he said and left.

Immediately I searched the room for Agee. He was up front, surrounded by people. Everyone was congratulating him on the speech. He looked so elated. Suddenly I felt desperate. Something awful had just happened to me, but it hadn't affected Agee. He was being exalted by his people while I had just been sullied. Before I left, I saw Heldman dart up to him. I was too far to hear what they said but after less than a minute I saw a disgruntled Heldman walk away.

Agee was surrounded by fans. I waited in the back of the room. After the crowd cleared out he came over to me. "What'd you think, Cunningham?" he said, beaming from the applause. "Didn't we do it?" he said, saying something about the strategy. I heard myself say, "Congratulations," but my heart wasn't in the words. "Did a man named Lou Heldman talk to you?" I asked. "Oh, yeah. From the *Free Press*," Agee said. "He asked some obnoxious question that I told him I wasn't even going to answer. But what did you think of the reaction to decentralization. Wasn't that fabulous?"

For the second time now, Bill Agee saw me cry. "What's the matter? Have I upset you? Didn't you like what I said about you?" "It was fine," I said. "It's just that reporter. I shouldn't have spoken to him." "Heldman? Don't worry about him. He's just an ass. He doesn't mean a thing." What a weird friendship this is, I thought If we were any other people, if we were two men, or two women, he could comfort me. But of course he couldn't, and I was grateful he didn't try. "Come on. Why don't you use the ladies room, take a few minutes to get hold of yourself, and then I'll meet you back here. The car will be waiting by the side door. We've got a plane to catch, you know. Guyol is waiting for us in San Francisco and those two reporters from *Fortune* are coming along."

Someone did reach out to comfort me then. It was Barbara, one of Agee's secretaries. "Are you crying, Mary?" she asked. She put an arm around me. "Don't let it get to you. They're just jealous. You've got so much going for you. You're so young. So pretty. So bright. They're just being mean." I thanked her and eventually ventured out the side door to the waiting limousine.

Lou, the driver, opened the door to the limousine. I got in. A moment of silence. And then, as we drove to the airport, Agee asked, "So, what did you think of the speech?" He was thinking about the speech when all I could do was think about that horrible reporter's face. "I just..." I faltered. "Oh, come on, Mary. You can't let these petty people bother you. You know the way to handle a thing like that? You tell 'em, 'No comment.' That's all and walk right out." "But why should I even have to deal with a question like that? Here I've just gotten a well-earned promotion and I can't even feel good about it. I've got to worry about this."

Oh, no, I thought. Here goes baby Mary again, crying into her milk. But I felt angry. "First letters to the board, then rumors around Bendix, and now I have to talk about this trash to the press. Where does it end?" Agee looked distraught. "Look, just for now, will you do me a favor? For me. Will you just allow yourself to feel good about this for just a few minutes? You're Vice President of Strategic Planning. The strategy that you worked on is coming to fruition. Let yourself enjoy that. Focus on the positive."

Two hours later we were on the plane, airborne for San Francisco. Little did we know what was about to explode at home.

# CHAPTER EIGHT

*T*hings surged ahead, with the inexorable speed of events that precede something very good—or very bad. Something much larger than Agee, than me, than any single individual, was happening, but we were too busy reacting to the immediate present to notice. We were actors being asked to read increasingly more difficult lines—but someone else was writing the script.

With the employees' meeting behind us, we boarded the plane for San Francisco—Agee, the two reporters from *Fortune*, and I. Somehow, they managed to persuade Agee to let them come along. "This is part of the story, isn't it?" argued Peter Bernstein, one of the two reporters. "And besides, it's time you'd only spend sitting on the plane anyway," said Wilton Woods, his sidekick. A private tête-à-tête with two reporters was the last thing I wanted. As far as I was concerned, they were all little Heldmans, and I was chary of them all. But Agee had other things on his mind. Namely, the strategy. Still on a high from the employees' meeting, he was only too happy to elaborate on it some more. He still envisioned that a straight business story on the strategy would appear in *Fortune* as the result of all this.

Once on board, the four of us started talking business.

Agee was happiest when talking about the new strategy. His enthusiasm was infectious, and the reporters furiously scribbled notes. But once they'd gotten down the highlights, they ventured onto more delicate fronts. "Let's talk about the people issues now. Surely this much change is bound to cause some upset in the ranks," Bernstein said. "With so much change, so quickly, you're bound to meet some resistance," Woods said. Obviously, they'd done their homework and spoken to Panny and his ilk. After a few minutes in which Agee explained the situation on his executive staff, one of the reporters asked how he could possibly move ahead on such a drastic plan with so few in the inner sanctum to help him. "There's been a vacuum at the top for a while now," Agee said. "Of my top management team, one retired early, one jumped ship, one tried a mutiny and one is too political to take any kind of strong stand. Still, that doesn't mean I can call a halt to everything. The timing of the strategy is crucial; interest rates and stock prices won't necessarily wait for me to clean up my executive staff. Besides," he said, nodding at me, "I have Mary to assist me. She's been my left and right arm throughout." Both reporters turned to me. Now that my name had been mentioned, the issue that was on everyone's mind, but that no one had dared mention until now was suddenly fair game.

"What do you make of the allegations that you entrusted your former executive assistant"—he looked right at me—"with too much power, too fast?" Bernstein asked. "I don't make an issue of it at all," Agee said, glad for the chance to speak up and defend me. "If a young man of similar talents had been in her position and similar events had occurred, I'd have done the same thing." He then launched into his belief in meritocracy. "When I was twenty-nine and a young executive at Boise-Cascade, someone entrusted me with the same kind of power," he said. "Why shouldn't I do the same with Mary? She's just as talented as I was and more capable than the rest of my team. Her situation is the same as mine was," he said.

"No it's not," Bernstein said. "You were a young *man*. She's a young *woman*." "And an attractive one," Woods piped up. "Is that a reason not to promote her?" Agee asked. "Should I make her wait another five years even though she's better able to do the job than the rest of the people on my executive staff—men who are twice her age? I don't think that's fair. That's bending over backwards in the other direction." "Theoretically you're right," Bernstein said. "But practically, you're wrong. You've got to take appearances into account. You know, how it looks to promote a bright, young and attractive woman one month after you get a divorce."

At this point I intervened. "Does that mean we should promote bright young women at a slower rate, and if they're attractive perhaps not even promote them at all?" I was tempted to suggest that perhaps I should dye my hair gray and gain ten pounds. Maybe that would make everyone happy.

"Just imagine how it looks when an attractive young female hops into a limousine with the chairman," Bernstein said. "Let's face it. People are going to get ideas." This really provoked my ire. "Do you mean then that the female executive shouldn't ride in the limousine with her boss, even though that may be the only free hour the chairman has to talk?" "I don't know," Bernstein said. "A young male executive wouldn't think twice about doing it," I said. "Why penalize the woman?" We went on like this for almost an hour. Bernstein and Woods had long ceased taking notes. No longer was this an interview between "journalists" and their "subject"; we were now just four people, locked into a timely philosophical debate. "This is an incredible story," Bernstein said. "It's a story on all sorts of levels and it's embodied by the two of you." I agreed. There certainly was a story here, but it didn't exactly thrill me that I was it. This was my life, and I didn't like watching it become an "issue."

We checked into the Hyatt Union Square in San Francisco that evening. Since Bernstein and Woods had broached the issue, I started thinking that perhaps it did look funny to people that the two of us stayed at the same hotel. Hotels were often sensitive to all this and usually put us on separate floors. I had never thought twice about it before. Perhaps now I was going to have to do so.

I met Agee in the lobby at 9 A.M. the next morning. Together we drove to the Bendix Forest Products meeting near Fisherman's Wharf. Agee took his place behind the lectern and I took a seat on the side. The atmosphere was decidedly tense. Our two friends from *Fortune*, Bernstein and Woods, sat diagonally behind me. As soon as Agee started to speak, I did what I always did at these meetings—gauged audience reaction and took notes. Agee mostly talked about the strategic reasons for the divestiture and then introduced the principals of Kolberg, Kravis and Roberts. He thought the employees would feel better about the sale if they could meet and talk with the new owners in person.

About three-quarters of the way through his speech, someone tapped me on the shoulder. "Ms. Cunningham? Would you step outside with me for a moment? There's a message for you." I couldn't imagine what would be important enough to have me called out midway through

Agee's speech. I followed the messenger out of the auditorium, but before I left, I turned to look at Agee. He'd seen me get up and looked puzzled. I smiled reassuringly and walked out. Once outside in the hallway, the messenger handed me a note. "Urgent. Call DT at Bendix. Immediately." What could David Taylor want? I wondered.

I found a phone and called Taylor. "David? This is Mary. What's up?" "I'm afraid we have a big problem here in Southfield, Mary. A *big* problem," he said. "What is it?" I asked. "Let me read a headline to you from the *Detroit Free Press*, page one: 'Bendix Boss Slaps Down Office Gossip, Female Exec's Rise Not Due to Friendship, Agee Tells Staff.'" My heart pounded. "Go on," I said. "Read me the rest." "Chairman William Agee, who runs the 88th largest company in America, stood in front of 600 Bendix headquarters employees Wednesday and..." He got through two paragraphs when I told him to stop. "Oh, my God. This is terrible," I said, feeling the ground give way below me. "What should I do?" "I don't know," Taylor said. "Wait. It gets worse. They have a quote from when you first met Agee. They have you saying, 'It was like a meeting of kindred spirits, a meeting of the minds.'" "But I said that weeks ago. It had nothing to do with— David, is this legitimate? Can they write something like this?" "They can write anything they want," Taylor said. "Ever since those anonymous letters, they've just been itching to get the story into print. Agee's speech gave them the hook." "What do you mean, 'hook'?" I asked. "A reason to write the story," he said. "They couldn't just write, 'People at Bendix are gossiping about Mary and Bill.' They needed a better reason to put it in the paper. Agee's statement gave them the excuse."

"But you advised him to say something about it at the meeting. You and Bette Howe told him to say that. Did you know?" "Look, now don't get angry at me, Mary. I was just doing my job." I felt a little faint. "What did the *Detroit News* say?" I asked, trying to stay calm. "Interestingly enough, they just ran with the straight business story. About the strategy and the layoffs and all." And in a jovial aside, "I bet that reporter's getting his fanny chewed off for missing the real story," Taylor said, chortling. If it was a joke, I didn't get it.

"I can't believe it," I said, still a little stunned. "There's more," Taylor said. "They have pictures of the two of you that they cropped to make it look as if you're gazing into each other's eyes." Now I felt like crying. The idea of my photograph being cropped to fit some newspaper's idea of an alleged romance was too much. "I don't understand how the press can do something like that, David. Aren't there rules about this? Can't someone do something?" I said. "Look, Mary. It's no time to get philosophical about the newspaper profession right now. The phones around here have been ringing off the hook. Every newspaper in the country is calling. Look, tell the boss to give me a call as soon as he can. We need to do something about this."

I wiped my eyes and made my way to the front of the crowded conference room. Agee saw me enter and looked quizzical. I tried to smile and nod reassuringly. My expression assured him that everything was okay. He continued with his speech but by this time Bernstein and Woods knew that something was happening. One of them passed me a note. "What's going on?" it said. I couldn't believe they didn't know. Probably they'd made a call back to New York and already knew more about this so-called scandal than I did. I folded the note in my hands and sat back and looked at Agee. Not a word registered. All I could think about was that headline. "Boss slaps down office gossip." Suddenly I saw my whole career going down the drain. And I saw Agee's, and the strategy he was describing so lucidly just now, go right down with it. My first reaction, and it was probably one I'd absorbed from all those stories in *The Lives of Saints*, was, "Take me. If it'll save you and the company, I'll resign." It was a thought hatched almost instinctively in a moment of shock and fright, and I held onto it as if it would steer me through this terrible ordeal. On the pad on which I'd been jotting down notes, I slowly started writing the words of a resignation. Not *a* resignation. *My* resignation. I knew the only way Agee would accept it was if I made it irrevocable and unconditional. So that's what I wrote. That I was resigning, effective immediately, and that it was "irrevocable and unconditional."

Agee saw me engrossed in my writing. He knew by now something was wrong. As soon as he finished his speech, he stepped down from the podium and headed my way. People rushed up to congratulate him, but he moved past them. "What's going on?" he asked. "Yeah. What's going on?" Bernstein and Woods joined in, hovering about us. "I have something to give you, but not now," I said, glancing toward the reporters. "Why don't you talk to your well-wishers, and in fifteen minutes I'll meet you outside." The fifteen minutes seemed like hours. "Let's find some place to talk," Agee said, flushed, as he emerged. We found an empty room and I handed him my scribbled resignation. He read it and then he looked up at me. "Why would you do a thing like this," he asked, confused. "David Taylor called," I began. "It's all over

Detroit, the 'alleged relationship' between you and me. It's front-page news in the *Detroit Free Press*, and by tomorrow, Taylor says, it will hit every newspaper in America. And even then it won't be over. Taylor says the press will have a field day with this thing." I paused. Agee looked stunned. "You know I can't take this, Bill. I warned you before. I simply can't take it anymore. It's gone way too far."

He put his head in his hands. I thought he was thinking, but then I saw his shoulders shake and I heard his breathing change. When he looked up, I saw he'd been crying. I'd never seen Agee cry before. "Those fools. Those narrow-minded fools. You can't let them do this to you. You can't let them run you out of the company like this. It's not fair," he said. I knew he would say this, which was why I'd written "irrevocable" and "unconditional." I felt moved by his tears but suddenly cold to the argument. "Look, you know I can no longer do my job in this kind of atmosphere and neither can you. I've become a liability to you. They've made us into a laughing stock." "Liability? Laughing stock? Stop saying things like that," he said. "I can't stand it. I can't stand this whole thing."

"Look," I said, suddenly practical. "David wants you to call him. Newspapers are calling him from all over the country, and he needs to give them an answer. We have to come up with a response." "I already did that and look what happened." He stood up and pulled himself together. "All right," he said. "Let's see if we can't figure out a way to handle this. I'm sure we'll be able to do something. Let's go now. We need to find a phone."

When we got into the hall, Bernstein and Woods were there. Mercifully, they stood back. For once they had the sense not to speak. Agee went to phone Taylor. The news was grim. Taylor announced that the story had gone out over the AP wire and that by morning every newspaper in America would have our faces smeared across the front page. "He wants us to return to headquarters at once," Agee said after he'd hung up the phone. We canceled the rest of our appointments and made plans to leave immediately. But before we left, he stopped to make one more call. "I'm calling your mother," he said. "I'd like her to meet us in Detroit and stay with you. I think you might need her just now."

Out in the hall, Bernstein and Woods were waiting. I still had their note in my hands. They'd flown out with us in the company plane and obviously were expecting us to take them back. Agee and I thought that perhaps since Bernstein and Woods understood the situation, we might get at least one fair story out of this. While Agee and I made some last-minute arrangements, I pulled from my purse a pad that said, "From the Desk of Mary Cunningham" and jotted on it a note: "Peter & Will: Plans have changed—dramatically. We are returning to Detroit. If you would like to return with us—please do." Did we have any choice?

All was quiet in the plane. I went to the bathroom in the rear of the cabin and started retching. When I came out, I assumed Agee had told the two reporters what I planned to do, so I spoke freely about it. Apparently he hadn't. When they heard, they both blurted out, "Mary, you can't do that." "It'll only look like a confirmation of all those rumors," Woods said. "It'll be like Nixon. Resigning out of guilt." "What if I told you it would all blow over in a matter of days," Bernstein asked. "Would you stay then?" "You bet I would," I said. "I'd like nothing more. But can you convince me it will?" "Of course," he said. "The press will have a heyday for two or three days and then they'll forget about the whole thing. You'll see. It'll all be forgotten in a matter of days." I looked at Agee. "Do you agree?" "Absolutely," he said. I went to the back of the plane. I sat down. The lights dimmed and I put my head back. The next thing I knew we were in Detroit, and, thank God, my mother was there.

A car was waiting for us. "We don't need a chauffeur, thank you," Agee said, telling the chauffeur he preferred to drive himself. Bernstein and Woods had disappeared into a taxi and we were alone in the car. Don Harner, the chief pilot for Bendix, had given my mother a copy of the *Detroit Free Press* while she was waiting, so she had some idea of what was going on. Agee drove us to Foxcroft.

The minute I opened the door, the phone rang. "Is this Mary Cunningham?" a woman's voice said sweetly. "Yes." "I'm calling from the *Chicago Sun-Times*," she said, her voice dropping an octave, "and I was just wondering if you'd care to comment on . . ." I hung up. More Lou Heldmans. The phone rang again. "We've got to get out of here," Agee said.

The three of us got back into the car and drove over to corporate headquarters. It was ten-thirty at night, and only the security guards were there. Agee led us into his office and locked the door behind us. The buttons on his phone kept lighting up, but thank goodness we couldn't hear anything as they rang in his secretary's office. Agee sat in his chair. He seemed to appreciate the familiarity. In meticulous detail, he proceeded to tell my mother everything that had happened. He told her about Panny, Blumenthal, his ex-wife, about the board, about the letters, *et al*. He didn't leave anything out. I was grateful to him for the care he took in explaining it all to her, and for his direct and candid approach. "Mary wants to resign for my sake," he told her, "but I don't want her to. I want her to do what's good for her, not what's good for me."

My mother looked at him. "What do you think my daughter should do, Mr. Agee?" she asked. The buttons on the phone were ablaze. "I don't know, Mrs. Cunningham. For the first time in my life, I can honestly say I just don't know." I looked at him. The *Wunderkind*. It was hard for me to get used to the idea of Agee's not knowing what to do. For a minute he looked like a little boy to me, helpless and confused. I felt sorry for him. "I have an idea," I said. My mother and Agee practically jumped out of their seats. "You do?" they said, relieved at the prospect of a solution. "Let's call Bo," I said. "He's a street fighter. He'll know how to handle this."

It was after eleven, but Bo was up. I told him what had happened. "You must really be hurting," he said. "What should I do?" I asked. "I really think you should get the hell out of there. But knowing you, you'll probably stay because you feel you're needed." "I don't know if I can stay. I can't do my job in an atmosphere like this." "It doesn't look good either way, Mary. I think this is one of those rock-and-hard-place situations. If you leave, they'll say you're leaving because you're guilty, and if you stay, you'll probably be less effective, so it'll be a slow death." "What should I do, Bo?" I asked again. "I don't know," he said. "Let me think about this." "Would you talk to Agee?" I asked. "Sure," he said. "Let me put you on the speaker phone," I said. "Who else is there?" he asked. "My mom." "Say hello to her for me." "Hello, Bo," my mother said. "Hello, Mrs. Cunningham. I'm really worried for our Mary." "I am too, Bo."

Agee spoke into the phone. "I can't tell you how badly I feel about this, Bo," he said. "I can imagine how it must make you feel." "If you're thinking, Do I believe any of the stuff they're insinuating, God, no. I know Mary. If anything, I thought she'd be trying to convert you." That broke the ice. Everyone felt more relaxed. "Again, I'm just terribly sorry we're calling you so late and all, and especially with such bad news. I feel in some way I've let you down," Agee said. "Don't worry about it, Bill. I remember a year ago when you sat with me and tried to help me get a job. If there's anything I can do, just ask." "Well what do you think Mary should do? Resign or stay?" Agee asked. "I don't know. It seems like an impossible situation. People being what they are, I think they're going to slaughter her either way."

Oh, no, I thought. This is not the time for one of Bo's grim scenarios. "Can't you come up with something a little less ominous?" I asked, only partly in jest. "Afraid not," Bo said. "Come on, Bo. I really need your advice." "Okay, look," he said, knowing that I was desperate. "I'd be inclined to let it ride out for a few more days. See if the thing blows over. But if it goes on, then get the hell out. I don't think Mary can take much more of it," he said to Agee. "I think Bo's absolutely right," my mother said. "I agree," Agee said. "Listen, Bo, we can't thank you enough." "That's all right," Bo said. "Call me any time." "Thanks, Bo," I said, and we hung up.

"I think we all ought to get some sleep," my mother said. "You both go on. I've got some things to finish up," Agee said, nodding at the pile of newspapers and mail heaped on his desk. "Okay, Bill. Goodnight," my mother said. "Goodnight, Mrs. Cunningham," Agee said. "And thank you." "Goodnight," I said. "Mary?" he called to me just before I left. "Do you think I've failed you in some way?" he asked, his eyes probing mine. "No," I said. "It's not your fault. They would've found their 'hook' one way or another. Don't blame yourself. Look, it's late. I think we could all use a little rest." I walked into the hall, but before I left I took one look back. There was Agee, slumped over in his magisterial chair. The King of the Castle, except that now his castle was caving in.

When we pulled into Foxcroft I noticed a crowd of cars double-parked in the driveway. "Who are all these people?" I said, seeing a crush of people sitting on my doorstep. "Has there been an accident?" my mother asked. There were men and women with cameras and strobe lights and pads and pencils in their hands. Just then, one young woman ran up to me and pushed a microphone in my face. "I know it's late, Ms. Cunningham, but I was wondering if you cared to deny the rumors about the alleged romance between you and your boss?" The other reporters now converged on the scene. "I . . . I . . ." I was about to answer but my mother reached over and pulled me away from the crowd. "Leave my daughter alone," she said in the strongest voice I'd ever heard her use. People moved back now and the two of us walked up the stairs into the apartment.

I was back at the office at six-thirty the next morning. I found Agee in exactly the same position as we'd left him the previous night—slumped down in his armchair. Apparently he'd spent the night there. "Good morning," I said, knowing full well it was not. He looked up, surprised. "Good morning," he said. "How are you holding up?" "All right," I said. "It's a new day and I'm sure it'll be a better one." Little Mary Sunshine making everyone smile.

I went back to my office. The sight of all those papers on my desk sickened me. I decided to call my mother. I'd left her back at the apartment only twenty minutes ago, but I wanted to hear her voice. Perhaps she could reassure me of what I had tried to reassure Bill. "Hello, Mom?" I said. "Hello, dear, what's the matter?" "Nothing. I just wanted to reassure you that everything's going to be all right." "I feel the same way, dear. Today's going to be a better day." "That's right, Mom. I can feel it already." "So can I," she said. Any more good cheer and we'd both start to cry.

At eight-thirty one of the secretaries brought in some tea, and Agee and I began going through the morning newspapers. It was just as Taylor had said. Our pictures were splattered across front pages everywhere. *The New York Times*: "Romance Is Disavowed in Bendix Promotion." *The Wall Street Journal*: "Miss Cunningham's Very Rapid Ascent." The *Los Angeles Herald-Examiner*: "Behind the Scenes at Bendix: Peyton Place?" Agee had previously scheduled a 10 A.M. meeting with our friendly reporters from *Fortune*. He was still hoping for a good story on the strategy. I kept having to remind myself that although the rumors were all I could think about right now, he still had a company to run.

I tried to work the best I could for the rest of that day but it was hard. I kept traveling back and forth between Bendix and my apartment, where I went to talk with my mother. On several trips I'd had the vague sensation that someone was following me. I kept seeing the same gray Ford with the dented front right grille in my rearview mirror.

When I returned that afternoon, security called me in for a meeting. "We want you to try to be as careful as you can now, Ms. Cunningham. There've been a few phone calls that have put us on alert. The world is full of wacky people, you know. All of this press attention has made you a possible target."

That afternoon I busied myself with strategic affairs; I thought I'd better check up on my staff. "We want you to know we're terribly sorry for what's been going on," strangers came up to me in the corridor and said. But the events of the past few days had made me suddenly paranoid. Who knew what they really thought? I wondered. What did they say to each other when I wasn't around? "Is she really sleeping with him?" "Do you think they're telling the truth?" Ghoulish conversations like this kept playing through my mind. I felt as if I were eternally on trial. It seemed a right, almost a requirement, for people to pass judgment on me.

But the reactions from strangers weren't as upsetting to me as what was starting to filter back from the board. Agee, now, was obviously torn. He was starting to get "advice" from his friends, and it wasn't always proffered with my best interests at heart. People like Don Rumsfeld would call Agee and say things like "All right. So you piddled on the floor. But you don't have to have your face wiped in it. She's got to go." Pete Peterson of Lehman Brothers was about as subtle. "You're not going to like what I have to say, but I consider you a good friend," he said to Agee. "Get rid of her. Give her a nice fat settlement. She'll survive. She's young. She's malleable. You're not. You're forty-two and you've just been divorced. You've got a company to run. Think of your obligations. You've got 85,000 employees and a lot of money goes through your hands."

I started to think of this as the abortionists' school.

Their solution: "Do a little surgery. Get rid of the problem. Nice and clean. You've got to save your own neck." They didn't even care whether we were having an affair or not. They just thought Bill ought to get rid of the evidence. Fast. Naturally they were speaking only as Bill's friends. The fact that some of them had political ambitions and hoped they could ride into Washington on Agee's coattails didn't make them any less concerned about Agee's image. And me? I was expendable. After all, I was just "the girl."

Members of the board, too, were getting an earful. Neither Blumenthal nor Panny had stopped beating the drum, and the stories in the press only encouraged them to do more. "Terrible, what Agee's doing with this girl," people in the country-club crowd were saying. And all of this was duly reported back to Bill. From Harry Cunningham: "It's all over Bloomfield Hills. The board is starting to lose confidence. And the press isn't leaving it alone. This thing just isn't going away, Bill and I'm not sure how much longer we can go on like this."

Of course Agee's line to everyone was, "Stay calm. If we can all just keep our shirts on, this thing will die down. Just don't overreact." But I could see it was even getting to him.

After work on Friday, the three of us—my mother, Agee and I were sitting in my apartment. Agee had stopped by to see how the two of us were holding up. A few minutes after he arrived, he put in a call to Pete Peterson, returning a call he'd received earlier in the day. "Fire her?" we heard him say. My mother and I looked at each other aghast. "On what grounds?"

Suddenly, a thought that I hadn't even considered before entered my mind. I'll sue them, I thought. That'll keep them from firing me, I thought in my traumatized state. Sue them? the other side of my brain said. What good would that do? That would mean suing Agee and the company I had devoted myself to for the last eighteen months. Could I do that? My mind was torn. The ironies started leaping up at me at once. Sue the company whose strategy I'd written? For which I'd worked seven days a week around the clock? For which I'd spent every holiday and vacation working on management solutions? It was too much. By now I was thoroughly confused. Was Bendix my ally or my enemy? Was I on shore or an island, slowly being pushed farther and farther out? And where was Agee in all of this? Whose side is he on? If the board goes one way and I go another, where would he stand?

I was a good enough strategist to start hypothesizing the various possibilities, and many I envisioned caused me to feel alarmed. "Did you really mean all those glowing things you said about me, that one of the decisions you're proudest of is hiring me?" I asked him, desperate to be reassured. "That I have been your right and left arm?" I said. For by now I realized how awful my dilemma was. I was utterly alone. There was only one person with any clout in this company whose complete support I had, and I wanted to make sure that I still had that. "If they turn on you, Mary," he said, looking at me and my mother, "then as far as I'm concerned, they've turned on me. I'd resign, too." I heard him say it. My mother did too. We looked at each other, almost relieved. It was those words we had been waiting for.

Still, the story kept getting bigger. Board members kept calling, and I could see that neither Agee nor I could continue like this. It was wearing me down. What's gotten into me? I thought after hearing myself say something particularly sharp to Agee. This isn't the way I should speak to the chairman of the board. Still, I was angry. At Agee. At Bendix. At the press. At the whole world. I could see that staying at Bendix was no solution either, even with Agee's support. We had to come up with a plan—some plan that would preserve my dignity and my job and yet remove me from the eye of the storm.

On Saturday, in the quiet of my apartment, sipping tea with my mother, a plan streamed into my mind. I'd offer to take a leave of absence. That would give things a chance to simmer down and yet keep my job and position intact. It seemed like a perfect solution—the only equitable solution, as far as I could see. All Saturday I worked on a draft of a letter to the board requesting a leave of absence. In it I wrote: "As a result of the kind of media coverage I have received in recent days...and of the false innuendoes and excessive attention...I have been *rendered ineffective* at this point in time. I therefore am requesting from the board an immediate but temporary leave of absence." I added, "This interlude should not be construed in any sense as tantamount to a resignation, for I have rejected outright that option as not being in the best interests of either the company, other women, or myself." I signed it, "Sincerely, Mary E. Cunningham, Vice President, Strategic Planning."

On Sunday I called to inform Agee of my decision. He agreed it was the best thing to do. Agee informed the board of my request and a meeting of the Organization and Compensation Committee was quickly set up for Monday at 4:30 P.M. at the Equitable offices in New York, where board member Coy Eklund was president and CEO. Hoping that things would quiet down now, I encouraged my mother to return to Hanover. There was no point in putting her through any more of this. It was also decided that I should accompany Agee to New York. He wanted me nearby in case the board wanted to question me further. All three of us went to the airport that night.

"I'm not sure I trust any of these people, Mary," my mother said to me before leaving. "Bill?" I asked. "No. I trust Bill," she said. "It's just that—well, I'm not sure he sees what a dangerous position you might be in." I kissed her goodbye and then boarded my plane. All during the ride to New York, one phrase stuck in my mind. "Rendered ineffective." That was my phrase. It seemed to me the politest way of saying my guts had been torn out.

We checked into the Waldorf, but at the registration desk, Agee paused before signing us in to the rooms the hotel had reserved for Bendix. "Maybe we should be on separate floors," he said. Oh, my God, I thought. The very fact that he had to consider this disturbed me. I felt guilty of a crime I'd never committed. I agreed, however, that it was the sensible thing to do. Banished from where Hastie, Svec and every other senior Bendix executive traveling with the chairman stayed, I rode the elevator uneasily to another floor.

The next morning Agee went over to Lehman Brothers. I went too, as there was last-minute work to do on the Asarco deal. It was uncomfortable for both of us, to say the least. Dozens of bright-eyed young investment bankers would try desperately to keep from staring. It wasn't just "business as usual" as everyone tried hard to pretend. Of course I had a chance to see my friend Pete Peterson. "How are you holding up, dear?" he said. "Just fine, Pete," I said, fighting hard not to say anything more. "If I can help, just let me know," he said. "Joan and I are there for you." "Sure, Pete, thanks."

Later in the morning, Agee had a chance to confer with Peterson privately. Agee told Peterson about our decision to request a leave but Peterson was grim. He didn't think it was a good idea at all and told Agee the board wouldn't buy it. His theme continued to be surgery—fast.

After lunch I left Agee and went back to the Waldorf. The meeting was scheduled for 4:30 P.M. Just before the meeting, Agee called my room. "I'm not going to vote in favor of your leave of absence, Mary," he said. "Why?" I said, confused. "I think it would be an important vote of confidence for you if the board decides not to let you go. I don't know how the others will vote—but I believe there are some major principles involved here. Rumors shouldn't be permitted to dictate corporate policy like this, and sexual harassment of this kind shouldn't be given any credence. It makes me so angry when I think about it."

Now I put on my strategist's hat. If they didn't accept my offer for a leave of absence for that reason, it would certainly be a good signal, but I didn't want them doing anything on Agee's account alone. I wanted to know where I really stood. "I'd prefer it if you would keep your position to yourself until the last vote is cast," I said. "See where they stand. See if I have their support." He agreed to listen.

It was a long and lonely vigil, except that during the afternoon Bo came by. Neither of us said very much but occasionally we held each other's hands. It was the missionary versus the cynic again, except that now we were starting to switch roles. It was Bo now who predicted things would get better from here on in, and it was I who was starting to foretell my own doom. Finally, at about 8:30 P.M., the phone rang. It was Agee. "I have some good news." I couldn't think of either outcome as exactly good news. "What happened?" I asked. "Not only did the Organization and Compensation Committee of the board turn down your leave, but they're going to issue a statement that shows they back you firmly." I actually did feel a surge of joy. "Thank God," I said. Now I didn't have to be anyone's fall guy. Nobody was going to make me wear a Scarlet Letter for the rest of my life.

Now there were hours of elation. It finally seemed as if perhaps the nightmare would be over. In major stories, *The Wall Street Journal* and *The New York Times* reported the board's strong stand to back me up. The Organization and Compensation Committee of the board issued a statement: "The Committee has complete confidence in Ms. Cunningham, and it would be unjust for the Corporation to respond to speculation in the media by accepting her request." Phone calls poured in from civil liberties and women's groups, extending sympathy and support.

Gloria Steinem called me personally and offered to lend a hand. "I'd be glad to go speak before your board," she said. I told her I really appreciated the offer. "The way it's been reported, it doesn't seem that Agee is handling the whole thing particularly well," she said, referring to what was by now the famous comment, "... it's true that Mary is a very close friend of mine and my family...." "I'm not sure his western candor is going to help him out here," she said. Steinem knew Agee. He'd invited her to speak before the Bendix board several years ago; he admired her intelligence and she admired his down-to-earth Idaho ways. "Why, for instance," she asked me, "did he bother to call a special meeting to discuss the whole thing?" she asked. "He didn't," I said. "That's just the way it was reported in the press. It was just a routine annual employees' meeting designed to answer any and all questions Bendix employees had." "Well, then, how did the press get in?" she asked. Steinem was more savvy about these things than either Bill or I. "Our public-relations person encouraged us to invite them. He said it would look bad if we didn't." "Is he a friend of yours, Mary?" Steinem asked. I couldn't exactly say that he was. Perhaps he was less of a friend than I thought. "Well, one thing I can say," she said. "I hope to God that you two are having an affair, because you're sure paying the price for it."

Back in Detroit, I was congratulated by members of my staff. "You end up a net winner in all this, Mary," Matt Lord, a senior planner in my department, said to me when I arrived at work the next day. "But Agee's been made to look a little foolish." That was the part I couldn't understand. Didn't people realize that if he were having an affair, he'd never have raised the topic in the first place? I knew that he was just trying to be up front, as always. But no one else seemed to understand that.

Had nothing more been done, had no further words been said, the board's decision to turn down my leave would have put an end to this dreadful nightmare, and things might have quieted down. But such was not the case. For one thing, the press was still reveling in the event. Now the columnists and the weeklies were having their say. "Executive Sweet," *Newsweek* called their story. "Bendix Abuzz," said *Time*. The story seemed to have taken on a life of its own. Little snippets of information were finding their way into various gossip columns around Detroit and Washington, D.C. Agee felt that the information they carried could only have come from one source—Bill's ex-wife, Diane. "But how could the press get hold of information like this?" I asked Agee. "I don't know," he said. "But Diane's been playing the story to the hilt. She's now talking as if we had had a blissful marriage until you came along. And guess who's suddenly started visiting and calling her regularly? Nancy Reynolds. She even sent young Bob a present. And Nancy Reynolds is well-connected to the Washington press."

But it wasn't only Diane and Reynolds. There was a whole network of people still fanning the flames. People like Panny and Blumenthal wouldn't let this thing die. Panny used it as an excuse for his falling-out at Bendix. And Blumenthal appeared to be only too happy to see Agee squirm. He kept feeding stories to Harry Cunningham and other directors who were on both the Bendix and the Burroughs boards.

I had only been back to Bendix for a day when Agee came into my office with the bad news. "I've polled several members of the board, Mary, and they are losing confidence in your ability to remain at Bendix under the circumstances," he said. "Why now?" I asked. "Just four days after their vote of confidence? What's going on?" Agee responded, "The thing just seems to be getting bigger. Everyone's talking about it. Everywhere any of the directors go, Harry Cunningham, Mirabito, Purcell, they say people ask them questions. Or don't. Which is worse. Because everyone knows what's on their minds." "Then why didn't they give me the leave in the first place? Wouldn't that have made things easier?" Agee stared into space. "I'm not sure they realized how much media play the story would get. I'm not sure anyone did."

That afternoon I received a call from Jack Fontaine, one of the company's attorneys. "We need to talk," he said. I agreed to see him. "I'm not sure this thing is working," he told me over lunch. "The newspapers are still carrying on with this and it doesn't seem to be quieting down. If anything, it's getting worse." "What do you expect me to do, Mr. Fontaine?" I asked, not certain what he was getting at. "Are you sure the right thing to do is for you to stay?" he asked. I had a queasy feeling the right answer wasn't "Yes." "The board's given me its vote of confidence, and I intend to try now and make it work," I said. The fact that he was suggesting I do otherwise only made me more determined to stick to my guns. "I think I can handle it. I think I can still go on," I said. "It's not that simple, Mary," he said. While I detected an effort to soften the message, there it was: "You may not have the choice. Perhaps you need to be reminded that you can always be *made* to fail."

I went back to my apartment distressed. It seemed as if I were living on a roller coaster, one minute up, the next minute down. It was during the present down cycle that the phone rang. "Mary Cunningham?" It was a woman's voice. "This is Gail Sheehy. Do you remember me? I interviewed you some time back, before you ever went to Bendix." "Yes, I remember," I said. The last thing I wanted was to talk with anyone associated with the press. "Look, Mary," she said. "I know about all those other stories. But I know who you *really* are. I know what an ethical, honest person you are. If we could just talk for twenty minutes."

I remembered our previous talk. It was just before I'd graduated from Business School. Sheehy was working on her new book, *Pathfinders*. She wanted to talk to bright, successful young women, and I was a sucker for such interviews. Besides, I was pretty impressed as well. After all, this was the celebrated Gail Sheehy of *Passages* fame.

I was flattered that she had chosen me as one of her subjects. I remember we spent three hours talking at Maxwell's Plum in New York, during which she asked me all about my background and my family. I had no qualms about talking—even about the areas of my childhood that were unclear or uncertain—since she assured me that all of it would be strictly confidential. She reminded me that all of the characters in *Passages* were kept anonymous and that she would do the same in her next book. We had a good talk, and I remember leaving and feeling somewhat pleased. She described me, at the time, as someone who hadn't quite found her path yet, which, in retrospect, seemed right.

I thought she might be the person who could help me out of this. "Well, I don't know," I said. "I'm a little wary about speaking with anyone in the press." "Look, none of those reporters out there writing about you really know you," she said. "I do. I know what an honest and ethical person you are. If I could write an article to tell your side of the story, it might really help." Help. I certainly needed that. "I wouldn't need much time," she said. "Just maybe twenty minutes with you and twenty minutes with Agee. I'm staying at the Michigan Inn. I can be at your apartment in no time."

I called Agee. I suggested he should speak with her for a few minutes. "This may be someone who will finally tell them what's really happening. She'll tell them the truth," I said. "All right," he said. "On your recommendation, I'll agree. Have her come to my office." Sheehy came to Foxcroft and we had a brief talk. She said she would write an article as soon as possible to correct the distortions and shed light on the bigger issues. She also talked with Agee. They spent about a half hour together.

The next day she called again. "Can I see you for just another twenty minutes? I just need a few more quotes." "Look, I'm sorry. I've given you enough time," I said. I was getting impatient. The idea that this was even a story still irked me. I wasn't thinking about Sheehy's article now; I had too much else on my mind.

Now even Agee and I were starting to drift apart. No longer did he report to me on the various meetings. His comments seemed guarded; so were mine. I started to feel a sense of distrust. The following morning he called me into his office. "There's another meeting of the board scheduled in New York," he said. "What's it for?" I asked, on edge. "I don't know, but it doesn't look good," he said. I could tell by his tone that I was not to ask him anything more. We both agreed I should fly to New York to be ready if and when the board convened. Agee would meet me out there later in the week. Besides, I was eager to get out of Detroit. The pains in my chest were getting worse, and I was rapidly losing weight. Again I called my mother and again she agreed to meet me, this time in New York.

All during the plane ride to New York I thought about Agee. Horrible scenarios ran through my brain. How would he respond if they wanted him to fire me? How would I want him to react? I didn't want him to slit his own throat. What would that accomplish? I felt like an insect imprisoned under a jar. At first the walls of the jar seem like protection but then they begin to seem like barriers. I felt that this protective jar was starting to suffocate me. But I didn't know in whose hand this horrible jar was. Was it the company's? The board's? Agee's? My own? Who was protecting me and who was trying to snuff me out? The board, who'd refused my leave and now seemed to be changing its mind? Agee, who'd encouraged me to stay, to keep on, through all the turmoil, even after those first terrible interviews I'd had with Jacobson and Svec that very first day?

I checked into the Waldorf on Wednesday, October 1. When I arrived, Herb, the concierge, took both my hands in his. "I just want you to know I believe in you," he said. "And if there is any way I can make your stay easier for you, please let me know." I was grateful for the support and at the same time I wondered what kind of nightmare this was where people were coming up to me and telling me they were on my side. What side? Who was the enemy? What had I done wrong?

They were terrible days, those days my mother and I spent cloistered in our room in the Waldorf, waiting to see what was going to happen next. Mother kept ordering up food, and I kept resisting it. And in my constant state of nausea, how could I enjoy those elaborate meals? Everything at the Waldorf seemed over-adorned. There was always silverware we didn't need. Three spoons with every dish. Garnish on everything. Even tea and toast was made into a lavish feast. Just the sight of the silver cart sent me into the bathroom, retching. But to leave the room was unthinkable. I didn't want to face any reporters or the stares of strangers. Besides, I had gotten so thin that none of my clothes fit. All I wore was a pair of white pajamas with navy piping which I came to view, not without affection, as my prisoner's garb. My mother, just to have something to do on one of those endless afternoons, went out to Saint Patrick's and on her way back, stopped in at Saks to see if she could buy me another pair. The only pajamas they had were silk and very expensive, so she bought me a small cosmetic case instead. When she came back in the room to hand it to me, I burst into tears.

I was almost thankful to have an absorbing project to work on. Having put off the typing of my annulment petition for almost a year, I decided to concentrate on finally getting it done. In my distraught state, I convinced myself the words might even hurt less. With the kind of media probing that I had experienced recently, I was worried that Bo would be drawn further into this. I knew I'd been putting off the inevitable for too long. Business at Bendix kept getting in the way. But now it couldn't wait any longer.

I rented an old Royal typewriter for twenty-five dollars a day from the Waldorf and busily started to answer the questions on the petition: What were the circumstances of your decision to marry? Did anything influence your decision? Was your state of mind clear and calm when you made the decision? I thought back on the dingy South Bend hotel room, the fear we felt amidst the racial threats in Indiana during that awful autumn, and of Bo's depressed state over his friend Johnny Coates's drowning. I typed answers, day and night, so that the Catholic Tribunal in Brooklyn, New York, might grant me what I believed I deserved and what Bo and I agreed would be best: an annulment. Thank goodness my mother was able to focus more on the immediate matter at hand. She made the one practical suggestion of our nightmarish vigil. "Mary, I think you should find a good lawyer to represent your interests." A few phone calls to a close family friend in Hanover came up with the name Tom Hagoort, an excellent lawyer with Cleary, Gottlieb, who agreed to represent me in the Bendix matter.

Agee arrived in New York later that week, but he was

mostly incommunicado. He spent most of his time holed up in the Bendix suite with various directors and investment bankers. We kept in touch by phone, but on Friday morning he asked if he could see me. We agreed I'd meet him in the Bendix suite.

"We're having some big problems, Mary," he said. I was bleary-eyed from lack of sleep. "I don't know if you can understand or appreciate what I'm going to say to you, but I've basically been informed that one of us has to go." "What are you trying to say to me?" I asked him, suddenly all too awake. "Just that. That one of us has to go." I paused a moment, searching his face for a clue. "Are you asking me to leave?" I said, feeling panicked. "I would never ask you to do that," he said. "Is that because you know you don't have to?" I said. "No," he said. "I'd never ask you to," he repeated, with emphasis on the ask. "I think I'd better go back to my room," I said. "Would you like me to come to your room to talk?" he said, trying to be conciliatory. "No," I said. "I don't think that would be a good idea."

I went back to my room. Sobbing, I told my mother what had happened. She was furious. "What has this man done to my daughter?" she kept saying. I had seen signs of it coming, but now it was all too clear: Agee and the board were moving in one direction: I was moving, or being pushed, in another. What I feared most of all was all too true: I had lost the person for whom I had run myself ragged during the last year and a half, the person I had served even when it was at my own expense. I had lost not just a boss, but my hero, my mentor. And I had lost my best friend.

Jack Fontaine called next. I knew he was only the

messenger, but I was starting to have strong desires to shoot him for all the bad news. The purpose of our "chat" was for Jack to see if I would do anything as drastic as sue the pants off the company. Short and to the point, he laid out my three options. "You could resign quietly," he said. "Which would be the best thing for Bill." He knew where I was vulnerable. "You could stand strong and refuse to resign," he said, "in which case you could be made to fail." I'd heard that one before. "Or you could wait and see," he said, at which point I completed the thought. "And force the board to fire me," I said. "Yes," he said. "And then I could sue." "You could sue," he said. "But the person that would create the biggest problem for would be Bill. The board and everyone at the company would then be angry at him for bringing this misfortune upon them all. Furthermore, it would make you look very bad too. After all, who will the public be more likely to believe, an entire board of distinguished directors or an angry young woman who's been fired?"

I felt again like the insect in the jar and started gasping for breath. I was being cornered. "Excuse me, Jack, I think I need to think about this in my own room." "Look, Mary. You have seven days to think about things and make up your mind as to what you want to do. Otherwise the board will have to take matters into its own hands. And Mary—" "Yes?" "I just want you to know, I'm sorry this..." I'd had enough false sympathy for one day and without waiting for him to finish, went quickly back to my room.

I told my mother about the meeting. The news came as not too great a surprise. "What are you going to do?" she asked. "I'll tell you what I'm going to do," I said. For once I was letting my anger come out. "I'm going to bring the whole house of cards down on them. And of all people to give me the ultimatum—how ironic that it should be Jack Fontaine, the *son* of a former Bendix chairman. You'd think he'd be more sensitive to the charge of favoritism. I'm going to sue every one of them. I'm going to expose the kind of people who are directing companies like Bendix...." My mother put her hands on my shoulders. "You can't handle a lawsuit now, Mary. Besides, do you want to put yourself through all that agony? Can you imagine what the press would do to you while covering a lawsuit like this? There are limits to what you can endure." Before I could answer, the phone rang. It was Agee. My hero. He wanted to know how I was. I told him about my impending lawsuit. "Please don't do that, Mary. I can understand why you might want to, but it won't help anyone, least of all you," he said. "Look, why don't you come down to my suite and we'll talk."

In a blaze of anger I stormed into his suite. "What are you going to tell me to do?" I asked. "Sit back and let myself be fired?" "I'm not saying that," he said. He looked as distraught as I was. "I'm just saying that a lawsuit is irrational. It's self-destructive. If you sue, you'll be branded as a troublemaker for the rest of your life. No corporation in America would hire you. Besides, that's not the way you play if you're a team player." "A team player?" I said, stunned. So it was I who wasn't playing with the team in mind? I'd had enough of this. Exhausted, angry and humiliated by all of it, I went back to my room. I wanted time to think. Alone. Talking with Agee only made me more angry and prevented me from thinking straight.

A lawsuit. I'm sure that's what people expected me to do. And I could have. It would have made quite a case. But what good would it do me, really? Sue the company whose dramatic new blueprint for change I'd help write? A Pyrrhic victory at best. The whole notion didn't sit well with me. I wasn't that way. I believed in loyalty. My mother raised me to be that way.

I woke up the next morning with one thought on my mind. If I were going to be made to resign, I'd have to have another job. To leave Bendix and not have another place to go would seem like sudden death. I'd be an untouchable. No one would hire me with a stigma like that attached to my name. With the compulsive energy with which I was now doing everything else, I started frantically thinking about getting myself another job—not a job in business, but something that would allow me some time and space, to gather my thoughts, to recover, so that if and when Bendix took me back, I'd have gained something from the experience and be that much more useful to the firm. In addition, without a job, how was I going to repay my $20,000 loan?

I was a tornado that weekend. I flew first to Cambridge, where I went to speak to a few of my former professors and to Bendix board member Hugo Uyterhoeven, hoping for some advice. He took me for a long walk in the woods near his home. He was very understanding, but not optimistic about what his colleagues on the board might do next. While I was at Harvard, I found out about a visiting professorship program at the Business School. I thought this would possibly work as an interim measure. "Why don't you talk to the faculty member in charge of this?" one of my former professors said. "He's the person who does the screening, and I'm sure he'd be glad to discuss it with you."

The only problem was that the professor was in California and wouldn't be back for several weeks. I didn't have several weeks. The board would be meeting on Tuesday. In my frenzy, I decided I had to take the matter into my own hands. Instead of waiting for the professor to return, I flew out to California to meet with him. I talked to him about the position over dinner at the airport hotel. He thought I'd make a fine candidate for the post. But he advised me that there was already someone slated for the post—Alonzo McDonald, someone I'd then never heard of. He was completing his tenure as Hamilton Jordan's Chief of Staff in President Carter's Administration. Anticipating my next question the professor pointed out there was yet another problem with my seeking this position. "The wheels of educational bureaucracy don't move that fast," he said. "We surely couldn't decide anything like this until next spring." Next spring? I didn't have until next spring. I hardly had twenty-four hours.

I flew back to New York on the redeye flight. I felt burned out. There was nothing I could do. My frenzy was only a means of forestalling the inevitable. When I got back to my room, Agee called. He told me the Organization and Compensation committee was planning to meet at ten-thirty the next morning to review my case. He was going to try hard to convince the board not to create another media event and to just let things calm down. A session with the full board strictly on business—Agee still had to get board approval for the $330 million sale of the 20 percent Bendix owned of Asarco—was scheduled for 1:30 P.M. My fate, I knew, would be decided by then.

Now things moved quickly. Agee called at ten the next morning to tell my mother and me he was on his way to the meeting. It was his way of showing us his concern. "Pray hard, Mary," he said, trying to comfort me. But even he was surprised by what happened next. At 11 A.M.

he called to tell us the turn events had taken. Apparently the board, or the small part of it that was actually present that morning—Harry Cunningham, Mac Baldridge, Jack Purcell, Coy Eklund, and J. L. Scott—was now taking things into its own hands. They had summoned a series of Bendix executives as "witnesses" to appear before them to talk to them about me. Except that now they weren't even going to allow Agee to stay in the room. "We're no longer sure you're able to be objective about this whole thing," Cunningham told him. I was starting to get the picture. I wondered if Bill was. Imagine—the chairman of the company being expelled from his own board meeting.

From his station in the hall, Agee described to us by phone the proceedings of this strange kangaroo court. Not surprisingly, the one woman on the board, Jewel Lafontant, wasn't there. It sounded like the Salem witch trials to me. I was to burn at the stake, but first there was to be a parade of "character witnesses." From his post outside the door, Agee watched as Joe Svec, Larry Hastie and others walked in and out of the room. After each session, the "witness" would re-emerge and shake hands with Agee. "I gave you my full support, Bill," each of them said. Finally Agee was summoned in and his calls back to our room stopped. There was nothing for us to do but wait.

At 1:30 P.M., the second meeting was scheduled to take place, but still no word from Agee. My mother and I continued to wait. If only we had been card players, or capable of watching TV, perhaps the time might have moved ahead more quickly. But we were not. We talked. We held hands. We paced in our ornate hotel room. We watched the clock. I knew the fact that I hadn't heard

from Agee for so long meant something was wrong. At
4:30 P.M. the phone finally rang. It was Agee. I could tell
at once the difference in his voice. It was stiff, cold, oddly
formal. There were other people with him, it was clear.
"Mary? This is Bill Agee," he said. "I'm in the lobby of
the Waldorf with Jack Fontaine and Hugo Uyterhoeven,
and the three of us would like to see you. Could you meet
us in the Bendix suite at once?"

"They want me to come downstairs to meet them in
the suite," I told my mother. "He didn't give you any
news?" she asked. "No. I suppose I should change," I
said, looking down at my creased white pajamas. Obviously I couldn't go in those. I walked over to the closet
and searched for the smallest thing I could find. I had lost
fifteen pounds during the last month and none of my clothes
fit. I pulled out a tan skirt. A size six. But it, too, hung
on me. When my mother saw how loose it was, her eyes
filled with tears. "Give me the skirt," she said. She took
a pair of scissors from her travel sewing kit and made
another hole in the belt. "There, that's better," she said.

Like a robot I rode down in the elevator and then
walked down the hall. It was a year and a half ago that I
first walked down this hall. I was nervous then, too, but
what a different kind of fear. That one foreshadowed excitement; this one foreshadowed doom. Jack Fontaine
opened the door. The other two were seated. I looked at
Agee. I searched his face for meaning, a sign, an expression, something that said, "Mare, I'm still there with you,"
but in vain. There wasn't even a glimmer. He sat as if in
shock. I looked at Uyterhoeven. He looked tired and
defeated. I looked back at Fontaine. He had the executioner's grim sense of purpose. Obviously he had been
designated spokesman for the group.

"Mary," he began, "the board has spent a long time deliberating over what has happened and we feel..." Many more words were expended but in effect Fontaine was telling me, You're a plague. You have seven days to get out of here. If you don't, we'll execute you.

"What is it you want me to do?" I asked, when he finished his lengthy apologia. "The most sensible thing for you to do at this point," he said, "is to quietly resign. We have all—" he emphasized the word all—"agreed that this is the most expedient thing for you to do. No one is actually accusing you of the allegations or rumors that have appeared in the press. But Bendix can't afford any more publicity and as long as you stay the headlines will continue. We simply feel it is no longer viable for you to remain and do your job efficiently at Bendix." "I will need some time to think," I said. "Fine," Jack said, reminding me that I didn't have much time to think. I shook his hand. I shook Hugo's too. But I could only look at Agee. I couldn't stand the thought of touching his hand.

I went back to my room and reported on the meeting to my mother. The news came as not too great a surprise. Then Agee telephoned. He wanted to tell me what had happened. I agreed to see him in his suite, blindly hoping he could somehow explain it all.

"I didn't expect it to play out this way, Mary," he said, looking desperate. "Neither did I," I said, stone-faced. "I just wanted to tell you what happened when I stopped calling you—after 1:30 P.M. It was because the board had taken matters into its own hands. I walked into the room, ready to start the regular meeting so we could approve the sale of Asarco, and Harry Cunningham stood up and said, 'Bill, I think you better sit down. We're going to take over now for a little while.' And then it happened.

They told me—not asked me—that they had come to a decision. The whole thing was absurd because not all the members of the board were there to hear the so-called 'character witnesses' that morning. People kept running in and out of the room. Coy Eklund had to go off to another meeting so he wasn't there for much of the meeting. Only a handful of the board was there for the whole proceeding. It looked to me as if the Burroughs contingent of the board—Cunningham, Schwartz, Mirabito—and a few others had managed to take over the helm. I couldn't do anything. They wouldn't let me speak. When they finally did let me talk, it was only to open the matter of the sale of Asarco."

I heard Agee's words but I didn't let them fully sink in. I could grasp the dynamics of it, but the only fact that mattered to me was that I was being forced to resign and Agee wouldn't—or couldn't—step in to help me.

When Agee finished, I went back to my room, had a quiet dinner with my mother and went to bed.

I woke the next morning knowing what I had to do. I wasn't about to wait seven days to see what the board would really do. I called Tom Hagoort, my lawyer. We reviewed the facts of the case. Then I called Agee. "I've made my decision," I said. "You have?" "Yes," I said. "Please summon whomever you need to convene a meeting." "Well, I'll get Fontaine and myself. Do you want Hugo there?" "Yes," I said. "Get Hugo. And I'll have my attorney with me." "What does that mean?" Agee said, slightly alarmed. I enjoyed hearing the alarm in his voice. "Nothing I care to discuss with you now," I said. "We'll see you in the Bendix suite. Noon?" "Noon's fine," Agee said.

Hagoort and I went to the suite. This time I decided to be a lady. I walked first to Agee and shook his hand.

Then I shook Fontaine's and then Hugo's. "Please be seated, gentlemen," I said. I loved those few seconds before I spoke. There was fear in that room and I could sense it. But I hadn't come to make threats or engage in recriminations. I knew what I had to do, in the end, and I began.

"I've been advised that there are a lot of actions I could take against the board and I've considered them," I said, watching everyone's eyes on me. "But if I acted now, in anger, I'd probably regret it later. I know that. I did at one time care very much about this company and I guess I still do," I said. "I was raised to care about loyalty and I still do." No one stirred. "I do not intend to sue Bendix. Nor do I plan to wait and then have you fire me. I was hoping I'd have another job to move into, to spare me the humiliation of this 'stigma,' but I don't. So there is nothing left for me to do but resign. But I want you all to know I'm doing this for two reasons. The first is, I believe in the strategy and do not want to stand in the way or distract further attention from having it carried out. And second, I believe in your chairman." I felt my voice crack. I couldn't look at Bill as I said this. "I believe in Bill Agee. And I believe in what he's doing for this company. And I don't want to do anything that would 'render him ineffective' as the events of the past weeks have done to me. Where are the papers? I'm prepared to sign."

"I admire your attitude, Mary," Jack Fontaine said. "You've truly acted with dignity and courage." Fontaine looked at Bill. "Is there anything you want to say?" Agee shook his head and looked down. "All right, then, Mary," Fontaine continued. "You've spoken to your attorney, I trust, and you understand the terms of the settlement?" "I do," I said. The company was basically giving me a year's salary, plus a bonus and my vacation pay. The total was $120,000. "And you also understand that if you sign this, you will be giving up your right to sue Bendix or any member of the company." "Only for things they've done in the past, not for any defamation of my character that might occur in the future. Is that right, Tom?" I looked at my attorney. "That's right, Mary." Fontaine continued, "Then it's all settled. There are press releases that need to be written this evening. The board, no doubt, will have only the highest praise for you. Here are the papers. Read them and then please sign."

I read the resignation statement. I kept thinking, Hand me the pen already. I can't take any more of this. My last hope was dissipating. No one was going to dull the executioner's blade. I took the pen that was proffered and signed. There were several copies. I stood up to leave and shook Jack Fontaine's hand. Then I shook Hugo's. "I can't believe it's come to this," he said. And then I shook Agee's. It was more of a grasp than a shake. He seemed to cling to my hand and hold on to it. I turned to leave. My lawyer, Tom Hagoort, put a comforting arm around me. "I've known grown men who cry at meetings like this," he said. "So if you want to, Mary, please cry." "That's all right, Tom," I said. "I'm done crying."

Agee came into my room later that afternoon. Immediately he went over to my mother. She was packing to leave for the airport. "Mrs. Cunningham, I hope you know how badly I feel about all of this. I want you to know what a strong daughter you have. She has handled this whole episode with real courage and dignity," he said. "I'm just so sorry it all had to happen. I never expected it to play out this way." "I'm sure my daughter didn't expect it to play out this way either, Mr. Agee," my mother said.

She looked at Bill, and then he turned to me. I got up and walked my mother to her cab.

That evening, a group gathered in the Waldorf suite to draft statements to the press, Tom Hagoort returned to offer his support—as much emotional as legal. Pete Peterson and Joan Ganz Cooney Peterson came by. "I think you made the right decision," she said, taking me in her arms. Pete Peterson almost looked sheepish. For the next few hours, Agee worked on his statement about me. Peterson, who was a masterful political draftsman, said it was too "gushy" and edited it. I nodded at most of what was read to me. Then the board's statement was called in, and it was effusive in its praise. The warm words left me cold. It was getting late, but I wasn't eager to leave. I feared the thoughts I might have when I went back to my room alone. It was the first night my mother would not be there.

It was midnight and we were still drafting statements. I worked on autopilot. I didn't feel anything. I just sat there and helped because it had to be done. Joan ordered some wine. Everyone was tired. It was time to go to bed. It dawned on me then that it was over. Now I was totally alone.

"Can I see you before you go?" I asked Agee before he left. "I'm sorry, Mary. That will be very difficult. I'm leaving for Michigan at the crack of dawn."

"Bill, I don't think you understand. I just gave up my job for you. I'm asking you, can I see you?"

"Of course. Sure. We can have a quick breakfast before I go. Meet you at the suite, seven A.M. Okay?"

I nodded and walked numbly back to my room.

The next morning, over breakfast, I asked him what he thought I should do. "After all, I don't have a job. I don't even know where to go without the press following me. I can't go home. My mother has already suffered enough seeing me like this."

The thought of spending another day in the hotel sickened me. Going back to my apartment in Michigan would provide no escape. Returning home to Mother, defeated and disillusioned, conjured up an image of myself I couldn't bear. But one thing was certain—I had to get as far away as possible from the prying media. If only our family had some mountain retreat. And then I remembered: "What about the place where you were when Svec and I came to visit you on our way back from Seattle? That private retreat of yours way up in the mountains of Idaho? No one from the press would find me there. Do you think I could stay there for a while?"

"No, Mary. I don't think so. I'm afraid that I'm going to need it."

"Well, do you know of any place like that? Don't you have any advice for me? What I should do? Where I should go?"

"I wish I did. I'm awfully bruised myself. Look, I'm really sorry, but..." Someone was knocking on the door. It was a porter. He'd come to take Agee's luggage. "I've got to leave now for Detroit. I hope you understand."

"Is that all there is to it? I'm on my own?"

"That's right," he said. "I really don't think I can be of much help to you. It seems I've only brought you trouble. You're better off on your own now."

# ADDENDUM

On October 9, 1980, the following press releases were issued by David O. Taylor, director, External Communications, The Bendix Corporation.

From Mary E. Cunningham, Vice President—
Strategic Planning, a statement announcing her resignation:

I have submitted my resignation, effective today,
as an officer of the Bendix Corporation. I very much
regret this action because I have enjoyed and ben-
efited immensely from this association. Nonetheless, I am convinced that the unusual convergence
of events beyond my control has substantially im-
paired my ability to carry out my responsibilities as
a corporate officer of Bendix. I appreciate that just
a week ago a committee of the Board, following
widespread publicity given to unfounded rumors,
gave me its unanimous support and declined my
request for a temporary leave of absence. However,
since the Committee's action, I have become even
more convinced that the continued association with
Bendix is no longer practicable. I am grateful for
the many supportive communications from the business community and others concerned with the right
to be judged on merit alone. I remain committed to
that principle and believe that I can best serve it in
an environment in which I can continue to succeed.
I take great pride in having participated in developing strategies which I am confident will enable
Bendix to reach even higher levels of performance.
I am equally confident about my own future.

In response to Ms. Cunningham's statement, the board
of directors of Bendix issued the following statement:

The Board of Directors of the Bendix Corporation today has reluctantly accepted the resignation of Mary E. Cunningham. The Board has the highest regard for Mary Cunningham as an executive and as a person. We appreciate very much the important contributions she has made to the company and to the development of its strategies for the future. However, we understand and concur with her appraisal of the difficulties which would confront her in a continuation of her present role. We are pleased but not at all surprised about the number of professional opportunities that have been presented to this gifted individual. We are confident that she will continue to be highly successful.

From William M. Agee, Chairman of the Board:

Mary's departure from Bendix is, and will be, an important loss to the company. She has made an outstanding contribution during her tenure and her exceptional intelligence, intellectual honesty and integrity will be sorely missed. The maturity, courage and professionalism with which she has addressed and resolved this difficult situation are testimony to her unique qualities.

# CHAPTER NINE

*Thus began the worst period* of my life. The emotions I experienced were exactly like those one lives through during the worst periods of grief. First, shock and disbelief. "This is your life, Mary Cunningham," I kept hearing a voice inside my head say, an echo of the old newsreel clips we watched in grade school. But I couldn't believe it. This wasn't really happening to me, was it? Then came the anger: "How could they? How could he? How could any of them?" And on, *ad nauseam*. I asked myself these questions a dozen times. And because there was so little I could do about any of it, I then felt helpless, and in the wake of the helplessness, despair. Complete and utter despair. In the past, my faith had always saved me. I could always go that extra step, "spiritualize" the hurt, so to speak, and then be free of it. But this time I couldn't get there. I just couldn't take that extra step. Which of the saints, I wondered, had ever lived through a mass-media event? Which of the saints had ever been the victim of a corporate powerplay?

I stayed at the Waldorf for about a week. I had no other place to go. The morning after I resigned, I lay in bed, weighed down by despair. It wasn't until late afternoon that I dared venture out. I knew the story would have hit the newspapers and daily tabloids by now, and for some masochistic reason I needed to read them. How bizarre! Following my life every day as if it were a comic strip. "Oh, Miss Cunningham, we're so terribly sorry for you," the elevator woman said as she took me down to the lobby. Her comment made me wince. I didn't want to be pitied; what I wanted was to be left alone—ignored. The elevator door opened out onto the lobby but the crowd and the noise threw me. I rode down one more floor to the lower Towers lobby but couldn't find any newspapers there. I braced myself and decided to brave the crowd on the main floor. At the newsstand I saw my name again as front-page news in both *The New York Times* and *The Wall Street Journal*: "Woman Quits High Post at Bendix Amid Controversy Over Favoritism" in the *Times*, and "Bendix 'Reluctantly' Accepts Resignation of Miss Cunningham" in the *Journal*. There was my picture on page one of the *Times*. I wondered if anyone in the lobby saw me stare at my own face. When I saw that people around me were looking at me, I hurried back to my room. Two reporters followed me, and as I walked down the corridor to my room, a third started to move toward me from the other end of the hall. I quickened my pace. What was this— some sort of macabre spy movie, in which everyone in the corridor was converging on me? I sped toward my room, ignoring the chorus of "This will only take a minute, Ms. Cunningham." Once inside, I slammed the door and bolted it behind me. But even that couldn't keep the press out. The minute I sat down the phone started ringing. "This is so-and-so from *The New York Times*." . . . "This is so-and-so from *The Wall Street Journal*." . . . "This is so-and-so from the *Washington Post*." . . . "Would you care to comment on whether sex discrimination played a role in your case?"... "Did you or didn't you have an affair with Agee?"... "What do you make of the actions of the Bendix board?" There were even job offers coming in, but what did I want to hear about these now? I figured they came either out of sympathy or to use me as good PR. The world was pummeling me with questions, but I didn't even have answers for myself, let alone the rest of the world.

"Fresh air, Mary, you need some fresh air," my mother told me over the telephone later that day. On her say-so I ventured forth. It was an unpleasant ordeal. Walking to early-morning Mass at Saint Patrick's was fine. The streets were blissfully deserted at 7 A.M. But walking back was another story. People did more than stare. Young women were the most vocal in their approach. They walked right up to me and said things like "You have my support." Older, middle-aged men, however, looked askance, although some seemed mildly amused. A few actually said to me, "You look much prettier in real life than you do in your pictures." They thought I'd take it as a compliment. In a two-block radius, ten people came up to me to talk. But it was worse back at the hotel. Clusters of reporters hovered by the door. Like vultures they moved in on me the moment I approached. Voyeurs, all of them, asking questions that betrayed an utter lack of discretion, not to mention compassion. "What are you going to do with yourself now that your professional life is ruined?" one of them probed, sticking a microphone in my face as I tried to make my way through the lobby. Just what I wanted to hear, when inwardly I was wrestling with the same question. I managed to make it back to my room without giving them any more of their wretched "good copy." Once safely behind the gilded doors to my room

in the Waldorf Towers, I realized I was no longer here by
choice. I was being forced to remain inside.

It wasn't just reporters who called. Friends called as
well. My mother and brothers kept calling. I couldn't get
my mind off the experience even for an hour. In my present state the efforts to help by people I loved only depressed me. I tried to call Bo, but that only reminded me
of one more failure, one more ending, one more loss. As
if for confirmation that this was really happening, I called
my office number at Bendix. One of the two secretaries
Agee and I had shared answered. Her voice only reinforced my despair. She reminded me that they were all
there, in my office, where I should have been right then.
Our already awkward conversation was cut short by
Marie's having to get off the line to take Agee's dictation.
For the first time I wished we hadn't had common offices
and secretaries.

My older brother, John, was livid with rage, and his
protective anger only inflamed mine. And of course Father Bill was morally indignant about the way the press
was handling the story and outraged at the political ex-
pediency that had guided the Bendix board. Still, he tried
to inspire me to rise above my anger. "Pray for those who
have hurt you, Mary Elizabeth," he said. But I was hardly
ready to do that. I couldn't forgive those who had tres-
passed against me. I just couldn't turn the other cheek.
Not this time.

I don't know how I would have survived had it not
been for my mother. I spoke to her, often twice a day,
and again she encouraged me to go out and get some
exercise even if it meant just walking around the block.
I ventured forth a second time. By now I was getting used
to the pattern. In restaurants it was always the same. One

person would notice me and recognition would suddenly light up his face. Then, one by one, all the people at the table would discreetly turn, then quickly avert their eyes. Then the whispering would start. But it was the laughter that often followed that really hurt. "I just want you to know we're with you, dear," an older woman said to me one morning on the steps of Saint Patrick's. "Many good people believe in you." It was soothing to hear kind words, but anonymity was what I really craved. I simply wanted to be the old Mary Cunningham again, the Mary Cunningham no one knew. It would have been such a relief had some stranger bumped into me on the street and said, "Oh, excuse me, lady," and hurried on his way.

"Come home, dear. Please come home," my mother implored me during one of our daily talks. She could always tell when my mood was the most bleak. "We want you nearby. You've always wanted to do things on your own but now's not the time. I'm really so worried about you." But I couldn't. I didn't want to face all those people on Main Street who always respected me for the values my family had instilled in me. And I didn't want to lead a trail of newspaper reporters straight to my mother's door. I could just imagine the kinds of questions they'd hurl at my ninety-one-year-old grandmother Bombi. "Do you think your granddaughter slept with her boss? Would you describe your granddaughter as a 'good girl'?" But apparently they'd already found their way to Hanover. "I don't know what to say to these press people," my mother confessed to me later during our talk. "They got Bombi on the phone. I don't know quite what they said but she's very upset. She's been asking all week what's been going on with Mary Elizabeth."

Most of the time I sat in my room, I spent in writing.

It was the only thing that made me feel better. I thought it might help me unravel my feelings. Going back over what I had written, it was as if I had experienced a death. And I had. The death of my job. The death of my privacy. The death of my friendship with Bill Agee. And worst of all, it seemed even the death of my faith. I was angry at God. Why had He let me down? As soon as I realized what I was feeling, I panicked. If I couldn't rely on my faith, what could I rely on? If I didn't have my faith, what would be the purpose of living? I had always linked faith in God to faith in people and faith in myself, but now even that was starting to disintegrate. I was becoming very hard on myself. I'm a failure—an embarrassment to my family. Worse yet, I'm a big sham. If my faith can't hold up under fire, then what good am I? I don't deserve to live.

Only one thing made me feel good in all this brooding and that was that I had at least been loyal, and when the chips were down, had stood up for my friend. I had not betrayed Bill Agee. I had been tested and I had withstood the test. My friendship was that deep. But no sooner did I think about that than more destructive thoughts would come pouring in. Why, then, if I'd been such a good friend, hadn't he done the same for me? I wondered. Maybe I didn't deserve it. Maybe I hadn't earned it. And that pushed me even deeper into despair. I started to think I must not be good enough to deserve anyone's loyalty and trust. It awakened in me long-forgotten feelings I'd had about my father. Why hadn't he stayed? Why after all those years hadn't he tried to get in touch with me? Didn't he miss me? Wasn't I good enough? I must not be worthy, I decided. He probably never cared for me as much as I'd cared for him. And I believed that was to be my fate.

To be betrayed by all men, except for Father Bill and my brothers. First, my father. And now Agee. Even Bo. Why hadn't he come up to Boston with me when I went to Business School? Why hadn't he followed me out to Detroit as he promised he would? Maybe I wasn't ever as important to him as he said I was. Was that my fate? To give more than I'd ever get back? That's what I'd always been taught love was all about, but should love feel this bad? My imagination was running wild. I thought maybe my brothers and Father Bill would now leave me too; maybe they'd be too ashamed of me.

There was a ray of hope in all this, and it came in the form of letters. Hundreds of them. An avalanche poured in each day to the secretaries' office at Bendix. Agee had instructed Barbara and Marie to save them for me. "If only you could see them, Mary, you'd feel much better," said Marie, who read a few of them to me over the phone. First a few—then hundreds of people sensed my need for help and wrote to tell me not to give up. They offered me encouragement in the form of books, invitations to come stay in their homes, and, above all, personal accounts of their own similar professional nightmares. What moved me the most were the hundreds of letters from other women, women from fifteen to ninety-three, who poured out their hearts to me, who said they'd had similar experiences but hadn't shared them with anyone until now. I realized then how common was this particular "accusation" as a weapon in corporate warfare—especially for women finally promoted from the less powerful to the more powerful ranks. Letter after letter told of the same experience—the undermining of professional credibility in the wake of rumors and speculation. Many of the other letters I received were from people who were deeply spiritual. They encouraged me to rely on my faith. Strangers, absolute strangers, wrote, "You don't know me, but if you're ever in Toledo, my wife and I want you to feel free to stay with us." Or, "Please come see us if you're ever in Lincoln City. We'll hide you from the press."

Still, the letters couldn't overcome my despair, and in between readings I entertained some ghastly thoughts. Maybe a lobotomy. One that would remove that part of my brain that kept reliving the final weeks at Bendix, kept replaying the scenes in which the board locked Agee out while conducting its kangaroo trial, or in which Agee sat there mute, as I signed away my job. I knew it was wrong to even consider such an option, but my mind pursued it anyway. Perhaps there was a way I could do it so that no one would know. An overdose? Too obvious. Hanging? Too gruesome. I could walk out into the street and let myself get hit by a car. That was it. An onrush of cars on Park Avenue would quickly put an end to all this. Kill off the media version of Mary Cunningham.

It was during one of these moments that my younger brother, Frank, called. He sounded so jovial, so happy. "Hey, Mare. How's my good Bean?" (It was our nickname for each other.) "Not so good, I'm afraid," I said. "I just can't get hold of myself, Frank. I feel like everything's ruined."

"Do you know what I think?" he asked. His voice was so cheerful it caught me off guard. "I think what you need right now is a little California sunshine. Why don't you come on out and stay with me for a while?" Frank was then living in Costa Mesa, California. "We'll have a few cookouts, catch some sun and swim in the Pacific. You'll love it. You'll see. In a few weeks you'll feel just like new." His easy manner disarmed me. It was the perfect antidote to my gloom. It was the first twinge of hope I had felt in days. "You won't believe this, Frank, but you just saved my life. You really did." He laughed. "Just get yourself on out here fast. I miss you, Bean."

I'd read about the resort and health spa at La Costa and made arrangements to stay there. It was an hour's drive from Frank's house. When I told Agee's and my secretaries I was going, they were thrilled. "That's the spirit, Mare," they said. For the time being, Slaughter on Park Avenue would have to wait.

As is the custom at La Costa, I was met at the airport by a limousine. I'd had my fill of those, but my spirits improved when I saw my room. It was decorated in soft shades of yellow and green: good, healing colors.

I looked like a walking advertisement for why someone might need to stay at a health spa. I was underweight and underfed and looked like a waif in my drooping tan skirt. All my summer things were still back in Southfield, and I wasn't about to go back there to get them. Frank must have realized this, for he arrived later that afternoon bearing gifts—a pair of corduroy pants (size four), a summery blouse and a pretty ribbon for my hair. It was just what I needed.

The first thing I did was get my hair done. The woman in the salon suggested I wear it in a French braid. I hardly recognized myself. My new disguise gave me a good idea. "Aren't you Mary Cunningham?" one of the less discreet patrons asked. "You know, more people think I look like her," I said with a smile. "We do look an awful lot alike, don't we?" I was already finding considerable relief in simply dismissing the Mary Cunningham that had been created by the whole Bendix episode.

The sun. The hot tubs. The nourishing meals (I must have been the only guest not on a diet). I was beginning to feel better already, but my newly found peace was shortlived.

No sooner had I settled into luxurious oblivion than I received a call from Gail Sheehy. She'd been trying to reach me for days. I was astonished that she had found me here. "I just wanted to check a few more facts with you for the series." "What series?" I asked, alarmed. "The five-part series I've written about you." She sounded much more businesslike than she had the last time we'd spoken. "I thought you were writing an article, not a series," I said. "Well, we decided to make it into a series. It's going to be syndicated nationally. Every major paper in America is running it," she said. "Don't worry. It's very sympathetic. You'll love it."

I wasn't so sure. How could she write a whole series from a twenty-minute interview? "What does it say?" I asked. "Well, the part that's running tomorrow is about your childhood, your alcoholic father, your brother who died and your upbringing by your mother and Father Bill." "What?" I asked, stunned. "That's confidential information I gave you three years ago, when you were interviewing for your book *Pathfinders*. That was supposed to be strictly confidential." "Well, I couldn't exactly have blocked it out of my mind. But don't worry," she said. "You look very good. I think you'll like the article."

I tried to remember what we had talked about during that first interview.

I couldn't recall our conversation exactly, but I did remember having the distinct impression that Sheehy had some rather elaborate theories about my upbringing that she seemed to be weaving together from a meager handful of facts. "What do you say about my family?" I asked. "Well, just what you told me. About your being the youngest of three children, your father, his drinking, how he killed your little brother in a car accident...." "What?" I said, unable to believe what I'd just heard. "He didn't kill my little brother in a car accident." I thought back to our conversation. I remembered telling her of my uncertainty about the exact circumstances of my brother's death. She had made me feel comfortable sharing theories I'd had as a child, since she reassured me that this was merely "deep background material" for what was to be a book that would not use names. Since that interview, I had learned that my older brother had, in fact, died from spinal meningitis.

"You can't print that kind of thing about my father. And besides, it's not even true. You promised that material would be kept strictly confidential." I felt the anger welling up inside me. Yet another betrayal. I knew I'd have to call my mother and prepare her for this. "When is it running?" I asked. "Tomorrow," Sheehy said. "Read it first and then tell me what you think."

It wasn't hard to find. Both the *Los Angeles Herald-Examiner* and the *San Francisco Chronicle* splashed it across their front pages. I held the papers with trembling hands and started to read. I couldn't believe what I was reading. The story was full of inaccuracies. It said my older brother, Richie, had died in a car accident and that I was the youngest of three children. I wondered what my younger brother, Frank, would think about that. But it wasn't the inaccuracies so much as the distortions that really upset me. Having spent with me a maximum of three or four hours about a year and a half ago, and only twenty or thirty minutes just a few weeks back, she had "psychoanalyzed" the members of my family as if she'd known them for years. It was pop psychology in its most disgusting form.

But aside from the inaccuracies, what bothered me most was the tone. Here was my life as soap opera, written by a journalist I hardly knew. And the style of writing made it seem as if Sheehy was right there with me throughout it all—on the plane, in the board room, strolling the beaches of California. If this was what they called "new journalism," I'll take the old.

My family was up in arms. My mother probably even felt worse than she let on because she didn't want to further upset me. "There are no ethics in this profession, are there?"

But the person who was most disturbed, and rightly so, was my father. The series roused him out of years of virtual silence from his new life down in the South. "Why should my new wife and son have to live with this hanging over their heads?" he asked. He was so enraged he threatened to sue Sheehy. Father Bill had to be called upon to dissuade him. "The last thing Mary Elizabeth needs now is to be tied up in a lawsuit," he said. "Besides, it'll only help Sheehy get more of the attention she's after."

Only Frank cheered us up. With his kind heart and generally sanguine outlook he saw only the good parts—and there were good parts in what Sheehy had written. "I don't think it's so bad," he said. "I think it's kind of neat that you're the subject of a five-part series." He pointed out that at least she was one journalist who had come close to getting the Bendix story right.

I had been so upset by the breach of privacy, I hadn't been able to appreciate what friends acknowledged was a decidedly sympathetic slant. I had to admit that her articles did at least defend my virtue and emphasized my role as a professional. If only she'd stopped there.

Frank and his friends were a wonderful elixir. Their good humor and their easy, joking manner were just what I needed to lift me out of my depression. But as the weeks wore on, I grew tired of the easy California lifestyle. I'd had enough jokes, enough hot tubs. My escape phase was over. I knew I had some problems, and I was starting to feel ready to face them.

At the end of my stay at La Costa, my older brother, John, called—just at a point where I was feeling especially low. I had called Barbara and Marie at Bendix to collect my messages—Agee and I had the same phone number, since our offices had been right next door—and it bothered me that Agee never even bothered to pass on a message asking how I was. It was at this point that John called, urging me to come visit him. "Why don't you come and stay with us for a while, Mary?" he said. "It's well into autumn, and Keene looks so beautiful this time of year. Remember how you used to love walking in the woods, kicking the leaves?" To be home in New England in the autumn—I could feel the snap in the air. But I wasn't sure I was quite ready to face Hanover yet. How would Main Street react to the new press version of the "controversial Mary Cunningham." But John persuaded me. He sounded older, wiser, almost paternalistic, and I thought a talk with him could do me some good. "You'll stay with Jane and me and the kids in Keene," John said. "And we can visit Mom on the weekends." That sounded satisfactory to me and I agreed to come.

John met my plane at Logan Airport in Boston. As there were ten years between us, we'd never really been close before, but during the two-hour ride along New

Hampshire's beautiful winding roads lined with green pines, we got to know each other again. It was like discovering I had a new brother. It was good to be with his family, too. Jane, his wife, who hailed from a long line of Yankees—her father had been a Supreme Court Justice in New Hampshire—held her emotions in check and made me feel right at home. And although John's two boys, John Junior, who was fourteen, and Amos, who was thirteen, didn't know quite what to make of their frail young aunt, they were respectful and polite. But it was Lizzie, John's ten-year-old daughter, who made me feel most at home. With her little girl's intuition, she sensed how needful I was, and during the rest of my two-week stay, she declared herself my loyal protector.

Jane cooked a pot roast that first night, and I realized how long it had been since I'd eaten a home-cooked meal. All those restaurant meals and room-service trays—if I never saw another sprig of parsley in my life, I wouldn't mind. The food was wonderful and so was the talk. After dinner, John took me aside. "Now I want you to feel free to talk to me any time," he said as we sat by the fire. Even if you have to wake me at midnight, please do. The only way to unleash the pain is to talk it out." I was grateful for his advice and concern. I'd never seen this side of my brother. Later that evening, Jane showed me to my room. Lizzie had already seen to it that I was supplied with a menagerie of her favorite stuffed animals.

Just before I got into bed, John peeked in to say goodnight. "Remember when you were little, Mare, how you always had to sleep with a light on?" He laughed and turned out the light. "John?" I said, as he walked out the door. "I still do." And he came back and turned on the bathroom light. "Good night, Mare," he said. "You'll be in my prayers."

As soon as I was alone, despair closed in around me. It was late October and I was in New England, and something about both those things made the events of the past few months seem so much worse. I was home and everything around me was dying. I started to cry. Tears seemed to cover my whole body. Lizzie, stopping in to say goodnight, saw my head buried in the pillow and heard my sobs. She put her hand lightly on my heaving back and in her little girl's voice said, "Don't worry, Aunt Mary. Everything's going to be all right." After a few minutes she climbed into the bed next to mine. "I'm going to stay right here with you until you feel better, Aunt Mary. I'm going to pretend I'm your roommate and sleep here tonight." And she did. Every night, she slept right next to me, my personal little bodyguard.

John encouraged me to talk, and after some initial reluctance, I did. We walked and talked, but always I hit the same stumbling block—Agee. "Could he really let them cut me out of Bendix so easily?" I said. "Could he really be back there working as if I never existed? How could he even speak to those people after what they'd done to me? And what about me? Doesn't he care at all about my life? He said I was his friend. But what kind of friend would drop his loyal aide-de-camp, just like that?"

John, hearing the hurt and confusion in my voice, tried to get me to see it from Agee's point of view. "Think of what he must be going through. He probably feels terrible about all that has happened. And besides, I'm not sure he had that much choice. Could he really have saved you? Was there anything, really, either of you could have done?" I heard John's words, but I was still too wounded to let any of them sink in. And when he suggested I talk to Agee, confront him face to face with my questions, the notion made me sick.

"Now I don't want you to get alarmed, Mary," he told me one day. "It's not that I think you're slipping or anything. I just think it might do you some good to talk to a psychiatrist I know—Dr. Wolterbeek. He's a good friend of Jane's and mine and he might be able to help." I'd heard John mention the name before—Wolterbeek worked for the University system in New Hampshire—but the idea of seeing a psychiatrist upset me. I'd never been to one before. Besides, I thought, how could anyone understand all that had happened? It wasn't just a simple, passing emotional trauma. It felt more complex and telling—like a Greek tragedy. Still, I decided to give it a try, but only for a few sessions.

It felt good to get in the car. Driving made me feel back in control of at least some part of my existence. And I took satisfaction in the fact that I could follow John's directions and find my way along back-country roads to Dr. Wolterbeek's house. It was a beautiful house, a lovely old farmhouse sprawled out against the rolling New Hampshire foothills. Dr. Wolterbeek's wife greeted me at the door and invited me in to wait. "He's just out in the barn milking the goats," she said. The kitchen was warm with the smell of freshly baked bread. She gave me milk and cookies and I spoke with her teenage daughter until Dr. Wolterbeek returned.

Once inside his office—it was a cozy den more than an office—Dr. Wolterbeek encouraged me to open up. He said he'd read about the case but hadn't followed it carefully. What a relief, I thought, to find someone who hadn't read the details of my gruesome experience. He sensed my relief and smiled. It was so easy to talk to him. He was so warm, such a good man. He just seemed to understand. "Do you think I'm ever going to feel good again?" I asked him at the end of our first hour's talk. "Well, it's not like a business strategy," he said. "There isn't any grand solution. But I do think you'll feel better. Over time."

We covered a lot of ground in those two-hour sessions. His questions were penetrating. He knew how to draw out my deepest feelings. After only the second meeting with him, I could already see the progress I was making. I was starting to understand so many feelings—about myself, about my family, about the cast of characters I'd come to know in the Bendix experience.

Driving home from Dr. Wolterbeek's that night along the dark, winding road to my brother's home was the first time that I felt strong enough to face up to the kinds of questions the doctor had been encouraging me to ask. I wanted desperately to unravel the complicated emotions this experience had brought on. I admitted to myself that I had entertained suicidal feelings. I pushed aside the guilt long enough to ask myself exactly what thoughts preceded these moods. I knew all too well. I thought about the allegations that had been thrown at me, and I realized that these were the worst I could possibly experience. My upbringing, my mother's ruined marriage—they would have made unbearable the kind of affair people were suggesting. And the public exposure made me feel as if control over my life had been taken completely out of my hands. What people said and thought about me no longer had anything to do with who I really was. I didn't have control over my job, where I lived, even who my friends were. And my privacy was destroyed. I started to recall the frustration of trying to tell other people about this agony, and they'd always counter, "In another five or ten years people won't even remember your name." That only made me feel more desperate. What was I supposed to do during those five or ten years? Wait around until this fictitious public persona disappeared? And why should I? Wait out a sentence for a crime I never committed?

I was starting to lose control. But then I recalled Wolterbeek's final words of advice before I'd left his home that evening. "You'll adjust, Mary," he said, "but it's going to take time. Don't be impatient with yourself." I believed him. I knew that I would feel better, and slowly I could already feel my faith returning. In my stronger moments I was even beginning to see that if I could just survive there would be an opportunity for personal growth in all this. Perhaps others could also learn from my experience. And perhaps I would learn that there was something quite universal in what at first seemed like such a lonely kind of suffering.

Ten minutes more and I would be in John's driveway. I was beginning to wonder if this self-analysis was really such a healthy process. But my mind pressed on. I knew there were other thoughts that preceded my darkest moments. And these were more complex. I recalled the face of Agee, his office, his company—and how I had believed in him. Tears welled up. I felt that I'd been betrayed. I heard my voice break the silence of the lonely car ride home: "I laid down my life for you, Agee, and afterwards you didn't even care." I reviewed the familiar scenes one more time. Agee being excluded from the crucial board meeting (could he really have allowed that to happen?), Agee, sitting there, mute, as I signed away my job, and then, the next morning, hurrying back to his own job in

Detroit after I'd asked him for help. The hurt and anger were almost too much.

Eventually I was able to talk more about the feelings and less about the event. That night by the wood stove in his den, I opened up. My brother and I picked up where my car ride left off. "He does seem to stir up in you a lot of feelings reminiscent of your childhood," John observed. We went back, as far back into my childhood as our memories allowed. We talked about my father, my feelings of loss, and how natural it was, coming from my background, to serve and be devoted to someone like Agee. John reminded me that I'd seen my mother do the same thing. I began to realize why it was especially distressing for me to see the world turn a professional devotion into something seamy and sordid. The combination of my talks with Wolterbeek and my brother John loosened me up. I found myself recalling incidents I'd never even talked about before. And soon I was starting to speak more freely about the event, the feelings, and even my hopes for recovery.

At the close of what Dr. Wolterbeek and I both sensed would be our final healing talk, he offered his opinion that I was now strong enough to take on the next important step—to confront Agee. "Ask him all those questions you have been asking me," he said. "You have a right to know the answers." It was the second time I'd heard that suggestion. I had ignored it the first time, when John made it. "I'll stay right here with you when you speak to him," Dr. Wolterbeek offered. After all, he didn't know Agee and had no idea what he might say. "But you have to be prepared for his answers, whatever they may be," he cautioned. I wasn't sure I could do that. Dr. Wolterbeek suggested he call Agee and arrange for the three of us to talk. "But what will he think, hearing from a psychiatrist? He'll think I'm weak or that I've flipped out," I said, alarmed. "He won't think that," Dr. Wolterbeek said. "We'll just let him know you're having a difficult time, as anyone would."

I sat in the den while Dr. Wolterbeek went into the next room to make the call. I was dreadfully nervous. What if Agee said no? What if he said he was too busy? I knew I wouldn't be able to take that kind of rejection a second time. After about twenty minutes, Dr. Wolterbeek returned. "Mr. Agee was very glad I called," he said, smiling. "He's been extremely worried about you. He'll be only too glad to fly out here and talk with us," Dr. Wolterbeek said. "Frankly," he added, "he sounds as if he could use a few sessions himself."

It was arranged that Agee would fly in the following Saturday and that Dr. Wolterbeek would meet his plane. Our meeting was scheduled for 4 P.M., but when I arrived at the farmhouse a few minutes after four, only Annica and Mrs. Wolterbeek were there. "They must have been delayed," Mrs. Wolterbeek said. "Why don't you come inside?" I followed her into the kitchen and the three of us chatted while Mrs. Wolterbeek made jam. "Looks like we're in for a big one," she said, pointing out the window. The sky was growing darker and the wind was blowing hard. Four-thirty. Five. Still no sign of them. I felt my resolve weaken as the minutes ticked on. What if Agee had decided not to come? What if he decided at the last minute it wasn't worth it? Or, more likely, that one of his crucial business meetings was more important. At five-thirty I got up and went into the den. The whole notion started to seem absurd. And yet the amazing thing was that instead of feeling angry, I started to feel sheepish. What right did I have to request that the chairman of the board fly in and see me like this? Who was I to summon such a meeting?

At around six o'clock I heard a car pull into the driveway. The front door slammed. I looked up, and there was Agee, walking into the den. In a flash, I felt the old scenes run through my head. The betrayal. The silence. And then, Agee telling me, no, I couldn't use his retreat house. Did I really want to speak with this man? And yet, how quickly the anger dissipated when I saw this wraithlike figure come up to me and grasp hold of both my hands. "Mary, it's so good to see you," he said, still holding my hands. I was astonished at how pale and haggard he looked. He must have lost at least twenty pounds. "You know I've been really worried about you," he said. "I've wanted to call but I didn't know what to do, I didn't know what I would say." His eyes filled with tears, and unexpectedly so did mine. How awful it had been, not just for me but for him, too. For both of us.

We talked for a few minutes and then Agee took off his jacket and sat down. Dr. Wolterbeek cleared his throat. "I think this ought to be a session with just the two of you," he said, getting up. "I'll be out front if you need me."

"You can't imagine what life is like back at Bendix," Agee started in. "I'm so grateful you're not there." That was a new way of looking at it. "How do you deal with it?" I asked. I could see from his pallor and dark circles, not very well. "I immerse myself in the strategy," he said. "I make up my mind when I go in in the morning to ignore the petty comments and the nasty looks and just do my job. For the sake of the strategy."

It would have been so easy to go on from there, to talk about business like we did in the old days, but I knew I had some questions to ask, and if I didn't ask them now, they would haunt me forever. I interrupted him. "Why didn't you stand up for me that day? Why didn't you speak up for me before the board?"

He looked almost shocked. "You don't realize what it was like," he said. "There was no way they were going to listen to me. It was over before it began. It was a charade. Just a mock trial designed to legitimize something a few powerful people insisted on seeing done." "Then why didn't you stick with me? Tell them if they did this to me, they'd lose you too." "Just walk away? Forget about the strategy? That's just what certain people would have loved to see me do," he said. "Then I really would have looked foolish. Like my priorities were warped. Like all they were trying to insinuate about us was true." I could feel my anger building. I cut myself short. "But why not call? At least talk to me? See if I'm okay." "You don't know how much I wanted to, Mary. But I couldn't. You've got to understand. Up until a few weeks ago, I couldn't even have stood seeing you. You reminded me of the biggest failure in my life. Your voice would only have deepened my own sense of helplessness."

I thought about the past few months, and how awful they had been. How many times had I played in my head his promise to me and my mother that if I were forced to resign, he would too. And yet, I saw that he had his own nightmares too. Worse, I saw that he was blaming himself for events that were beyond his control. And yet, he still had a company to run. He couldn't just fly off to La Costa as I had. He didn't have the support of a loving family to back him up. I decided not to press him with more questions. But I could tell there was more he wanted to say.

"It's been awful," he said. "Rather than quiet down, things at Bendix have gotten worse. Blumenthal and his coterie are still gloating. Most of the directors still have confidence in me but some fissures are starting to show. And then on the personal front—" he rubbed his eyes— "Diane's been milking this for all it was worth. She's been talking with neighbors, calling old friends, even visiting my parents in Florida to explain away twenty years of problems in our marriage. And she's been using the girls to do a guilt trip on me, and even Bob's becoming confused. I don't know exactly what she's been saying about you or me but she's a pro at manipulating people to feel sorry for her and she's succeeding."

For an hour he spelled out the grim details of his personal life. If such a thing were possible, his situation seemed almost worse than mine. Diane—"Vernor Court," he called her, a reference to the Bloomfield Hills estate she had won in the settlement—apparently had succeeded in rallying his entire family against him. After all, how could you have much sympathy for a man "running around with his twenty-nine-year-old executive assistant?" "She's been calling my sisters and a lot of my old friends whom she hardly talked to before. They all think I'm the bad guy now." "What about your parents? They knew the two of you had separated several times over the years." "I know," he said. "In August they rejoiced when I told them we were finally getting divorced. They knew we'd both been miserable. They'd always criticized her and felt we were mismatched. But when this story hit the papers, suddenly it gave her an excuse. She could use you to make people feel sorry for her. Then she could make it look as if all along it had been my fault." How quickly people believe what they hear, I thought. I quickly changed the topic.

"How's the strategy going?" I asked, hoping to steer us to safer ground. "Not very well," he said. "I'm having trouble with the board. Blumenthal's still fanning the fires and everyone on the board is angry and upset. Some of them are still trying to blame me—you—for the whole media incident." The idea of Blumenthal, the board, even Diane, still using me as the scapegoat for all their problems caused my heart to pound. I could feel myself start to explode. "I won't take it," I said, suddenly losing control. "I'm not going to sit back and take it. Not from that board. Not from Diane. Not from anyone," I said. "Listen, Mary. We'll handle it. Okay? There's not much we can do right now." I'd heard these phrases before and they only made me feel more enraged. But I caught myself. Agee looked so tired, so sick. Did he need yet another person railing against him? Both of us had been hurt, and when I realized that, it softened my anger against him.

"Have you had anything to eat?" I asked. "No, but I'm really hungry. How about you?" "Starved."

We had a quiet dinner with the Wolterbeeks. Agee told me he would have to leave soon. "I know you're still my friend," he said, when the two of us were alone. He was waiting for a similar statement from me, but I couldn't give it to him. Not yet. But I did tell him it was good to see him—something I could and did feel. We had a friendship, and however imperfect, I was glad to see it hadn't died.

In the next few days, strands of our conversation played through my mind. It took a little time for its significance to seep in but I could feel it start to have an effect on me.

For one thing, I realized it wasn't only I who'd been hurt; it was Agee too. And that seemed to lessen my anger. At last I began to realize that not every divorce was my mother's all over again. Sometimes the woman is every bit as wrong as the man. For the first time, my sympathies started to shift from the left-behind wife to the long-suffering husband. In addition, I realized that Agee wasn't as able to save me as I'd once believed. Had he stormed off in protest, that probably would have confirmed in the eyes of certain members of the board and much of the press-influenced world that we had been having an affair. But finally, and most important, I saw that he cared. And he did care. I could tell from the way he walked up to me the minute he came in. And he cared that he had hurt me. This hardly alleviated my immediate problems, but it did allow me to see Agee in a less villainous light. At least he was still my friend, and however poorly that friendship had fared in the last few months, at least it still existed. It was its sudden death that had been so hard to take.

I spent one more week with John and his family in Keene, but by the end of the week, I felt it was time to go back. Back to the battle. Back to New York. Back to the real world. I had had a career knocked out from under me, but I was not about to let it die. I had a purpose. I was going to go right back out there, get myself another job and start at exactly the same point where I'd left off. I wanted the same title, the same salary or better, and the same kind of position. That would say more than any words that it wasn't Agee's "poor judgment" that had gotten me where I'd been.

It was November when I checked back into the Waldorf. In some odd way it seemed only right to launch my job campaign from here. I gritted my teeth and got down to work. But before I could attend to reestablishing my career, there was some unfinished legal business pending. My lawyer, Tom Hagoort, had encouraged me to confront Sheehy on what my family and I believed to be a serious invasion of my privacy. I finally summoned the courage to make an appointment with her at which my attorney and I could formally address my legal grievances. But at the appointed hour, her receptionist informed us flatly that she was "unavailable." I was sure this aborted meeting signaled the last of the glowing Sheehy stories. She'd already gotten what she wanted.

In the last several weeks, I'd received, unsolicited, more than two hundred job queries. I divided these into three piles—the good, the bad, and the if-all-else-fails pile. I'd also received letters from dozens of headhunters eager to hunt mine. I knew it would be a real plum for any of them to boast, "We placed Mary Cunningham." But I didn't want to be used in that way. I loathed the idea of reading a profile of myself in some company's magazine. Nor did I respond to firms who spoke to me about The Cause. "Let us help you show the world..." I was through with crusades for now. I simply wanted to get a job on the basis of my abilities and get back to work. Period.

Thus began another round of interviewing. It was the Great Harvard Business School Job Hunt all over again, but how things had changed. Receptionists never just buzzed me in; they stood up and shook my hand. Not once was I asked for a résumé. As one executive quipped, "You probably have the best publicized résumé in the country." Jokes like this made me laugh, but only because if I didn't laugh, I would surely cry. I was still a fired executive and my self-esteem was low. But what was worse was the awful sense of *déjà vu*. Every job I interviewed for reminded me of the one I'd lost. Here was a secretary who looked like one at Bendix. Here was a personnel officer who reminded me of one at Southfield. And yet, like a new pair of slippers, none of the jobs I considered ever felt as comfortable as the old. In what job would I feel the same excitement? In what job would I be able to accomplish the same things? And then, all the reminders of Agee—in truth, few people I met were as impressive.

Still, I stuck to my purpose. I bought new luggage and three new size four suits (I still hadn't gained back all my weight) to psych myself up. I threw away my Bendix briefcase. That era had ended. I answered any and all questions as best I could. "Do you really think that you are healed enough to go back to work?" was the most commonly asked. "Probably not yet," I answered honestly. "But I plan to be by the first of the year."

It was Gerry Roche, chairman of the executive-headhunting firm Heidrick and Struggles, who really helped me get back on my feet. He set up a brainstorming session between me and a group of his firm's most seasoned headhunters one afternoon in the Sky Club, atop the Pan Am building. It was hard walking into that room, my first business conference à la Bendix since my name had become front-page news. "Why don't you tell us a little about yourself, Mary," he began as everyone in the room went still. I was nervous at first, but after a few sentences, I felt myself at ease. Gone was the Harvard Business School argot; I was too experienced for all that. Comfortably and naturally, the words seemed to flow right out of my mouth. Again, I had Agee to thank. Apart from my tumultuous exit, the job had been an incredible learning experience—so much experience telescoped into so short a time.

When we were alone, Roche said to me, "I didn't know whether to expect some loudmouthed, Harvard Business School clone or a blond bombshell, but I'm glad to see you're neither. Anyone with half a head knows that what was printed in the papers isn't the whole story," he said. He may have been flattering me, but in my vulnerable state I was eager to drink in the praise. "Even when affairs do go on, no one makes them front-page news. Someone was fanning that media event. And more important, most people know you took the bullet for Agee," he said. "That makes you a real asset in corporate America. You're loyal. What chairman of the board wouldn't want that?"

I felt encouraged after our talk. I hadn't formally applied for any job yet but I had made the rounds. I started to feel more confident that by February, my self-imposed deadline, I'd be back at work—Mary Cunningham, somebody's VP.

In the midst of all my interviewing I'd managed to move myself out of the Waldorf. I wasn't terribly happy in my new home—yet another carton-filled apartment, this time in Brooklyn Heights—but at least it wasn't another hotel room, and now with the prospect of work before me, I wouldn't have to be there very much.

About a week before Thanksgiving my mother called. "It would be so good if you would come home for the holidays, Mary," she said. "We miss you and I want to see that you're well." A part of me longed to go home but another part of me held back. I had put my mother through so much grief, given her such cause for worry, that I couldn't bear the idea of bringing any more of my problems home. I wanted to see her desperately, but I decided to wait. I resolved not to return home until I was back on my feet. And I wasn't walking quite upright yet.

But there was something else on my mind. I still hadn't completed the business of my divorce, and it bothered me. I had filed my annulment papers with the Tribunal in Brooklyn Heights, and yet, when I arrived, the priest asked me rather matter-of-factly if I'd been granted my civil divorce. "Civil divorce?" I asked, feeling foolish. I didn't know I needed one. "The Church won't review your annulment papers until you receive a legal divorce," he said. I was perturbed. How long these things dragged on. The ritual continued long after the emotional "divorce" had been accomplished. I wanted to make the process as swift, as painless and as private as possible. Any civil action meant I was subject once again to the reporters' merciless probes. I called my lawyer and found out the details. He reminded me there were only two states in which a divorce could be obtained after only six weeks. They were Nevada and Idaho. A lot of good that did me here in New York.

A few days later I received a disturbing call. It was from Agee. He was calling from outside a doctor's office. "What are you doing in the middle of the day seeing a doctor?" I asked. "I've been told that I need to take a prolonged rest," he said. It wasn't like Agee to want or need a rest. "Is anything serious the matter?" I asked. "Well, I'm a little under the weather, I suppose." It took several minutes before he confessed that he had been walking around for weeks with what had been diagnosed as a severe case of mononucleosis. He sounded frighteningly depressed. "Is there someone taking care of you?" I asked. "No," he said. "That's why I'm calling. There are some things I want to talk about to you. I was hoping you would consider flying out to Idaho for a few days."

The request caught me off guard, and I stalled for time. What did he think? That I was still his executive assistant? "What about any of your friends?" I asked. "Could any of them come out there?" I thought surely a few of his old Idaho chums would help. "I don't feel like being pumped for gossip anymore," he said. "I'm just too tired. And besides, few of them understand. Too many want to talk about what they read in the newspapers." There was an uncharacteristic note of cynicism in his voice. "What about your parents?" I asked. "I'm not exactly the object of their concern these days," he said. "It's the 'abandoned wife,' not the 'runaround husband,' who gets the sympathy vote." "And your sister Jackie?" I asked. "Not on my side," he said. "She sides with the ex-wife too."

I remembered getting a call like this ages ago, at Notre Dame, from Bo. It was when he asked me to come out after his friend Johnny Coates died. I felt needed then, and I could tell I was starting to feel needed again.

"I'd like to help out," I said, not at all sure that I really did. "But it's risky. I mean, it wouldn't exactly be the best PR for either of us if the press got hold of this. You know what they could do with that little piece of information." "Well, that's up to you, Mary. If you're worried more about appearances than friendship, then perhaps you'd better not come."

I didn't like the way that sounded at all. Maybe this whole experience was starting to change me from a compassionate human being to a kind of unfeeling pragmatist. Maybe my reluctance was really a form of retaliation. I knew it was only right to help a friend in need—no matter how much that friend had let you down in the past. I remembered that he'd caught the first plane out to Wolterbeek's office when the doctor had told him I needed to talk. "Will you judge me badly if I don't come?" I asked, testing one last time. "I'm not in a position to judge anybody right now," he said. "My family's turned on me. Many of my friends are acting cool. And I'm still fighting the Blumenthal faction on my board." "I'm sorry, but I'm going to have to think about this overnight," I said. "I'm just so battle-scarred that I don't trust any of my reactions yet. But I promise to get back to you tomorrow."

As soon as I hung up the phone I felt confused. Part of me still felt angry and yet part of me genuinely wanted to help. After all, for eighteen months I'd grown accustomed to being at his beck and call to help him with any problem he had. And he had been my friend. Had been— but what was he now? Even more confusing to me was the nature of his request. What did he want from me? After all, who was I kidding? It wasn't strategy I'd be going out there to discuss. We no longer had any official professional relationship. Sure I could still offer business insights, but that wasn't what he was asking for this time. He wanted me to go out there as a friend. Was I still a friend of this man? Did I want to be?

And yet, there were reasons entirely apart from Agee that a trip to McCall might be good for me. When I had asked him, back on that awful morning, if I could use the house, the idea of secluding myself up in the mountains had a strong appeal. There was healing in that clear mountain air. Something about being in the mountains reminded me of the seclusion of a monastery. And how I longed for that kind of peace. Surely no one, not even the most persistent reporter (and I'd met some persistent ones), was likely to follow me there. And finally, something Dr.

Wolterbeek had said kept playing through my head: "You've got to confront the thing that disturbs you the most." And what had happened between me and Agee still kept me up at night; I wanted to get to the bottom of it once and for all.

I thought about the idea for another day and weighed the pros and cons. But the deciding factor was confirmed by a conversation with my attorney about finalizing my divorce. He reminded me that if I could spend six weeks in Idaho I could once and for all complete my divorce and in absolute privacy. Even if Agee got well and left, I could find a place to stay. The parents of one of my classmates at Wellesley had homes both in Boise and in McCall, and perhaps I could arrange to stay with them. The press surely wouldn't be able to cover my divorce way up in the mountains of Idaho.

I called my mother and told her what I was considering. She was concerned. "Are you sure you're emotionally equipped to finalize your divorce just now?" she asked. "I'm going to have to get it over with sooner or later. It's not fair to either Bo or me to keep letting it drag on. And this may be the last chance of it's being private." She said she understood the reasoning but still was concerned about my seeing Agee while I was there. "I know you've always needed to face your problems straight on—but this one may be too much for you. I'm not sure that either you or Mr. Agee are in any condition to help each other. You've both been through so much." "I know, but no one else can possibly understand the other's hurt as well as we do. In that way, we can help each other better than anyone else." A long pause. "Just remember, Mary. Don't feel you have to stay out there the full six weeks just to see your divorce through if things become too unpleasant," she said. "I won't," I said, knowing her need for reassurance. And with a mixture of emotions, some of which even I didn't understand, I packed my things and left.

I landed in Boise International Airport a few days before Thanksgiving. Agee's older sister, Carolyn, met the plane. If Agee looked bad when I'd seen him at Dr. Wolterbeek's office, he looked worse now. Only three weeks had passed but he looked as if he'd been through the Hundred Years War. His skin was gray-white. A rumpled white sweater hung on his emaciated frame. How different he looked from the suntanned, exuberant executive I'd seen step off the Concorde in July of a year and a half ago.

Carolyn was a few years older than Agee and very animated. Agee called her "Frisky." Unlike his younger sister, Jackie, who was caught up in her own problems, Carolyn had taken at least an initial interest in her brother's plight. It seemed that up until now she had always been in the shadow of Agee, the fair-haired boy. She seemed only too happy to enlist Agee in her cause. "Aren't they incredible?" she said, referring to their parents, while the three of us had dinner in Boise. "To turn on their own like that?" I remained silent, except to offer some banal comment about parents and children. But the whole discussion made me uncomfortable, and I was relieved when Carolyn left to drive home. I was not used to a family where sides were picked—and swapped—so quickly.

The drive to McCall was long and lovely. Two and a half hours of breathtaking sights—snowcapped mountains, towering pines and magnificent crystal-clear lakes. The terrain was much more stark and powerful than any in New England. But it was the stillness I loved. For so many weeks now—actually months—I felt like a cartoon character whose legs were running far apace of its body. Now, in the quiet of the mountains, I felt as if I could finally slow down. I was glad Agee was driving. I sat back and looked at the scenery, grateful for the chance to rest.

"It means a lot to me that someone is here with me," he said as we made our way deeper into the mountains. He paused. It was awkward. We both felt awkward. After all, what were we to each other? Friends? Enemies? Fellow sufferers? "Although if you hadn't come, I'd have understood," he hastened to add. "You have every right to still feel angry."

I groped for something comfortable to talk about and came up with business. It was a poor choice of topic. Much had gone on at Bendix since I had left, and Agee was extremely bitter about it and other matters—his ex-wife, his ex-friends. "I wish to hell I knew who my friends were," he said. "It doesn't seem quite believable they'd all scatter like this." I was surprised. It wasn't like Agee to be bitter about anything. The farther we drove, the more philosophical he became. "What a waste it's all been," he said. "What have I done, devoting the last ten years of my life to that corporation? For that matter, my whole life has been tied up in organizations of one sort or another. And for what? You do a great job, scramble up to the top. Make yourself sick earning bonuses to support your family so your ex-wife can collect it all in alimony and turn your children against you. In the end, what have you really accomplished? Was any of it worthwhile?" This was not the old Bill Agee speaking, the confident *Wunderkind*.

I saw how hurt he was, how wounded. I thought perhaps I should stop him, but he seemed to have a need to

get it all out. "Blumenthal, Nancy Reynolds—I can't believe what they've done. Panny I can understand. He's a
hurting dog, so naturally he's going to try to find excuses.
But what about the others? What's in it for them to see
me fall? And neither of them hardly knows you. Do people
just get pleasure being king-topplers? I wonder."

On this point, we both stood on common ground. If
strategy was what we'd shared in the past, we now had
something else in common, a certain cynicism as a result
of what had gone on.

Out of habit, I started to try to say things to console
him. Advice Dr. Wolterbeek had given to me that I had
listened to with disbelief I now heard myself telling Agee
with conviction. And the most curious thing was that as
I spoke to Agee, I felt soothed. It was the ultimate healing
experience, teaching someone else the lessons you yourself needed to learn. And how ironic that Agee, in needing
my help, should give me the very thing I needed to heal
myself: the chance to heal another.

As we approached the house, Agee seemed to relax.
He became aware of his role as host, and mine as guest,
and his remarks shifted toward the practical. "I'd better
apologize for the house, Mary. It's been months since it's
been cleaned." I didn't think he was exaggerating. He led
me on a tour of his ranch-style house. It was hardly in
tiptop shape. "Here's your room," he said, leading me in
to one of the girls' rooms downstairs. Inside was a lovely
antique bed and dresser. He told me the set had belonged
to his parents. "It was thoughtful of them to give it to
you," I said, hoping to point out something nice that they'd
done. "They didn't 'give' it to me," he said. "I bought it
from them." I decided to refrain from mentioning his family affairs from now on.

"Would you like to have something to eat?" he asked after I'd unpacked my things. "I'm not very hungry," I said. "But I would like a cup of tea." We sat together in the living room. Agee made a fire. Outside, I could see the top of Brundage Mountain in the light of a full moon. "You'll find it very soothing out here," he said. "Don't worry about me," I answered. "It's you who's got to get back on your feet."

I didn't get up until 11 A.M. the next day. I went to the kitchen and called to Agee, but apparently he was still asleep. I ate breakfast and then devised my plan of attack. First I gave the oven a good scrub and then I did an inventory of the refrigerator. There were all kinds of dead things in there. I was an expert at this kind of KP, having done it several times for my brother Frank. It wasn't until twelve-thirty that Agee appeared. His face was wan, and he looked as if he were all bones. Even his fingers looked spindly. "What do you say we get some groceries?" I said. "That sounds like a good idea, Mary, only why don't you drive into town yourself? I don't quite feel up to it."

It was fun driving into town. McCall, with its general store and snow-covered streets, looked like a little winter wonderland. I bought cleaning supplies and food for a week. When I got back, I made some soup while Agee read. He wasn't able to do much else. During the rest of the day, he paid very little attention to me. He seemed almost to ignore me. I began to wonder if I'd been foolish to come. I tried to convince myself that my presence did offer him some comfort but my doubts caused me to bring the matter up. We had one of our most personal talks. He told me he wasn't used to expressing his feelings, that it was embarrassing for him to admit certain things. But he reassured me that he was happy, "very happy," that I had come.

During the next few days, I cleaned while Agee dozed and read. The slow pace was good therapy for me as well. Occasionally Agee did business over the phone. I could always tell when he'd been talking to any of the Blumenthal-Burroughs directors on the Bendix board— he looked particularly weary and frustrated then. And then he would talk to me as he'd done in the pre-fiasco days. One afternoon after a long stretch of silence, he looked up from a book he was reading. "What do I need this for? If these are the rules of power, maybe I'm just better off taking a walk."

I was surprised by the sudden urge I had to take the other side. Here he was finally saying what two and a half months ago I would have given anything to hear, and here I was convincing him otherwise. "You've got to stay, Bill. What about everything you told me at Wolterbeek's office? You were right, you know. If you had left, it would have only confirmed those rumors as true. And what about the strategy? You can't just drop it because of a few petty men. It may have taken one kind of courage for me to leave Bendix—but it has also taken a special kind of courage for you to stay." The irony was that, despite my words, part of me wanted him to leave. What did he need it for? Such sniping and petty rivalry from a board that hadn't had the strength to back its own boss. Not to mention what they'd done to me. But I resisted the temptation. I believed it would be wisest for him to stay, in the long run. I wasn't sure he could handle what I'd learned about unemployment since October 8th. And besides, I knew there were other things bothering him. It wasn't just business that was eating away at him.

One wound led to another and he opened up about them all. He dredged up the whole matter of his divorce. Despite the years of unhappiness, I could see he still felt some guilt. "It stopped working a long time ago," he said, talking of his marriage. "We hadn't been happy together for years. Even at the beginning, we had practically nothing in common. But every time I tried to leave, I couldn't. I didn't want to leave the children while they were small. So I waited and immersed myself in business instead. But once the girls were grown up, it dawned on me that I wasn't helping any of us by prolonging the agony. There was no love there. Only indifference. How could that be helping anyone? Once Bob was old enough, Diane agreed it was long overdue. But then the newspapers started blowing the rumors about you and me out of proportion and before I knew it, everything had changed."

It was this, on top of the board's wavering, that hurt him the most. And yet, as the child of divorced parents, I could reassure him that one parent's leaving wasn't always the worst thing. We talked about this and other matters for hours, in between meals and strolls around the lake. Very little of what we said had to do with business or strategy, and yet our talks were as intense and fulfilling as they'd always been.

We had a quiet Thanksgiving. I cooked a turkey for the two of us. It seemed a little sad and lonely being there by ourselves. I missed Father Bill and the way he always said grace. I missed even the special way my grandmother made turkey dressing. But somehow it felt as though it all would have been different now if I were back at home. I had to do a lot more healing before anything would feel like it used to.

We took a walk after dinner and felt revived in the

fresh clean air. The wind felt good blowing on my face, but I could see it was too much for Bill. He was too weak to withstand more than a few minutes of cold air. That evening his mother called. I picked up the phone. "This is Mrs. Agee," she said curtly. "May I speak with Bill?" I watched as he spoke. The gist of their conversation, as it was later reported to me, was, "Son, how could you disgrace us like this?" I saw his face crumple. I felt the sudden urge to hug him, yet I was unprepared for the consequences.

The world had caved in around Agee, and in some way that altered my point of view. How could I too add one more burden to his load? After all, we were both survivors of the same bloody ordeal. And neither of us had come out unscathed.

We passed most of our days walking, talking and nursing each other back to health. Every morning we got on the scale—our daily "weigh-in." We made a little competition of it to see who could gain more weight the fastest. Bill had dropped from 175 to 150 but was starting back up to 155. My weight at its lowest had dipped to 98, but I was well on my way to 110. Slowly I was starting to regain my health. I took long walks around the lake and through the woods, and I felt the strength come back to my limbs. But Bill wasn't always strong enough to join me. Most days he just sat in the living room reading, an afghan wrapped around his knees.

We would talk for hours. We acted as each other's trusted companion. When one of us was down, the other pulled that one up, and vice versa. Helping Bill was therapy enough for me, but for him I played many roles—not the least of which was counselor. I listened while he talked about the torment he felt. His talking about his difficult childhood, his troubled marriage and his attempt to find satisfaction through work made me feel closer to him. How different our past experiences had been, and yet how similar were our views. If I were his psychiatrist, I was also his absolution. My being there and forgiving him released him from the guilt he had over the part of my experience he blamed himself for. And when I saw how guilty he did feel about it, it caused my own anger to subside. I was also his sounding board. Our long talks about the future gave him a chance to figure things out. He still had the strategy on his mind, and who better understood his concerns than I? Then, too, I was his nurse—but not a very satisfactory cook. We both joked about the meals I cooked—it was a miracle that either of us gained weight. And, finally, we were friends—friends who'd been through a terrible ordeal together, and now, either by force or fate, were the only ones available who could really help each other.

A few of Agee's other friends did call, and a few were in synch with the real Bill Agee. Bendix board member Jonathan Scott, former chairman of A&P and Albertson's, came by and cheered up both of us. And Bob and Mert Hendren, old friends of Agee's from his Idaho days, became like surrogate parents to us. "We weren't at all prepared to like you from the press reports out here, Mary," Mert Hendren confided to me one day. "But I'm so glad to know you as you really are and care for you so much." She gave my arm a squeeze. The Hendrens had a cottage near Agee's, and in the first week I'd arrived, offered me the keys. Mert Hendren, a beautiful little woman with sparkling blue eyes, was especially sensitive to my needs. "Don't forget, you still need some healing yourself," she said, encouraging me to use her cottage whenever I felt the need. "You may want to spend some time alone," she said.

I'd been there ten days when I felt the first naggings of conscience calling me back to New York. "I really should go back," I said to Agee one day. "I guess you should," he said without much conviction. I missed my mother and thought I'd like to go back to Hanover for at least a day. But it was Mert who reminded me I couldn't. "My brother is an attorney out here and they're pretty sticky on that six-week divorce rule, Mary," she said. "If you spend even one day outside of the state, they're likely to give you trouble." I pushed thoughts of Hanover out of my mind and decided to stay until the first of the year, when my divorce would be final.

One morning, without saying a word, Agee got up, dressed and quietly drove into town. When I came up-stairs, I saw all kinds of little presents sitting on the table. He'd gone into town to do some Christmas shopping. There weren't any shops to speak of in McCall other than the general store, so the presents he bought me were on a modest scale—a cake of soap, a ribbon for my hair. "We don't exactly have a Tiffany's in McCall," he said. We laughed. A few days later we went out to cut a Christmas tree. For fifty cents we cut one, but the effort wore Agee out. I suggested we go decorate it right away, but Agee declined. He rested while I did my best with what few ornaments I could make.

But the best Christmas arrived a few days later. It was my mother. Since I'd arrived, we'd spoken on the phone almost every day—our "fireside chats," we called them—but it was no substitute for the real thing. My mother knew I never liked to spend Christmas away from Hanover, so a few days later she did the next best thing—she flew out to Boise. It was wonderful to see her. She was relieved to see how much better I looked, although she was somewhat taken aback at the change in Bill. "What happened to him?" she asked when we were alone. I told her about his struggles at Bendix and how his family had virtually abandoned him. She was witness to some of the more vituperative phone calls he received from his grown-up daughters as well as his own parents and, as the available "mother" on the premises, tried to offer him some soothing advice. Naturally she was still wary about his effect on me; she did not want to see me hurt anymore and wasn't prepared to fully trust him yet. But in the course of their talks some of those doubts were allayed. Her only advice, which she gave me just before she left, was, "Don't lose sight of your own dreams, dear."

She needn't have worried. On January sixth, the day after my divorce was official, I flew back to New York. Even before I unpacked my suitcase, I started setting up job interviews for the next day. In the weeks that followed it seemed I did nothing else. Sometimes I had job interviews at breakfast, lunch and dinner. During one of these I was introduced by Gerry Roche to Phil Beekman, president of Seagram's. Beekman and I hit it off at once. I started to talk about my experience at Bendix but he cut me off. "Don't bother explaining," he said. "As far as I'm concerned, you handled yourself with dignity. You were loyal to the company and loyal to your boss. What I want to know is, what can you do for Seagram's?" That launched us into a discussion on strategy, where I was on terra firma.

That night I called an old family friend. "Phil impressed me. He seems like an exceptionally talented manager. And a caring man as well. Do you think I should accept his offer?" I asked my advisor over the phone. "Funny you should ask," he said. "I just received a call from Phil, who gave me rave reviews about you. I think he's a wonderful guy and Seagram's is a top-notch place to work. I think you two would work well together."

The next day, Beekman wanted me to sit in on meetings at Seagram's to see if I could function as part of the team. About midway through the day, Chairman Edgar Bronfman strode in. "So you're Mary Cunningham?" he said. "Did you see Ronald Reagan on TV last night?" "Yes, sir," I responded. "What did you think of his plan on cutting government spending and taxes?" I told him what I thought and Bronfman said, "Yes, I agree with that. Good comment. Phil?" he said, smiling at me, "do you think she's too smart?"

At the end of the day, Beekman said, "Do you want the job, Cunningham?" "I think I do," I said. "I'm pleased," he said. "Let me have a few words with the boss." The next day he offered me the job. "How does the title of Corporate Vice President of Strategic Planning and Project Development sound to you?" he said. It was the same title I'd had at Bendix. "Just fine," I said. "You'll have to report to both me and the chairman," he said. "Good," I answered. "Past experience has made me a little wary of reporting only to one man," I added with a smile. Beekman gave me twenty-four hours to think about the offer. That night I called Agee. "Do you think I ought to take it?" I asked. "It sounds great," he said. "Do I detect a little doubt in your voice?" I asked. "No. Just a little regret. I wish it were me offering you the job instead." "Those days are behind us," I said. "From here on we look ahead." The next day I told Beekman I'd like the job.

Naturally, nothing in my life was private. Within hours of my accepting the job, the *New York Post* broadcast the news. "Bendix Mary Lands on Her Feet." I appreciated that it was positive news, for once, but didn't quite like the tone. "Bendix Mary"! It sounded like "Hurricane Mary" to me.

Two weeks before I started at Seagram's, I made my official public debut. I gave a speech at San Francisco's prestigious Commonwealth Club. I had received the invitation to speak way back in November, and had been very hesitant about accepting the offer. I knew how difficult it would be to face the press if by the date of the speech I still hadn't gotten a job. Nevertheless, I took the risk of accepting the invitation in the hope that I'd have a job. Now, with my Seagram's offer firmly in hand, I was ready. I viewed the occasion as my "coming out"— the end of my period of hiding.

My brother John escorted me into the room behind the auditorium. It was customary at the Commonwealth Club to hold a press conference before giving a speech. I had never held a press conference before. From behind a small table covered with microphones, I looked out on a sea of reporters. I'd dealt with *them* before, however. "What's the nature of your relationship with Mr. Agee?" one of them harped. "I'm sorry. I'm not here to discuss my personal relationship with Mr. Agee. Next?" My voice sounded incredibly calm. "It's reported that you still see Bill Agee. Is that true?" "I'm sorry. I said I'm not going to talk about anything personal. I'll be happy to entertain questions of a general nature about the issue of women in business, but nothing personal. Let's turn our attention to the text of my speech, which concerns business and productivity." The more they baited me, the stronger I became. I felt incredibly at ease. At last I was taking control of my own life.

The auditorium was packed. Standing room only. Near record attendance. Well over a thousand people were there. TV cameras followed me to the auditorium door. As soon as I entered, a gentleman near the center of the room stood up and started to clap. In seconds, the whole room was on its feet. The room was electric with emotion. My speech was interrupted twelve times with applause, and at the end I received a five-minute standing ovation. In the crowd I saw my brothers, Frank and John. Both of them were crying. I felt a little like crying myself. Except there was nothing to cry about, I told myself. It was all in the past. It was time now for my life to begin. Time to close the door on those who wanted to pry into my personal life. As I told my audience at the end of my speech, "The business of Mary Cunningham is business."

# CHAPTER TEN

*Back in New York, I* returned to my new home in Brooklyn Heights. It was a small duplex in a brownstone on Garden Place. It had a winding staircase and hardwood floors, but despite the amenities, it never felt like home. I wanted something bright and cheery, not something dark and grim, no matter how charming it was. People told me that Norman Mailer lived around the corner, but that didn't do much to dispel the gloom.

Again I delayed unpacking. Cartons seemed to be the leitmotif of my life. Fortunately, I hadn't had to return to Southfield to get them. A kind-hearted mover named Jablonski took pity on me and packed up my things and shipped them East. The first night I moved into my new urban *pied-à-terre*, I found a big bouquet of flowers on the mantelplace. I thought they might be from Agee. How nice of him to think of this, I said to myself. But I was wrong. "Best of luck in your new home." Signed, "Mr. Jablonski."

Apartment life in Brooklyn wasn't quite my style. I bought a telephone-answering machine, but its only value seemed to be immortalizing on tape the words of obscene callers. I also had the pleasure of meeting my first would-be mugger. He followed me late one night from my car— Bendix had allowed me to use my company car through the spring—and chased me home. I ran up to my apartment and bolted the door, but the experience unnerved me. In my present state I couldn't handle any more traumas.

I knew as soon as I'd returned from Idaho that I was starting to miss Bill. I wanted to call him, to talk to him, and it wasn't just to talk business. We spoke on the phone a few times in those first months when I was back in New York, and I could tell a similar feeling was starting to develop in him too. He told me about his social life, his attempts to go out to dinner with people, and I felt myself cringe. And when I told him about my social life—however meager it was—I could detect a similar disappointment in his voice.

Not that it was much of a social life. I knew when I resettled myself in New York that I ought to try to have a more normal life, so I forced myself to go on a certain number of dates. But it was hard. "Come on, Mary. We're going disco dancing at Regine's," a friend would say. Sure, I'd think to myself. Dance at Regine's and read about it the next day in the newspaper. I fared little better at parties. No sooner had I added my coat to the pile of coats on the bed than I felt a strong desire to go home. Groups of people my age would be bubbling about their new jobs or their aspirations to become comptroller of some company, and I'd silently groan. Somehow I felt I had been through all this. I was their peer in every respect, and yet I felt so removed from them all. I was laden with history and they all treated me differently from the way they treated each other.

Bill and I continued to talk by phone, but the person he had the most conversations with that winter was my mother. He was concerned about me but wary of interfering in my life too much, so he often called her instead. At first I think he called her simply to find out how I was, but eventually he called to talk about himself. Since his own parents had turned against him, there were few people with whom he could share his problems. Besides, he liked talking to my mother. She was compassionate and yet levelheaded, and she gave him sound advice. For her part, whatever doubts she may have had concerning the final days at Bendix, she nonetheless felt a bond with him. All three of us had been through a tremendous ordeal together, and its intensity had inevitably made us much closer.

In March, I once again decided to move. How I dreaded rummaging through those cartons again. Each time I moved I was newly reminded of, and depressed by, the transience of my life. Would I ever have a home? Would my letters ever come without two or three forwarding addresses scribbled on the envelopes? I spent the first weekend in March packing (now that I wasn't working at Bendix I learned that there were such things as weekends). It was dusk and I was trudging still another box-load out into the street when I saw the figure of a man watching me from across the way. At first I thought it might be one of my brothers. I felt relieved. My mother knew how much I dreaded another move alone, and I thought maybe she had called Frank or John to suggest they keep me company. Thank goodness I don't have to go through with this by myself, I thought as I started to walk across the street. But no, it was Agee. He had come to my apartment to lend me a hand. "I was talking to your mother and she mentioned you might need a little help," he said. I felt a mixture of both embarrassment and relief. I was so glad to see him, and yet I was a little embarrassed at having been caught so unprepared. "I've been watching you for quite some time," he said, which only made me feel more self-conscious. I looked down at my dirty jeans and sweaty shirt. I'd always been mindful of my appearance around Bill, but I noticed now that I seemed to care in a different way. "Maybe I could help you finish and then we could go out and get some dinner," he said.

Of course we spent more time talking than we did packing. There was so much the two of us had to discuss. We hadn't really spoken in depth since our convalescence in Idaho, and both of us had things on our minds. Bill had been through more battles at Bendix, which he recounted to me in detail. It started to sink in then that perhaps I'd gotten the better end of the deal by having been forced to resign. I would be starting in a brand-new job—I was scheduled to begin my job at Seagram's next week—while Agee was stuck with his crisis-ridden board.

After a few hours of packing, we decided to take a break. He waited in the living room while I showered and changed. "That's better," I said, relieved to be out of my work clothes. "Where would you like to go?" he asked. I was chary about being seen in public with him. But then, why should we let the press dictate our lives? I thought. I knew they'd be looking to justify their "affair" nonsense with an "I-told-you-so" approach—but neither of us were going to cater to that element. We decided to hold our heads high and, like any other couple in New York, go out for a pleasant dinner. We went to a little Italian restaurant in the Heights, had a lovely meal and drank a bottle of red wine. For the first time, it started to feel as if we were a couple. I didn't mind at all. After dinner, Bill walked me back to my apartment. Both of us were a little uncertain as to what we should do. We had known each other for so long, and yet for us, as for any new couple, the moment felt awkward. I went into the cramped kitchen to make a pot of tea. When I came out, Bill came up to me and said, "I want to give you something I've been waiting to share for such a long time." And then we kissed. How natural and good it felt.

He stayed over that night; he slept in the den and I slept up in my second-floor bedroom. The next morning I couldn't wait to see him. I walked into the den and sat on the side of the convertible sofa. I took his hand. It was wonderful to watch him wake up. "You look beautiful," he said. And in his eyes, I felt perhaps I was.

We were old friends, but now, as lovers, we were new.

The first time we felt we were hiding something was that morning when we walked out the door. It was funny, feeling for real what people presumed we must have felt all along. And yet, wasn't it silly? Here we were, two divorced adults. What did we have to hide? In the cool March breeze, we set out for the Promenade. I could smell the arrival of spring in the air although there was still snow on the ground. Everything seemed possible on that radiant March day. A sudden impulse for playfulness possessed me and I gathered up a snowball and threw it at Bill. It was really more of a slushball. He bent down and threw a bigger one at me and we started chasing each other down a side street. By the time we stopped, we were soggy and red-faced. We walked the length of the street arm in arm. I felt happy and I could tell Bill did too. It was as if we were whole again—almost.

We must have looked as happy as we felt, for the maître d' of the Montague Café gave us ringside seats—right by the front window. We ordered salads and mimosas, telling stories and even joking with each other about some of the more dour things that had gone on. No sooner had I started to relax than I saw something disturbing out the corner of my eye. "Bill, don't turn toward the window," I said as vehemently as I could in a whisper, but instinctively he did. Flash. A bearded photographer snapped our picture. I turned and saw him smile as he prepared to take another. The snapshot had an instantly sobering effect. "We can't just sit here," I said. Bill looked stunned and angry. "Let's get out of here," he said.

We left the restaurant and walked briskly down the street trying not to look back, but the photographer continued to stalk us. Click. Click. Flash. He must have taken two dozen shots. "Just leave us alone," Bill said, choking on his rage. The man paid no heed. I started to run. "Don't run," Bill said. But I continued. Bill ran after me. We flew down the street and up my front steps. Once inside the apartment, I started to cry. "They're never going to leave us alone," I said. "Never."

My move from Brooklyn Heights was completed soon after that. I'd had enough of the Heights and the bohemian way of life. I wanted comfort and security now. The following week I was settled in a comfortable two-bedroom apartment in midtown Manhattan. I felt much more at home there. There was a doorman, and he treated me with respect. "Miss Cunningham?" he would say. "Mr. Agee is here. Shall I show him up?" "Yes, please do," I'd say and then he or one of his colleagues would escort Bill to my door.

I rented a two-bedroom apartment with thick tan carpeting and muted beige walls. It was a little more expensive than I could afford but I felt I owed it to myself. Why not live it up? Given my recent track record, who knew how long this present peaceful phase would last? I allowed myself the pleasure of a bubble bath after work and de-

veloped a taste for fine wines. I made a serious effort to
start to enjoy life. I invited a few friends from Business
School to visit after work. Several of them had been calling me when they found out I'd moved back to New York.
Phil Beekman, an avid sportsman, enrolled me as a member of both the Vertical Club and the Cardiovascular Club,
two no-nonsense health clubs. Bill was in New York frequently, and we went out to dinner or a play as often as
our schedules allowed. We had the pleasure of reading
about our dates in next morning's papers along with the
dates of rock stars and basketball players. Suzy Says...
"Bill and Mary were seen together walking in the park."
Or, "Bill and Mary stopped in at Haagen-Dazs for ice-
cream cones." We were learning what public figures must
have learned a long time ago. There's only one way to
handle the press. Ignore them.

Legally I was a divorced woman dating a divorced man,
but I could not forget that in the eyes of the Church I was
still married. Back in January, I had filed my annulment papers with the Tribunal of the Brooklyn Archdiocese, but I
still hadn't heard the results. The prospects for an annulment didn't look good. "Frankly, the odds are not in your
favor because of your renown," one of the priests confided
to me. "The Church doesn't want to invite any scandals."
And I knew, as a person of conscience, how seriously I'd
take its decision. If the Church ruled my marriage to Bo
Gray valid, then I would have to go back and at least try to
make that marriage work. As it turned out, that wasn't necessary. My annulment was granted in almost record time.
Given my strong religious background and my orientation
toward helping people, the Archdiocese judged that at an
impressionable young age I had mistakenly used the institution of marriage to try to help someone. I was granted my

annulment in April. Bo and I continued to be friends. After all, it was our marriage that had ended, not our friendship. And it was really a friendship more than a marriage that we'd had all along.

With the annulment, I felt a final burden on my conscience lift. Up until this point I had felt free to kiss Agee, even free to love him, but I still could not accept the idea of any great intimacy. Now I could. Despite the misery, I had always seen a strange humor in our situation. If all those people who assumed I'd been sleeping with Agee knew what I had to go through to finally get to that point, they would have been amazed.

That spring would have been a perfect time to be in love, but reverberations of the past kept coming up. At the Bendix shareholders' annual meeting, a well-known corporate gadfly named Evelyn Davis took to the floor. Three months after I had resigned, she still wanted to know about this "Cunningham affair." "I was having lunch with Nancy Reynolds the other day," Davis said at one point in her rambling tirade. "And I want to know exactly what did go on between you and this girl." It was clear who was still keeping that issue alive.

And of course Blumenthal was still up to his old tricks. "It's embarrassing," an insider on the New York social scene confided to me one afternoon, describing how, at a recent dinner party, Blumenthal had spent the better part of the evening droning on and on against Agee. "He just isn't willing to leave it alone," she said. "He seems almost obsessed with putting Agee down."

But it was more than just talk that was bothering Agee. If my resignation was supposed to have quieted things down at Bendix, it didn't. If anything, it was just the beginning of what had to be for Agee the worst spring of his life. The origins of the problem dated back to the fall of the previous year. About three days after my resignation, in an attempt to try to figure out what was really motivating Blumenthal, Agee met him for lunch. He didn't succeed in extracting any great confession from Blumenthal but he did leave with the impression that their luncheon had resulted in a temporary declaration of peace.

Within a week, the armistice blew up in Agee's face. The incident involved a last-minute attempt by Blumenthal to torpedo the Bendix Forest Products deal. For months now, Agee had been putting the finishing touches on the deal whereby Kolberg, Kravis and Roberts would buy out BFPC. Agee had been assured that the Equitable, of which he was a director, would lend $40 million in promissory notes to help K.K. & R. close the deal. It was good business for both Bendix and the Equitable. But just as the deal was about to close, who should arrive with last-minute fervent objections to the deal? Mike Blumenthal. In an impassioned eleventh-hour speech, Blumenthal, also now a member of the Equitable board, persuaded the directors that it would be a conflict of interest to go ahead on the loan. Up until this point, Agee had dismissed Blumenthal's rantings as petty child's play—dangerous but essentially limited in scope. Now it was affecting business, and that was serious. Only now did Agee understand the depths of Blumenthal's rage.

All throughout the months when Agee was recuperating from his illness in Idaho, a small group of directors, chiefly those with connections to Blumenthal's board of directors, continued their attempt to subvert Agee's authority. Under the aegis of Harry Cunningham, a close personal friend of Blumenthal's and up until that April a member of the Burroughs board, they committed the cardinal sin of management: they went behind the chairman's back and started interrogating his subordinates about him. "How do you think Agee's doing? Do you still have confidence in him?" Cunningham and some of his henchmen would ask people on Agee's executive staff. Questions like that have a funny way of undermining the very confidence they seek to gauge. People like Mace Reynolds and Lee Henry now started to wonder; "Gee, why is the board checking up on Agee? Is something wrong?" But although Agee's staff people were for the most part loyal, a small group of directors were not.

One in particular emerged at this point as Blumenthal's newly baptized aide-de-camp. His name was Robert Purcell and he'd been a member of the Bendix board throughout the Blumenthal reign. When it came to business, he and Agee had never seen eye to eye, although up until recently they'd gotten along reasonably well. Purcell tended to be tightfisted and conservative, whereas Agee had a more free-spirited style. Purcell was cautious, whereas Agee took risks. One of the "risks" Agee took, against Purcell's advice, was to buy and then sell Asarco, a transaction that eventually netted Bendix more than $200 million in profits. But it wasn't simply matters of business that fanned the flames. The source of Purcell's hostility toward Agee was somewhat more complex.

In April or May of 1979, when I was still at the Business School, Purcell had come to Agee with a strange request. He and Agee were scheduled to fly to France that spring on business, and Purcell, whose wife had died recently, wanted to know if the company would pay for him to bring along a woman friend. Agee said no. Company policy was to pay for spouses only. Purcell was piqued. After one of the meetings in Paris, Agee bumped into Purcell emerging from Maxim's with a woman on either arm. The incident must have humiliated Purcell, for it seemed that he helped feed the rumors linking Agee and me with a special fervor.

Once I'd resigned, Purcell escalated his attacks. Seeing that Agee was wounded and vulnerable, Purcell rallied the few dissident directors in an all-out attempt to get rid of Agee. As I was no longer available as a means for attack, he tried a different tack. It was Purcell's contention that Agee was merely "talking" strategy: he implied that there really was no strategy. Naturally Agee was wary of disclosing all his plans to certain members of the board because of a much more serious problem that was bothering him now—and that concerned the incestuous relations between the Bendix and Burroughs' boards.

A genealogy of the corporate ties of some of the directors made the cast of characters in *War and Peace* look simple. Alan Schwartz, Paul Mirabito and Coy Eklund were all members of both the Bendix and Burroughs' boards. Harry Cunningham had also been a longstanding member of both boards but he'd recently resigned as a Burroughs director due to an age restriction. However, he still lived within two blocks of Mirabito in the posh Florida resort of Lost Tree Village and had remained a close friend of Blumenthal's. A former chairman of K-Mart, he was also friendly with Purcell, who also was on the K-Mart board.

Interlocking directorates are common on many corporate boards, but the situation between Bendix and Burroughs made things in Southfield a bit tense. Conflicts or potential conflicts kept surfacing, not the least of which was

Bendix's interest in a possible merger with Burroughs. Agee first suggested doing something about the overlap in the fall of 1980. What prompted his concern was a conversation he'd had with Harry Cunningham in which he had mentioned that he was interested in asking Harold Schapiro, then president of the University of Michigan, to take a seat on the Bendix board. "Oh, is he available?" Harry Cunningham had asked. Not long after, Burroughs announced that Schapiro soon would be joining their board. Cunningham agreed the overlap was dangerous, but Purcell disagreed. He saw no reason to change things now. Had Agee not been sick at the time, he might have pursued the matter more vigorously then, but it was the fall of 1980 and he was walking around with a raging but as yet undiagnosed case of mononucleosis. He was not in a fighting mood, although by the following February he was.

What spurred the change was the strategy. Bendix now had a war chest of almost $700 million from the sale of Asarco and BFPC. With interest rates going up, it was a good time to be liquid, but in the back of Agee's mind was the ongoing issue of what companies should Bendix eventually merge with or acquire? On the detailed list of potential acquisitions candidates were Burroughs, Lockheed, RCA and Martin Marietta, among several others. The presence of Burroughs on the list made it impossible to discuss the full strategy with the Burroughs-affiliated members of the board.

Besides, Agee had reason to believe their loyalties weren't necessarily with Bendix. Every time he mentioned a potential acquisition candidate, he feared it would somehow find its way onto a Burroughs list. His fears proved well founded. The prior February, before Jerry Jacobson had gone across the street, Agee had had several serious meetings with him concerning Bendix's interest in Memorex. Guess what company Burroughs acquired not long after Jacobson joined the board? Memorex.

Another example surfaced around Bendix's interest in Wang. Warner and Swasey, a Bendix subsidiary, owned a healthy portion of Wang, which was a competitor of Burroughs. Mirabito and Schwartz suggested Bendix sell off Wang to solve their conflict of interest problem. Agee initially resisted, feeling it would be foolhardy to give up Wang so cheaply. The idea of making a business decision to alleviate a personnel one seemed highly inappropriate, to say the least. Enough pressure was applied and the vote was to sell Wang.

In addition to the obvious business problems involved, the Burroughs coterie was making life difficult for Agee at Bendix. Purcell was drumming up antipathy toward Agee. Mirabito, Cunningham and Schwartz were going along. Only Coy Eklund refused to be a part of their cabal. He was above that kind of power politics.

Clearly the directors could not serve two masters. Something had to be done. In late February Agee formally raised the conflict-of-interest issue to the members of the Organization and Compensation Committee of the Bendix board. The Committee agreed that it was high time for the issue to be resolved once and for all. Agee proposed that any directors who were on both boards should make a choice. The Committee voted to enforce the decision immediately.

"If you think it's a conflict, then I'll resign," Cunningham said moments later in the same meeting. He already had passed the mandatory retirement age of seventy, and in past conversations had told Agee he could have his resignation "any time Agee wanted it." Agee then received resignations from Mirabito and Schwartz as well. Eklund chose to remain with Bendix. However, later that night, Purcell met with Harry Cunningham and convinced him to change his mind. Agee was just on his way to the airport—he'd planned to hear my speech at the Commonwealth Club in San Francisco the next morning—when Harry Cunningham called. "I think I may have acted too hastily and would like to change my mind," he said. "Harry," Bill answered, "you gave me and the board your resignation. Your decision was accepted as final." "I'm not sure it is, Bill," Cunningham said. But Agee already had checked with his lawyers. An oral resignation was binding.

Now Purcell started throwing gasoline on the flames. He began openly working to garner the sympathies of the rest of the board. He mailed a letter Harry Cunningham had written lambasting Agee not only to each member of the board, but to key members of Agee's internal management team as well. This was unheard of in the annals of corporate etiquette—to attempt to discredit the chairman in front of his own executives. As soon as he found out, Agee scheduled a meeting of the full board. He distributed copies of the Cunningham letter and then proceeded to refute it. "You be the judges," he said to the board. The board gave Agee its whole-hearted support. Several members chastised Purcell for his behavior and suggested the possibility of his resigning. The issue was delicate because of Purcell's age. He was already approaching his seventieth birthday and several of the directors thought his retirement was long overdue. But Purcell wouldn't budge. He said he wanted to stick around to see if Agee really was serious about this "fictitious strategy."

As late spring approached, things started to calm down. In March of 1981, Agee hired Alonzo McDonald, Jr., a former member of the Carter staff, to fill Panny's old spot as president. And with most of the dissident members of the board gone, he could devote himself to strategy. But if Agee started to relax, I couldn't. Naturally, all through the spring, I'd had to live through this nightmare with Agee. The stronger the external forces against him, the closer we became. It was no longer Agee and the divisive elements of his board against me; the battle lines had shifted. It was now "us" against "them." And it made us closer. But at the same time, I wasn't so sure I wanted to be part of that "us." Here I was, just getting my sea legs at Seagram's, and I found myself back in my old Bendix frame of mind. It was as if I were still Agee's executive assistant. "How are things with Agee over at Bendix?" Phil Beekman would casually ask at work, and I'd say, "Oh, we're trying to get the strategy completed," and then catch myself. "We" were now Seagram's, not Bendix. Beekman laughed. "Don't worry," he said. "It took me two years after I left Colgate-Palmolive to stop talking about it as 'us.'"

But I didn't know if I'd ever get Bendix out of my system. And it wasn't as if my personal relationship with Bill was that smooth. There was a campaign being waged now, by various members of Bill's family, to try and push me out of his life. His parents, his sisters, even his daughters made it known—to both Bill and to me—that I was definitely persona non grata in his life. A part of me, rebelling from altogether too many months of abuse, was defiant. "Show them what I mean to you. Let them and everyone else know I'm more than just a girlfriend," I wanted to say. And yet how could I? Wasn't that just what the press wanted to see me do? Fortunately, my work at Seagram's required that I take a tour of some of the wine-growing regions of France and I decided now was a perfect time to go. It would give me some time alone, which I desperately needed. I wrote Bill a note. I told him I didn't want him either to drive me to the airport or to pick me up. I simply needed to get away from it all. While in Paris, I visited a priest at Notre Dame. He reminded me that love was a gift from God. Again I felt so confused. The past year's experience seemed to indicate that loving meant mostly being hurt.

That night I called Hanover. It must have been one of the longest overseas calls in history. "You sound terribly upset," my mother said after I told her how I felt. "Is there anything I can do?" I didn't think so but apparently she did. The next day she called Agee. "You called me once when you felt she needed me," she said to him. "Well, now I'm calling you to tell you the same. Mary loves you, Bill, but is still terribly afraid of being hurt. She needs some reassurance from you. If you want the relationship to survive her state of mind right now, I think you're going to have to start protecting her from some of the pain she's had lately. A good place to start is by being there tomorrow morning when her plane arrives." He was, which made me feel what my mother had anticipated. But it was clear that this was not to be one of the more even-tempoed relationships in history. Our courtship was to be marked by surges, both forward and back. The circumstances of our lives made that inevitable.

In the late spring Agee did something that was especially important to me. He quietly started to take Catholic religious instruction from Father Thurston Davis in New York. With all he'd been going through with the board and the upheavals at Bendix, I was amazed that he had found time for anything else. But probably that was exactly why he felt he wanted to do this now. He was feeling put upon and besieged. His life had taken a sudden turn for the worse, and he wanted to understand it. He wanted to learn more about forgiveness, to find a meaning in suffering, to figure out if it was possible to live a better life. The experience deepened our relationship and caused me to love him even more. Whereas previously Agee had kidded me about my vigilant attendance at Mass, now he asked if he could come along too.

He seemed to savor the healing process. In the midst of the whole fiasco at Bendix, he needed some lessons in both forgiving and being forgiven. The treatment he was receiving at the hands of his own parents and sisters only caused him to view with greater disdain his strict Protestant upbringing. His grandfather had been a Baptist minister and had bequeathed to his progeny a heavy dose of guilt. Now he was learning another way, one that emphasized forgiveness and healing. And he drank of them thirstily. Each time I saw him, I could tell he was gaining strength. I wanted to make sure, though, that he wasn't doing it for me. "It can only have meaning if you really believe in what you're doing, Bill," I said. "If I were gone, suddenly, you'd still have to feel right about what you're doing and strong in your faith. It's really a huge responsibility you're taking on." "I know, and I've never felt better about a decision, Mary," he said. "I feel very good about the whole discovery process." And I believed him. "Do you think Father Bill would be willing to baptize me?" he asked. "I think he would, but you'll have to ask him personally," I said.

We spent as much of that summer as our work would permit in Idaho, at Bill's summer house in McCall. He commuted from Southfield on weekends, and I stayed out there for several days at a time. As a strategic planner at Seagram's, I could afford to not always work at my office desk. My task was to mastermind a worldwide wine strategy for Seagram's and I used the peace and serenity around McCall to analyze the data I'd collected and to figure out a plan.

In late July, Bill was baptized. My mother flew out for the occasion and Bill's son, Bob, came to spend several weeks with us. At dinner that evening, Bill said he'd like to say something. All of us quieted down. "I just want you all to know what this has meant to me," he began. "For a few months I thought I was without family, friends or faith. You, all of you," he said, gesturing around the table, "have given all those things back to me. A family," he said, looking at my mother and Father Bill, "a true friend," he said, looking toward me, "and a faith," he said, and touched the scapular medal he'd been given during the baptism. Father Bill and my mother were radiant. "I don't think I've ever seen Mary Elizabeth so happy," my mother said. And Father Bill added, "And I don't think I've ever seen Bill Agee so happy either." Bill and I looked at each other. "I think it might be nice to take a little walk down by the lake," Bill said, smiling. "What do you say, Mary? Will you all excuse us?"

Bill and I strolled down to the water. We sat on the dock and dipped our feet into the cool, dark lake. "I really don't know if I can ask what I want to ask you," he said, sounding terribly apologetic. "So I'll understand if you say no." He took my hand in his. "The last thing I want to do is bring any more hurt into your life. I've already done enough of that," he said, staring at the ripples of water circling his feet. "And yet, sometimes I think I make you really happy. I know I do. I see it in your face." I looked at him. He seemed to be struggling so. "Other times, I know I'm just a bad reminder." "What are you trying to say to me?" I asked. So many times in the past I'd mistaken his intention. "I want you to be my wife. I want to spend the rest of my life with you. I can't imagine living my life anymore without you," he said.

I should have felt ecstatic. After all, this was the man I loved. But he seemed so unhappy now, even as he was proposing to me, that I could not just come out and say yes. "Why the sadness? Why do you seem so distressed?" I asked him. "Can you envision what the press is going to make of all this?" he said. "Just think of what they'll say. It'll be one more time where Mary Cunningham gets promoted and demoted in the same day." "Isn't it amazing?" I said. "This event just won't let go of our lives. And the event isn't really an event, it's a total fiction, and yet it continues to shape our lives." I started to dwell on it but I had to stop myself. This was a special moment for us and no fears should be allowed to lessen its beauty. I turned to Bill and we hugged and kissed. "It means a lot to me that you asked," I said. "You know what I want to answer, what I'd love more than anything to answer, but I can't yet. Not just now."

Our love blossomed and bloomed over the summer. Almost a year had passed since the media event and the wounds were healing. Whatever time we needed for recovery we had. I didn't tell Bill in so many words that I was willing to marry him, but he could tell from my actions I was. Quietly he began to investigate the possibility of his getting an annulment. Just as I'd dredged up all the past history of my marriage during that terrible period when I was locked in my room at the Waldorf, now Bill had to dredge up his.

The memories were not pleasant. Bill and Diane had known each other in high school but they hadn't exactly been sweethearts. He was a straight-A student, president of the student body, captain of the basketball team and well liked by everyone in school. Diane was much quieter. She was shy and hung around with a less academic crowd. It was during the summer break between Bill's freshman and sophomore years at Stanford when they decided to marry. He'd come home after his first year at Stanford and didn't want to have to return to Stanford in the fall. He equally dreaded the thought of returning to live with his parents. Both he and Diane came from families in which there was alcoholism. Bill tried unsuccessfully to live for a brief period that summer at home. It was at this point that they decided to get married. Bill's parents heartily disapproved. They saw him as marrying someone beneath their standards and to a person with whom he had little in common. His sisters complained she was stealing "their Billy." It was not a happy affair. The fact that they were unsuited to one another soon became clear. Diane became more reclusive at home and Bill dived into work. They grew farther and farther apart as the years went on. After ten unhappy years, Diane thought they might patch things up with another child but such was not the case. Even after Bob was born, the marriage continued to be one of pain and misery for both.

When the priest at the Boise Tribunal heard the story, he agreed that the circumstances in which they'd been married were far from conducive to making a true marriage commitment and bond. But it was Diane's politicking that backfired and may have given the annulment an extra push.

She had encouraged Carolyn, Bill's older sister, suddenly no longer on speaking terms with Bill, to talk to a priest in the diocese in which the annulment was being reviewed. Carolyn visited at least one priest to explain her unsolicited theory that Bill was having a "midlife crisis." The Church frowned upon this meddling. Bill was notified of this unusual effort to interfere in what was considered a sacred and private process. Bill contacted Diane to put a stop to it but she was in no mood for reasoning. "It's not that I want you back," she told him. "But I don't want you to be happy either." If Agee was ever going to feel sorry for what he was doing or sorry about the divorce, this experience prevented those feelings from surfacing. The Tribunal wasn't about to be rushed into a precipitous decision about Bill's annulment so we simply had to wait. In the meantime, we grew closer and more in love.

I was also getting closer to Bob. He spent a lot of time with us and continued his old habit of confiding in me. Bill liked the fact that I was bringing spirituality into the boy's life. I taught him to say grace, and he preferred my version to the one they'd taught him in school. "You don't have to say anything you memorize," I said. "You can just say what you feel. Say it from the heart. It feels more natural that way. Why don't you try? Just say one thing you're grateful for." He thought for a while and then looked up. "I'm grateful for you," he said. I was touched. I really did feel close to him and was glad he was feeling that way toward me. One day after lunch, Bill looked at Bob and said, "How'd you feel about having a second mom?" Bob smiled. "I would like it if it would be Mary." "You wouldn't have to call me Mom," I said. "That would probably feel funny, wouldn't it?" We smiled.

September 1 was my thirtieth birthday and I awoke

just as the sun was coming up to find Bill watching over me. "You're not very appreciative," he said. "What do you mean?" I asked. "For someone who graduated from Harvard and Wellesley you're pretty dense." "What do you mean?" I said. "What are you talking about?" "Just reach under your pillow," he said. I reached and felt something cold and jagged. I pulled it out from under the pillow. It was a gold ring with a spray of diamonds flowing over the band. It sparkled in the early morning sun. "It's beautiful—but I could never wear anything like this," I said. "Can you imagine me scribbling notes or writing a memo in something like this?" I held out my plain hands with their clipped and unpolished nails. "I certainly can," he said, slipping it on my finger. "Will you wear it?" he asked. "Yes," I said. "And I'm never going to take it off."

We kept our engagement quiet. Public-relations advisers were telling us this was the best thing to do, but I wasn't so sure. I didn't want to see us mocked in the press, but I didn't want to feel as if we were in hiding, either. And there was another problem that gnawed at me. Bill's annulment. "I have to ask you something, Mary," Bill said one day. "What if I don't get my annulment? Would you still marry me?" "No," I said. "I don't think I could." "Then we're not really engaged, are we?" he said. "Well, in a sense, we are," I said, "because I'd never marry anyone else. We just wouldn't be able to get married." He looked disturbed. "In the eyes of the Church you'd still be married to Diane," I said. "And if the Church felt you could still make that marriage work, then you'd have to try to make it work. And as your friend, I'd do everything I could to help you do that." I was serious about this, and Agee knew I meant what I said. Every week he checked the mail to see if the decision had come through. But the Tribunal was taking its time.

In the fall of 1981 I shifted my base of operations back to New York. I spent most of my time at the office or in my apartment, where I saw Bill. Things between us were never completely smooth. The press was always there, and trouble at Bendix kept both of us on edge. Every now and then we needed some time alone. During those periods I'd send Bill back to the Waldorf and cloister myself in my high-rise apartment.

In October I had to make another trip abroad for Seagram's, in preparation for completing the wine strategy by Christmas. I visited wineries in Germany, Italy and France. It was a rejuvenating tour, and when I returned I felt fortified to hear more about Bendix.

And, as usual, there was more. In November Bill received an interesting call from Nancy Reynolds, my old pal from Public Relations days. She had been in the news recently in connection with a nasty political scandal that had already made the pages of both the *Washington Post* and *The New York Times*. It had the potential to become a much bigger story unless someone with "pull" could quiet the press. It began in the *Washington Post*'s infamous "Ear" column, in which it was alleged that the Carters had made tape recordings of conversations in (or "bugged") Blair House during the final months of President Carter's Administration. Allegedly a conversation between Rosalynn Carter and Nancy Reagan had been taped. The story was a great source of embarrassment to the Carters, who threatened to sue the *Washington Post* for libel. The *Post* eventually had to print a retraction, as it turned out that the rumors of the Blair House bugging were untrue. In a follow-up article in *The New York Times*, Nancy Reynolds was exposed as "the mole," the person who fed the false information to Diane McLellan, author of the "Ear" column. Publicly Reynolds would "neither deny nor confirm" having played any role. And, miraculously, further mention of her name simply disappeared in future articles.

Nonetheless she felt it might be wise to call up Agee and set things straight. "I'm sorry if this whole episode has caused you or Bendix any embarrassment," she said. "The Reagans are furious with me and I can't have you down on me too." Bill accepted the apology, but once in a confessional mood, Reynolds went on to seek absolution for other, more personal crimes. "And I'd like to apologize for everything else too, Bill," she said, carefully choosing her words. "I hope if by any of my actions I've caused you any pain, you'll forgive me." She paused, hoping Bill would let on just how much he knew. Actually he had a pretty good idea of the supporting role she had played during the whole Bendix event.

From the start, Agee knew she hadn't been supportive of me. And during the convention he could see how she had tried to undermine my role. But it was after his divorce that she had really swung into high gear. Suddenly she became close friends with Diane Agee, whom in previous years she'd ignored. In a move that was obviously designed to annoy Agee, she had decided to send prime tickets to the Reagan Inauguration to Diane and a companion instead of to Bill. "What was that for?" Agee had asked her at the time. "Oh, I didn't think you'd really want the tickets anyway." Agee reminded her that her first responsibility was as an officer of Bendix, and that in sending his ex-wife the tickets instead of him she was deliberately creating an embarrassing situation. Another new person on Reynolds' social agenda was Blumenthal. The two of them had had lunch together just after I resigned—probably with champagne to celebrate.

"Only you know what you've done, Nancy," he now told her on the phone. "Well, I hope you'll forgive me. Please accept my apology," she said. And that was the formal end of the Agee-Reynolds friendship. It was apparent to both of us now how the *Washington Post* and other Washington-based publications had uncovered so many details of Agee's personal and professional situation in the weeks before I was forced to resign.

What a pleasure it was, in contrast to all of this, to immerse myself in the relatively apolitical atmosphere of Seagram's. On December 18, 1981, I had completed my worldwide strategy and was ready to present my report. Thank God there were no Jerry Jacobsons, no Bill Pannys here. Instead, I presented my proposed strategy for Seagram's wines to Edgar Bronfman, Phil Beekman and a handful of other top executives. "That makes a heck of a lot of sense," Bronfman said in his informal way when I'd finished. "But do you really think Seagram can move into the number two position in the wine industry?" I assured him that I did whether by acquisition or internal growth. I handed out a separate detailed analysis of each of the top five competitors in the wine industry and showed how vulnerable each was. Edgar seemed convinced that we could take over the number two position and finally turn around our wine profitability. "Your expansion strategy is very ambitious but I think it puts us on the right track," Phil Beekman joined in. There were objections, but they didn't seem as if they would set off World War Three, as they had at Bendix. There was rational discourse here, not petty sniping. Having learned the value of consensus, I suggested that everyone spend the next four weeks writing up their objections or questions, and then, in January, we'd reconvene to discuss them. Everyone agreed, and a January 20 date for a second meeting was set. It was almost anticlimactic—walking out of a staff meeting with neither the desire to kick or scream. So this was business. How pleasant it all could be.

Bill and I spent Christmas in McCall. It could have been a lovely time. After all, how different we were from those two skeletal creatures who could barely put up the Christmas tree the previous year. Physically we were both in much better shape, and it was not without some gratitude that we drank a toast in Mumm's, one of Seagram's best champagnes, and wished each other an uneventful New Year. But our mood was tempered by another disturbing event. On our way to the airport, David Taylor from Bendix PR read us in its entirety an article *Fortune* magazine was planning to publish on January 11. The article resurrected ghosts of Christmases past. This time the attacks were aimed at Bill—his management style, whether his troops had confidence in him, employee morale in the wake of the "Cunningham fiasco," etc. But what really shocked me—and Bill too—was that my name figured prominently in almost half the article. And I hadn't been at Bendix now for more than a year. Not a person from *Fortune* had tried to contact me. Nor had anyone asked me for my views. Par for the course. Not surprisingly, the man featured as the prime source for the article was Robert Purcell; what was not mentioned in the article, however, was that the true cause of this biased and defamatory version of the past year's events at Bendix had occurred back in August.

In August, the volcanic Purcell had erupted again. In a last-ditch effort to remove Agee, Purcell called a clandestine meeting of the outside directors. Coy Eklund, Jonathan Scott, Hugo Uyterhoeven, General Stafford, Jack Fontaine and Jewel Lafontant were there. Purcell outlined his complaints against Agee. But his plan backfired. His protest only served as an excuse for the outside directors to reiterate their total support for Bill, and once again to question Purcell's motives. "If you're that unhappy with Bill," one of the directors told Purcell, "then perhaps you ought to consider resigning yourself." That night, Purcell wrote up his resignation and handed it in the following day.

But it wasn't like Purcell to depart with only a whimper. The big bang was what he was after. "There is a question about whether a corporate director should talk about his reasons for resigning from a board," Purcell told *Fortune*. "The tendency is to leave and shut up. But on matters like this, I think it is appropriate for a director to speak out." And speak out he did. First he went to *The Wall Street Journal*. "Robert Purcell resigns from Bendix board citing lack of confidence in management." But of course the real story was that the directors at Bendix had lost confidence in Purcell. Then he went to the magazines. He took his collection of inaccuracies to *Fortune*, and the editors at *Fortune* were eager to swallow it. The editors asked Agee for his version, but gun-shy from his famous "just good friends" speech, Agee was hesitant about speaking to the press. Besides, the reporter already seemed to have his mind made up, as was obvious from the biased questions he asked. The result was a very one-sided version of the circumstances surrounding what *Fortune* immortalized as the "midnight massacre."

"In Detroit's firmament of economic gloom," the article

began, "Bendix Corp. shines like the morning star. . . . Yet when Robert Purcell, 70, quit the Bendix board in August, he cited 'loss of confidence in top management.' For top management, read Agee." The article was downhill from there. Basically a mouthpiece for Purcell, it suggested that these three white knights (the Burroughs affiliated directors) were out to rescue Bendix from the villainous and hardhearted Agee. The inaccuracies were one thing, but what bothered Agee the most was that so little emphasis was given to his incredible track record at Bendix. "I can't understand how they can do this" he said after reading the article himself a second and a third time, hoping Taylor had skipped over some good parts. "We're one of the most prosperous companies in the country. At a time when other companies are going bankrupt, we've got half a billion dollars in the bank not to mention record earnings. Record earnings for 1981. Ditto for 1980. Not to mention '79, '78, and every other year that I've been chairman. Imagine," he said, pacing back and forth. "The country's in a recession. The automobile industry's in its death throes. And Bendix never had it so good. And what do those editors do? They focus on 'problems,' and fictitious, distorted ones at that. And who's their source? A guy who obviously has an ax to grind. Don't those editors know better than that? Aren't they more savvy than to swallow his bait? And why didn't they ever quote all the directors and executives who reported to me the positive comments they had said to the reporter? Instead, they'd rather quote 'unnamed sources' and fired former executives."

Those were Agee's chief complaints. Mine were all too familiar. Naturally, no article on Bendix was complete without titillating references to me. Only this time a full third of the article was about me. I'd never even been contacted for an interview on the story and here was a fullblown warped version of my career at Bendix. Some of the more sordid subheads in the story, as it was reprinted in the *Detroit Free Press*: "It all started with Mary." And once again, the old smoking guns: "They worked long hours together, traveled extensively, shared hotel suites. . . ."

So obvious was the one-sidedness of the *Fortune* piece that even the Bendix board felt compelled to write a letter stating their backing of Agee. Pete Peterson wrote one too. The first version of the letter the board drafted said something to gainsay the unfair insinuations the *Fortune* article made about me, but at the last minute Don Rumsfeld persuaded the board to scrap it. "It'd be better for Bill," he said. "We don't want to create another media event. Leave Cunningham as part of the past." Apparently it was more convenient now to treat me as merely incidental. But what bothered me most was Bill's reaction. So outraged was I by the fact that he was willing to accept the Rumsfeld approach that the whole fiasco nearly split us up.

"How can you just sit back every time my name gets dragged through the mud for your damned company?" I asked. "Why act as if you have your tail between your legs? Why don't you tell them it's not enough to write a letter to the editor correcting only the misstatements about you. Don't you care about my reputation too?"

What bothered me most was the hypocrisy of it all. The board, trying to ease its conscience, wrote "a private and confidential" letter to me at Seagram's, apologizing for any reference in the article that implied they hadn't meant the positive statements they wrote at the time of my resignation. They wanted to take this opportunity to reiterate their support for my valuable contribution to Bendix. Why were these people always so gallant in private and such cowards in public? And why did Agee just accept it? He was fighting to save his reputation as well, but why was it mine that never seemed to matter enough? The old anger was surfacing and I knew I'd better stop before I suffered a relapse of October 8th. But it seemed to me, as long as people kept resurrecting the Bendix "affair," our relationship was destined to fail.

Maybe—but we had come too far together to give up on each other now. It took a few weeks for the *Fortune* wounds to heal, but by then we received some good news. Agee had been granted his annulment. Apparently the Tribunal in Boise had agreed that the circumstances around Agee's decision to marry were as suspect as those surrounding mine, and it granted him an annulment. Both of us were tremendously buoyed by the news. We decided to marry in June. No longer would I have to see myself depicted as Agee's "friend," "alleged lover" or "protégé/mistress." I would now be his wife. And yet the irony was that by marrying Bill, even a year and a half after leaving Bendix, I would probably convince some people that I had been all those other things after all.

Of course we couldn't exactly announce to the world our wedding plans as other couples might. I was determined to keep the press out of this event, so we took some extra precautions. Only nine other people knew the exact date, time and location of our wedding. We were probably the only couple who first consulted our public-relations directors on the subject before we told our family or friends. Everyone agreed it was best for us to keep our decision under wraps until June. For now, it would have to be business as usual for both of us.

\* \* \*

And it was. In February I made a speech before the Young Presidents Organization at its 1982 annual meeting in Maui, Hawaii. Among the four keynote speakers, I was certainly the least illustrious. My colleagues were former Presidents Gerald Ford and Jimmy Carter, and Democratic National Chairperson Robert Strauss. My subject was business and productivity, and I did find ways of injecting a few words on equal rights. "How many of you received the adoring gratitude of your own daughters whose education you have unquestioningly paid for and whose professional paths you've publicly and privately supported?" I asked. I knew the show of hands would be sizable. "But how many of this enlightened group have urged their *wives* to pursue an educational degree or career opportunity that would give her personal fulfillment outside her home and greater economic independence?" A much smaller show of hands. I went on to make my point, showing how these quirky human prejudices take their toll not just in purely economic terms. It was good to speak before such a prestigious group. The male skeptics in the audience at least had the chance to see I had more than half a brain, and I was glad for the opportunity to speak on my own in front of Agee. He'd never heard me speak before and I think he was proud to see how well I did.

Back in New York, Bill and I continued to immerse ourselves in our jobs. At Seagram's I was next asked to present the wine strategy to the Seagram's board of directors in March. It was well received, and shortly afterward Edgar Bronfman set up the Seagram Wine Company, and named me executive vice president of the unit. Agee was barreling ahead at Bendix too. During the past six months, with interest rates falling, Bendix had started to acquire small amounts of stock in selected undervalued companies. One was RCA. The plan was to go up to, but not to exceed, 9.9 percent by February. According to SEC regulations, a company has to make public its purchases if they exceed 5 percent. To this end, Agee flew to New York in March for a meeting with RCA Chairman Thornton Bradshaw. "Our intentions are to buy more than five but not to exceed 9.9 percent," Agee told a disconsolate Bradshaw. The Bendix bid came at what was not the best of times for RCA. The company had only recently disclosed to its shareholders that it had lost $106.8 million the previous year and was in the midst of a complex and troublesome reorganization. The announcement of the Bendix purchase sparked rumors of a pending takeover bid, which naturally alarmed Bradshaw. Vulnerable and threatened, Bradshaw spent the weekend locked up with some of his aides, who, we were told, advised him to play dirty.

Just how dirty, no one could have guessed. On Monday, when Bendix went public with its purchase, Bradshaw was ready with his comeback. "The purchase of RCA stock by Mr. Agee's Bendix is not welcomed by RCA," he said. And then, in a statement that caused Wall Street to stand still, "Mr. Agee has not demonstrated the ability to manage his own *affairs*, let alone someone else's."

Every major newspaper in the country ran the titillating quote. Once again, I had to read about myself as the shadowy figure in Mr. Agee's past. All the more important financial stories of that day were shoved aside so that newspapers could have some fun with Bradshaw's dig.

But if the Bradshaw comment knocked me down, another jab to the stomach kept me from getting up. An article written by John Holusha in the March 11, 1982, *New York Times* said, "He [Mr. Agee] has conceded that he was romantically involved with Mary E. Cunningham...." I couldn't believe it. Was my vision right? Was I going crazy? I managed to summon my voice to call Agee from the living room where I was reading the *Times*. He denied ever having said anything of the kind to the *Times* reporter. "What are you going to do about it?" I shrieked. "I don't know, Mary. I'll have my lawyers look into it. We'll see what we can do."

I started to shake. This on the heels of the Bradshaw episode. "What am I—some sort of crude joke anyone can play with whenever it's a dull press day? What do you really care?" I began on the Waldorf ashtrays. I threw them at the gilded mantelpiece and watched as they fell to the floor in a hundred bits. Then I took the message pads, the pens, the pencils, the lamp. I think I must have thrown every item in that suite. Bill grabbed hold of me so that I couldn't move. Suddenly, I was convulsed in tears. "Bill, if you sit back on this one," I told him later that night, "you can have Bendix and your whole damn company. I'm through. With all of it." Agee couldn't believe the rage. He had rarely heard me swear, and the rage he'd just witnessed still shocked us both. The same day, he contacted his lawyers and they quickly extracted a retraction from the *Times*. The newspaper agreed to print the retraction, and our lawyers dropped their plans to sue for libel. But the retraction was of little consolation to me. The *Times* allegation had been printed in a story that began on page one of the business section, and the retraction buried in a small blurb under the index. What a travesty—"All the news that's fit to print."

At work the next day, an editor from the *Times* business section called to apologize personally. But I was hardly in a conciliatory mood. I chewed that poor man out for every sensational distortion and unethical move the press had made for the past year and a half. After the phone call, I passed Edgar Bronfman in the hall. Just an hour earlier he had stopped by to tell me how pleased he was with the new wine strategy. And now he saw me on the verge of tears, rushing to the ladies room. "Just hang on, you've just got to hang in there, Mary," he said, putting his hands on my shoulders and shaking me. "You've got to go on and not let it get to you." After all he'd been through in the press with his own personal troubles not so long ago, Edgar Bronfman well knew the meaning of endurance. "You can't give in to them. You just can't."

And I didn't. The next week I was initiated into the New York Economic Club at a meeting which coincidentally fell on Saint Patrick's Day. Who should I see in the receiving line but Thornton Bradshaw himself. "Aren't you Mary Cunningham?" he asked. The crowd around us, which included Pete Peterson, among other Wall Street celebrities, stood back. "Yes," I said. "My name is Thornton Bradshaw," the man said. I had recognized him from his picture in the paper. "How do you do, Mr. Bradshaw," I said. "I think I owe you an apology," he said. "My wife was appalled at the crudeness of my published statement, although I must say, it wasn't my idea. My advisers suggested it." I thought this was rather dastardly, trying to pass the blame off on one's underlings. But I refrained from saying so. "Frankly, Mr. Bradshaw," I said, "your comment surprised me more than anything else. It didn't fit any of the nice things Bill Agee had to say about you."

"Good show, Mary," Pete Peterson said afterward. "You handled yourself like quite a lady." "And, as usual, you handled yourself like a cad," I felt like telling him, but I refrained. Although I had good reason to say it. Peterson was on the board of RCA but had been on the West Coast the weekend Bradshaw drafted the statement and had come back to town too late to stop it—or so he told Agee.

In May I was invited to speak at the Women's Economic Club of Detroit. Naturally I was fearful of returning to the "scene of the crime," but I decided that unless I faced my old ghosts, they'd haunt me forever. "As I'm sure you can understand," I said, in my address before a record crowd of over three thousand, "I have been anticipating this day with somewhat mixed emotions." The topic of my speech was, of course, women in business, but I made ample opportunity to deliver what I felt were certain well-justified criticisms of the press.

It was filmed by "20/20" and had such a long standing ovation that Barbara Walters commented to her cameraman that it was the closest thing she'd seen on film to a Billy Graham revival meeting.

More than a few dignitaries from both the rival *Detroit Free Press* and *Detroit News* newspapers were there. After the speech, *Detroit Free Press* editor David Lawrence came up to shake my hand. "I owe you a significant apology," he said. And he did. The next day, the headline in the *Free Press* said, "Now it's Cunningham's turn," and on another page, the paper printed almost the entire text of my speech.

It was in this triumphant mood that Bill and I let on to our closest friends that now we were really more than "just friends" and that, in a week, we'd be husband and wife.

I think most women planning a wedding wonder if their hair will look nice or what dress to wear. My biggest concern was whether the press would be there. For that reason, Bill and I decided to be married in a small private ceremony at Saint Mary's Cathedral in San Francisco.

Our wedding was planned for June 5, but we flew in a day and a half before. Bill was nervous that the marriage-license bureau would be closed, which it wasn't, and I was afraid something would go wrong in reserving the altar, which it didn't. The morning before, we decided to walk to Saint Mary's, a beautiful cathedral on top of a hill, which had a special significance to us. It was almost two years ago, in August of 1980, that Bill and I first went inside Saint Mary's. We were in San Francisco for our Bendix Forest Products meeting with Jack Guyol. Before the meeting, Agee had asked me to have breakfast and go over the agenda for the meeting with him. I'd asked if he'd excuse me so I could attend early morning Mass. I'm not sure why, but he asked if he could go with me. "If you like," I said. The priest gave an unusually powerful sermon that morning, about being tested. The sermon was about the cross and suffering and how it can come into any of our lives, often when we least expect it. "When it does, it will test your faith," the priest said. All during the sermon he kept looking straight at me. "Do you know him?" Bill asked me afterward. "No," I answered. But I knew why he'd asked. It was almost frightening the way the priest kept addressing his warnings to me. The testing certainly did come to pass. But now almost two years later Bill was telling me he'd like it if we were married there.

As we were walking up the hill to the church, a red-haired reporter emerged from the bushes and said, "You wouldn't by any chance be Philip Agee?" "No," Bill said, declaring emphatically that he was not the ex-CIA agent who'd written the best-selling exposé of the CIA. "Well,

I know you're Mary Cunningham," he said, looking at me. "And I bet you're here to get married," he said. The San Francisco papers had printed such speculation that morning. Bill and I looked at each other, smiling. "You sure you're not here to get married?" "If we were," Bill said ironically, "I'm sure you'd be one of the first to know." We walked a little farther up the hill when I paused, hearing what seemed like thunderous applause in the distance. "What's all the commotion?" I asked. Our persistent reporter, still on our trail, answered, "Mother Teresa is speaking. That's why I'm here. I'm covering her speech." I quickly turned to Bill. I couldn't believe she was speaking here exactly twenty-four hours before we were to be married at that very altar. The coincidence was too much. How many times had my life almost taken her path. And then, when I came nearer and heard her words, it was almost as if she were talking directly to me. She was speaking of marriage and the divine nature of love. "To love is to forgive," she said. To love is to forgive, I thought.

That night we had a small private dinner in the Presidential Suite of the Pacific Plaza Hotel. My mother, Father Bill, my sister Shirley and her husband, Dick, and my brothers Frank and John and John's wife, Jane, were there, as were our good friends Bob and Mert Hendren. No one from Bill's family had been invited for fear they'd leak it to the press, but the friends and family gathered provided enough love to sustain us both. It was a beautiful evening. All the hurt, all the suffering only seemed to have reinforced the bonds between my family and us and between Bill and me. The other couples there felt it too, Bob and Mert Hendren, John and Jane, and Shirley and Dick. Not one of the toasts was less than inspiring. Even Frank, usually so cheerful and jolly, was quiet and serene.

At nine the next morning we gathered at Saint Mary's. My mother looked radiant. She wore a lovely peach gown that Bill and I had bought for her the day before. (She had been unable to buy a gown herself because she felt "nothing was good enough for you children.") I wore a white lace gown and had put a sprig of baby's breath in my hair and in my mother's belt. Bob Hendren was Bill's best man and my matron of honor was my mother. We were married by Father Bill. Just before I said "I do," I looked at Father Bill and then at Bill. I knew this was right. "I do," I said. "I do," Bill said. We were now, finally, husband and wife.

It was a relief to be married. Even the press started to leave us alone. Having successfully protected the privacy of our wedding day, we even felt comfortable enough to gather our closest friends and strongest supporters in a post-wedding reception at the Versailles Room of the Helmsley Palace in New York. We paused a moment before the first dance, cherishing the freedom of our new bond and the delight reflected in the faces of our friends.

We spent much of our time that summer commuting between Michigan and New York, but we had long, pleasant weekends that summer in McCall. For once, all seemed well for both of us at work. I was immersed in implementing the wine strategy at Seagram's and Bill was moving full speed ahead at Bendix. In addition to buying shares of RCA, he had spent most of the spring accumulating positions in Gould, Lockheed and, most recently, Martin Marietta. His sense of timing, as usual, was impeccable. Just at the time Bendix was buying, stock prices were going down and interest rates were going up. It was a perfect time to move out of cash and into stocks. As the weeks passed, Martin Marietta looked more and more as

if it was going to be the target company. A merger with
Martin Marietta would make Bendix one of the top twenty
aerospace companies in the U.S. And it was Agee's conviction that what Martin Marietta was producing—missiles, guidance systems and computers—would be the hot
items of the next decade. Furthermore, Martin Marietta's
stock was nice and low, in the low twenties, and with
Agee's impeccable sense that the market was soon to take
off, now was the time to buy.

On August 12 to 14, the bull market indeed started to
take off. By August 24, Bendix had accumulated 4.9 percent of Martin Marietta stock. Papers announcing Bendix's intent to acquire control were filed with the Securities
and Exchange Commission.

September 1 was my thirty-first birthday, and Bill and
I decided to spend it with my mother at the Cape. "How
are things going with Bill?" she asked one afternoon while
we were sitting out on the porch. "Really fine now," I
said. "I believe we'll finally be able to settle down and
live a more-or-less quiet life like other people do." I had
barely finished the sentence when Bill came flying out the
door. "Guess what," he said. "What?" I asked, hoping to
hear that our tomato plants had bloomed. "Al McDonald
just called." "Why did he call us out here?" I asked,
knowing that only the most crucial phone calls came to
my mother's summer cottage on the Cape. "Martin Marietta just did the most unbelievable thing. They decided
to fight back and buy our stock," he said. I knew the
business implications of this but more important, I knew
what it meant for our own lives. Peace was over. Martin
Marietta and Bendix were now at war.

# CHAPTER ELEVEN

*Three distinct misimpressions were* generated by the press during the most intense periods of the Bendix-Martin Marietta-Allied wars. One was that I, Mary Cunningham, functioned as a sort of Lady Macbeth, whispering evil stratagems into my husband's innocent ears. The second was that Bendix was the big bad wolf out to gobble up poor harmless Martin Marietta for its own greedy ends. And the third was that what Bill Agee did during the whole ordeal was bad for business, bad for the country and bad for the American Way. All three are neat and tidy apothegms, but untrue. The truth, actually, is more interesting.

I knew from the moment Al McDonald called us at the Cape that the recent peace we'd been enjoying was short-lived. For Agee to decide to attempt a friendly takeover of Martin Marietta was one thing. But for Martin Marietta, a company merely two-thirds the size of Bendix, to fight back by trying to take over Bendix was another. It seemed totally irrational, but one thing was certain—that it would dominate our lives for the next few weeks. And it did.

Even in the days before Martin Marietta announced its kamikaze plan, Agee had been working diligently on the tender offer. Although I was not directly involved in any of his business activities—I had plenty of my own at Seagram's to occupy my mind—he periodically surfaced from Southfield to bring me reports of what was happening at the front. I had more than just a passing interest in all of this for two reasons. First, I was his wife, and was naturally concerned about my husband's business. And second, and probably more important, as Agee's former chief strategist, I'd had more than just a hand in the strategy that had resulted in the Martin Marietta bid. After all, I was a strong advocate of putting the name Martin Marietta on the original list of target acquisitions. So I watched the whole ball game as more than just a fan.

Bill's first order of business was to get the approval of his board. The board that Agee presented his plans to was a slightly altered board from the one that I'd faced during the last of my Bendix days. After the exodus of Purcell and the Burroughs troika—Schwartz, Mirabito and Cunningham—a few new faces had come aboard. Former astronaut Tom Stafford and Mobil Oil Company chairman William Tavoulareas joined the roster of new directors. For weeks now, they and the rest of the Bendix board had carefully reviewed the vital statistics of three companies, RCA, Gould and Martin Marietta, and all had agreed that Martin Marietta was the one to pursue. A merger with Martin Marietta would firmly hoist Bendix into the stratosphere of the high-technology companies. Martin Marietta made missiles and other high-technology products for the military and commercial markets, and in the early 1980s, for better or for worse, that looked like a good place to be.

Of course, little did Agee or anyone else at Bendix take fully into account the military minds of the men at Martin Marietta. Considering themselves merely "an extension of the Defense Department," as Martin Marietta chairman Tom Pownall had once said, they viewed the world in military terms. Their lives were spent in contemplations of missiles, guns and wars, and they thought of business in those terms too. Fight unto the death. Might makes right. But it was only after it was too late that Agee and his comrades realized their misjudgment of the no-holds-barred military mentality. They hadn't taken into account that in business, as in anything else, personalities and cultural norms, not P/E ratios and maximizing share-holder value, sometimes rule the game.

So when the idea of making a tender offer for Martin Marietta was proposed, it received rave reviews. "A brilliant strategic fit," said Donald Rumsfeld, who had inside knowledge of the defense industry and also was a buddy of Mel Laird, who sat on Marietta's board. Bendix President Al McDonald had connections with Griffin Bell, the former attorney general who also sat on the Martin Marietta board. McDonald urged Agee to act quickly. He knew the stock market was starting to soar and wanted Bendix to get the best price.

Personal factors also played a role. McDonald, who had been a managing partner of McKinsey & Co. before he had come to Bendix, had been president for just over a year now, but under Agee he had little opportunity to exert control. He wanted to graduate from chief-of-staff-type roles into operational management. A merger with Marietta would give Agee so much to do that he'd need McDonald on the operation's side. Bill Purple, head of the Bendix aerospace division, naturally was in favor of the plan. He had one word for it: "Terrific." And it was.

Despite the personal reasons why many directors approved the bid, it made solid sense from a business and economic point of view. And as Hugo Uyterhoeven pointed out, Martin Marietta had not been successful in its diversification program. Agee knew that over the past four or five years, the bulk of the company's capital had been allocated to the cement and aluminum businesses. Almost $800 million had been invested in these two businesses, which were either losing significant profits or were only marginally profitable. With better management, future capital might be more efficiently invested and those areas might be improved upon as well. Any director with the brains and vision of Agee would have seen this as an excellent move, and if there were other serious objections, no one raised them then. One director did raise the question of whether the board thought Marietta would resist. "Do you think they'll fight?" one of the directors asked. "You can't ever rule it out," another said, "but it seems unlikely." In fact, the only real problem anyone anticipated was antitrust, and Bendix already had its teams of lawyers working on that.

Agee was very much concerned that the deal not be hostile. He was well known in the business community for doing only friendly deals and was willing to push that policy only as far as engaging in what is commonly referred to as a "bear hug." Instead of declaring out-and-out war, he made sure Martin Marietta understood his willingness to negotiate any and all terms. He sent a letter and also telephoned Pownall shortly before the announcement in an attempt to communicate his open negotiating position. Pownall ignored both.

On August 26, 1982, in what was a surprise move to most of the people at Martin Marietta, Bendix registered with the Securities and Exchange Commission a $43-a-share tender offer for 45 percent of Martin Marietta's common shares. The release explained that Bendix would acquire the rest of Marietta's stock in a favorable swap of Bendix stock.

When a corporate takeover is announced, all of Wall Street takes note. Investment bankers and merger-and-acquisitions specialists in the big law firms start feeling their fingers twitch. Millions of dollars are to be made in these transactions. And the irony is, it doesn't really matter to the investment bankers and lawyers who wins and who loses. They get their million-dollar fees as long as the game is played. And the longer the game, the higher the stakes. Not to mention the thrill of the battle. If Martin Siegel of Kidder Peabody can put one over on Jay Higgins of Salomon Brothers or Pete Peterson of Lehman Brothers, so much the better. As it was, Bendix was no longer doing business with Lehman Brothers. Lehman Brothers represented RCA and after the last (and rather unpleasant) interchange between Bradshaw and Agee, Bendix decided to seek its investment banking advice from someone other than Pete Peterson.

At the start of the Martin Marietta takeover, Bendix employed Jay Higgins of Salomon Brothers, a well-known name in the field. But by the end, when Martin Marietta started to move in on Bendix, an adviser with more experience on the defense side was needed. Agee decided to add Bruce Wasserstein of the Mergers and Acquisitions department of First Boston to the team. Naturally, these investment bankers were playing their own game. It seemed to me they were often more concerned with which of them would get credit for a certain maneuver than they were with being a coordinated team. And although they were working for Bendix and Agee, they seemed to know their counterparts on the other team a bit too well. There were times when there appeared to be more friendship between Wasserstein and Martin Siegel, the investment banker masterminding Martin Marietta's game, than between Wasserstein and Agee. Networking played a role in this industry too. I was told that was just part of the game. At least it was then.

It was important to Agee to keep his offer for Martin Marietta friendly, so the first thing he did just before the bid was announced was to try to contact Martin Marietta chieftain Tom Pownall personally by phone. But Pownall was not in a talking mood. Then Agee tried a letter. It went unanswered. A military man, Pownall was a fighter. The advice he received from his subordinates was not even to speak to Agee. Perhaps they feared straitlaced Pownall might be vulnerable to Agee's rationale. So the response Bendix received in the wake of its offer came through the newspapers. Martin Marietta wasn't interested.

Yet that was typical in corporate takeovers. The company being courted played hard to get, hoping to elicit a higher price. But when Agee heard the news that Martin Marietta was launching its own counteroffense tender offer for Bendix, that struck him and everyone else as more than a little odd. Also, it came as a complete surprise. When Agee received Al McDonald's phone call at the Cape that afternoon, he was stunned.

Wall Street observers—and there were many; after all, what else is there to write about during a sleepy September in a non-election year?—called it the Pac-Man strategy. You gobble up your opponent before he can take a bite out of you. The idea that Martin Marietta might pursue such a strategy had crossed the minds of a few of Agee's advisers but none took it seriously. "It would be so irrational they wouldn't consider it," was the prevailing view. "They'd have to borrow too much money and it would put their entire company in serious debt. No responsible board would approve such a move." So when news of the counteroffer came through, everyone was incredulous. Jay Higgins, Bendix's investment banker from Salomon Brothers, dubbed it the "Jonestown Offense" to illustrate how self-destructive a response it was. As a joke, Higgins kept packets of Kool-Aid on his desk.

As surprised as he was by the counteroffer, Agee was put at ease for two reasons. First, it confirmed his notion that the two companies were, in fact, a good strategic fit. Martin Marietta must have perceived that too. And second, antitrust, the problem that up until now he'd worried most about, obviously, was no longer an issue. If Martin Marietta was making an offer to buy Bendix, then clearly it could no longer try to block our bid on antitrust grounds.

Naturally, Bendix refused the Martin Marietta offer. Obviously no one at Bendix was interested in selling Bendix, and second, the offer was "insultingly low." In these situations that phrase is always used, but the Martin Marietta offer, by everyone's analysis, really was. They were offering a two-tiered bid that averaged out to a purchase price of only around $60 per share for the entire company. (The deal Agee eventually negotiated brought Bendix shareholders $85 a share.) But what bothered Agee most about the Marietta counteroffer was that it was a two-tiered offer, which, in the business, is regarded as a dirty deal. A two-tiered offer means you offer more money for the first half of the stock and less for the rest. The higher front-end price causes a stampede of arbitrageurs and institutional investors to sell their shares, regardless of what's good for the company. Once those shares are sold, the bidder owns a controlling number of shares of the company and then can pay the lower price to the remaining stockholders, usually the widows and orphans. In essence, the big boys on Wall Street get rich and the widows and orphans lose out. The two-tiered offer was a tactic Agee abhorred. The Bendix board viewed it as unfair. But to Martin Siegel, the investment banker from Kidder Peabody who was running Martin Marietta's show, it was merely one of the tricks of the trade. Siegel, handsome, smart and thirty-four, kept a paperweight on his desk with a tarantula inside. It was his way of letting his clients know what kind of a fighter he was.

To show Martin Marietta that Agee meant business, he unilaterally raised his offer. He pushed his price up from $43 a share to $48 a share. If Martin Marietta considered his initial bid too low, Agee wanted them to know he was willing to negotiate. The $48 a share offer represented a 60 percent premium over the original market price, which was under $30 a share just before the acquisition rumors pushed the price up. Furthermore, Agee's wasn't a two-tiered bid. But the better financial offer and signal to negotiate did little good. Agee still had no idea how strongly committed Martin Marietta was to fighting the bid. He found out soon enough.

Enter Harry Gray, chairman of the mammoth United Technologies Corp., a company bigger and mightier than either Bendix or Martin Marietta. Harry Gray and Tom Pownall were friends of a sort. Both men belonged to an all-male club of defense-company executives called the Conquistadors. It was the kind of place in which men arm-wrestled and didn't eat quiche. In the field of corporate takeovers, Pownall couldn't have found a better friend. Harry Gray was known as a "shark" for his role in previous takeover battles. Pownall wanted Gray to step in and help Martin Marietta in its counterraid. Most companies that are the object of corporate takeovers search for a white knight to come and buy them on more favorable terms. But Pownall was looking for someone to help him in his attack on Bendix. He was looking for a "gray knight," so to speak, and he found it in the guise of Harry Gray.

The deal struck by the two "conquistadors," was that Gray would make his own $1.5 billion bid for Bendix stock, similar to the one Martin Marietta had made. Gray had nothing to lose and everything to gain. He probably figured that no matter what happened, he'd get a piece of Bendix, a firm he'd been looking at for quite some time. And Martin Marietta, who, on its own, had neither the muscle nor the finances to stage a raid of Bendix, now did, with United Technologies. The two conquistadors agreed: if either of them acquired Bendix, they'd divide the spoils between them.

It was foul play from Bendix's point of view. Two kids in the playground ganging up against a third. But who was talking about being fair? Agee first learned of the two-against-one strategy from his friend Felix Rohatyn, an investment banker with Lazard Freres. Lazard Freres represented United Technologies, which Rohatyn knew was hungry for the chance to fatten itself on Bendix. "You'll be getting a call from Harry Gray," Rohatyn told Agee. And sure enough he did. For the first time he realized the possibility that Bendix could be eaten up.

And there was more foul play afoot. When two companies are locked in a takeover struggle, the various investment bankers and lawyers on either side scramble for inside information about the rival firm. Any tip can change the odds. Martin Marietta and United Technologies didn't have to do much scrambling. On more than one occasion, people from Burroughs had been in to see Martin Siegel at Kidder Peabody. Word was out that Blumenthal himself had met with Siegel, and, while Agee was no longer surprised by Blumenthal's antics, still he felt wounded. And then it was also discovered that a former Bendix executive was also working hand in hand with United Technologies and was relaying information to Harry Gray's team about Bendix. No one was safe.

Our lives were now consumed by this corporate war. Our headquarters were Suite 4509 in the Helmsley Palace. Bill had sequestered himself there since Labor Day. The suite was convenient to Bendix's new New York headquarters in the General Motors Building and only a few blocks from my office at Seagram's. But it was hardly a place one could call home. Round the clock Agee held meetings there with his team of lawyers, investment bankers and subordinates. Hardly had I put my makeup on in the bathroom when I'd hear the troops start coming in. Agee's best hours of work were done in the morning, so from 6:30 A.M. on, his entourage would sit in our living room at the Palace and plan their strategy. As one of Agee's former business strategists, I was invited to listen to these breakfast talks. At nine, I'd pull myself away and immerse myself in the far more pleasant world of wines at Seagram's. Occasionally during the day, my secretary, Adrianne, would interrupt me at a meeting to say, "Your husband's on the phone," and I'd know from one look at her face whether it was urgent. At noon I'd return to the Helmsley to join Bill and his advisers for lunch. Occasionally, just to take a break, he'd come over and meet me at Seagram's and we'd go out for lunch by ourselves. And every night, no matter how tired we were, I'd return to our suite only to find the place still crawling with advisers. Investment bankers, lawyers and corporate counselors were everywhere I looked. Again it was room service, hotel meals and late-night consultations.

And of course, once again, Bill and I found ourselves the focus of the public eye. In his case, it was entirely appropriate. After all, he was one of the principal players in all of this. But me? Not that the frequent mention of my name in the newspapers surprised me by now. I'd had it explained to me by one of the blunter journalists with one of the leading newspapers—"They use your name whenever the story starts to lose its luster." I was getting used to the fact that everywhere that Mary went, the press was sure to go.

Three events were going on now: Bendix was trying to buy Martin Marietta. Martin Marietta was trying to buy Bendix. And Martin Marietta's ally, United Technologies, was also trying to buy Bendix. What would decide who would win? One crucial factor in all of this was time. Initially it looked like Bendix had the edge. When a company announces a tender offer, federal regulations mandate that it must wait fifteen business days before it can actually buy the stock. Bendix announced its tender offer on August 25, which meant it could buy Marietta stock on midnight of September 16. Since Marietta announced its tender offer five days later, on August 30, it couldn't buy Bendix's stock until midnight, September 22. And of course United Technologies couldn't acquire anyone until September 28. Naturally, if Bendix acquired Martin Marietta first, the first thing it would do would be to call a special shareholders' meeting and vote to have Martin

Marietta stop its raid against Bendix and terminate its agreement with United Technologies.

But a legal loophole—and this entire episode was full of legal loopholes—seemed as if it might cost Bendix the fight, at least on this front. The Bendix legal department had not alerted Agee to a peculiar interplay between Delaware and Maryland corporate law. Delaware law (Bendix is incorporated in Delaware) says a majority shareholder can convene a meeting without giving notice to the other shareholders. But Martin Marietta is chartered in Maryland where a majority shareholder cannot convene a special shareholders' meeting without giving the other shareholders ten days' notice. That meant that even if Bendix bought Martin Marietta stock first, it couldn't call off Marietta's raid until at least five days *after* Martin Marietta could call off Bendix's. But since nothing like this had ever happened in the annals of business affairs, it was anyone's guess what the courts might rule. In the meantime, both sides sent their attorneys to court. It was, in any event, a race against time.

Agee tried repeatedly to contact Pownall both by phone and in writing. He wanted to try to de-escalate this if at all possible. The essence of his communiqués was to remind Pownall that "anything and everything is negotiable." Admittedly, Agee was bewildered by Pownall's silence. If it actually came to pass that Bendix bought Marietta, and Marietta in turn bought Bendix, the two companies would be crippled in debt and tied up in legal wranglings for years. Agee called this outcome "the unthinkable." "I'm prepared to sit down and come up with an agreement that's mutually satisfactory," he wrote in a letter to Pownall. But Pownall wasn't interested. "I can find no useful purpose to be served by a prompt meeting with you," the Marietta chieftain wrote back. It was the Tet Offensive mentality all over again.

Not far into September, a subcommittee of the Bendix board, organized by Jack Fontaine, worked out the terms of an employment contract to protect the executive staff, should the company change hands. Not that anyone was thinking it really would, but it's customary in merger-acquisition battles to put these safeguards—the press likes to call them "golden parachutes"—in place. The Bendix plan guaranteed the sixteen top officers of the company three years' salary and, as is customary, the chairman five. But no one was thinking the "parachutes" would need to be unfurled. Who ever thought the battle would go that far?

Meanwhile, psychologically we were on an emotional roller coaster practically every day. If in the morning there was good news from somewhere, by nightfall there was bad news from somewhere else. The phone rang every fifteen minutes, and each time it rang, my adrenalin surged. This corporate battle was wreaking havoc with our bodies. Bill was afraid to sleep too soundly at night for fear that if the phone rang he'd be caught off guard.

The evening of September 9, I walked into our suite at the Palace, and as usual, the whole crew was there—the crew, being Bendix President Al McDonald, investment bankers Bruce Wasserstein and Tony Grassi, our attorney from Fried, Frank, Harris, Shriver & Jacobson, Arthur Fleischer Jr., Agee and me. Everyone seemed in a pretty good mood. "Why the cheerful spirits?" I asked. "It looks like Martin Marietta doesn't have enough shares of Bendix to fill up its proration pool," McDonald said. The reason it couldn't was because of SESSOP, the Bendix Salaried Employees Savings and Stock Ownership

Plan. SESSOP held roughly 4.5 million shares of Bendix stock, or approximately 23 percent. In the trade, this was known as an excellent "shark repellant." It was highly unlikely that Bendix employees would tender their shares over to any hostile raider if management was opposed to such action. The trustee for SESSOP was Citibank, and both Bendix and Citibank agreed that the SESSOP shareholders had not voted to tender their shares to Marietta.

But at 9:30 P.M. the phone rang. It was the voice of Bendix's attorney, Hal Barron. "I'm afraid I have some bad news for your husband," Barron said. "Just one moment, Hal, I'll get him." Agee was in the midst of conferring with Fleischer and Wasserstein. "What's up?" Agee said. When Agee got off the phone he looked stunned. He turned to us and said, "Citibank's just tendered all their shares of Bendix employee-held stock. That means Martin Marietta will now have enough to buy." Everyone was incredulous. "How could they do that?" McDonald asked. No trustee ever tenders employee-held stock to an unfriendly raider without the shareholders' explicit consent. But it didn't take long for Agee to figure things out. Who sat on the board of Harry Gray's company, United Technologies? Bill Spencer, president of Citibank. And who was on the board of Citicorp, the parent company of Citibank? None other than Harry Gray. Not only was Gray on the Citibank board, he was also a member of the Fiduciary Committee of the board, the very committee that is empowered to review such decisions "on behalf of the shareholders." It was back to interlocking directorates.

The next morning Al McDonald came stomping into our suite at the Helmsley. "Just look at this," he said, waving *The Wall Street Journal* in Agee's face. "This says the Marietta pool is overflowing," McDonald shouted, "when what it should have said was 'Marietta fails to fill its pool.' This is unconscionable, to vote our employees' stock without ever polling them." Had Marietta not been able to wrest control of the SESSOP shares and fill its pool, the psychological advantage to Bendix would have been enormous. Fleischer immediately put his attorneys to work. But Agee knew that by the time anyone resolved the dispute, the matter was likely to be academic.

Not long after the Citibank surprise came another, equally disturbing. "Gentlemen and Mary," Art Fleischer said one evening after I'd just gotten back from Seagram's. "The strangest thing's just happened." Nothing could surprise me now. "Martin Marietta appears to have dropped its qualifiers." This was indeed strange. So bullish was Marietta on going ahead with its self-destructive plan that it was actually trying to bind itself by law into purchasing a controlling portion of Bendix shares. This meant that even if Agee and Pownall came up with a settlement, Marietta would still be bound to commence with its doomsday plan. Shades of Dr. Strangelove. "This is crazy," Agee said to me that night. "No responsible board would allow any management to do such an irrational act." I started to wonder about these military men. No wonder our Defense Department was having problems.

I was getting homesick. Agee and I had bought a condominium in Michigan back in the spring and I was longing for a night at home. I'd have loved to sleep in my own bed, eat a home-cooked meal, sit around our living room and watch TV. And although McDonald, Fleischer, Wasserstein *et al.* were perfectly nice, how pleasant it would have been to spend an evening without them.

Luckily, the week of September 13 we had an excuse to leave town. Bill and I spent the next few days at home, but by Tuesday morning it was back to the races. We landed at LaGuardia. Agee went back to the Helmsley, but for me it was an especially hectic day. I was met by a Seagram's car and whisked to one of Seagram's private planes in White Plains. There was a Seagram's board meeting in Montreal and I had a major presentation to make. I had worried that the distractions of the last few weeks would affect my report, but my fears were needless. Presenting complex stratagems to a roomful of executives seemed like child's play. "Great job," Beekman and both Bronfmans told me after my presentation. And for a few hours I actually forgot about Bendix and remembered the pleasant world of wines.

I was back in New York the next day. September 16 was a big day at Bendix headquarters. It was the day when Bendix could go ahead and buy Marietta's stock. To expedite the decision-making process, the Bendix board now delegated authority in the Marietta war to five of its members—Agee, McDonald, Tavoulareas, Stafford and Scott. The group authorized Agee to go ahead and buy 70 percent of Martin Marietta's stock. However, earlier in the week, U.S. District Judge Joseph Young of Baltimore had ordered a ten-day freeze to give both sides time to reflect. But at 9:30 P.M., word came through that a U.S. Appeals Court had overturned Judge Young's freeze, thereby freeing Bendix to buy the Marietta stock. So dismayed was Martin Marietta by this development that, according to McDonald, it was trying to rouse Supreme Court Chief Justice Warren Burger from his bed to overturn the appeal. With no one certain what might happen next, the atmosphere in Suite 4509 at the Palace was tense, to say the least. If nothing new happened, Bendix would buy Martin Marietta stock at 12:01.

At 10 P.M., Bruce Wasserstein suddenly asked to use the phone. "Who are you calling?" McDonald wanted to know. "I just want to check in with Siegel," Wasserstein said obtusely, referring to Marty Siegel, his counterpart at Martin Marietta. "What do you need to call Siegel for at a time like this?" asked McDonald, already wary of the informal network of alliances among the investment bankers. So many unpredictable developments and side agreements had already occurred that no one had much trust in anyone anymore. "I promised I'd call Marty every hour. He's expecting my call," Wasserstein said. Alonzo's face turned red. "You bastards," he said. "You're sending signals to each other again. It would be one thing if you'd let your own clients in on your game plan. This whole negotiation is just a big game to you. You don't care whose side you're on. You're on your own side, throughout all of this." "Easy, Al," Agee said, trying to calm McDonald. "He's on our side." But McDonald was in a rage. And I knew how he felt. None of the investment bankers had been very candid about their strategies or much good at predicting events so far; they seemed most adept at taking credit for ideas they gleaned from their clients. They also had an uncanny way of knowing exactly when to become invisible when things weren't going well. I could sense that Agee was also starting to lose faith. "I tell you what we're going to do," McDonald said, "we're going to sequester you. No more calls until midnight." Wasserstein looked uneasy.

What none of us had been clued into was that Wasserstein was driven to reach Siegel because he had been negotiating privately with him the terms of a possible settlement. Without authorization from either Agee or McDonald, he had been working out a plan by which Martin Marietta would pay Bendix a certain sum to buy back all the stock that Bendix had bought, in effect, thereby terminating Bendix's acquisition effort.

The next hour seemed interminable. But, about an hour before midnight, McDonald acquiesced to Wasserstein's request to accept one call from his associate, Tony Grassi. With McDonald right at his side, Wasserstein still managed to defy his client's request for confidentiality. Wasserstein asked Grassi to pass to Siegel a not-so-cryptic message: "Just tell him we're drinking champagne"—the implication being: Bendix is going ahead and buying the Marietta shares. Between 11:45 and 12:01 the phones to the bank were ordered cleared. Finally, at midnight, Agee made the call. He authorized the bank computer to spend a billion dollars for the purchase of the Martin Marietta shares in the Bendix pool.

But things were far from over yet. Now that Bendix had bought, would Marietta buy? If so, what Agee feared— "the unthinkable"—would come to pass: two companies that owned each other and a legal nightmare that would take years to untangle.

In the meantime, Agee began working on another front. There was another way Bendix could delay Marietta's takeover and that was to have another company, a partial white knight, make a bid on Bendix. According to federal regulations, if a second company bid for Bendix, Marietta would have to wait an additional ten days before it could purchase the Bendix stock. Fleischer called this "the Great

Extender" strategy. Already feelers had been sent out for a partial white knight. One of the most promising so far was New York City real-estate developer Donald Trump, who was interested in purchasing Bendix's block of RCA shares. But no one knew if Trump could raise the $100 million in time. Nor was Fleischer certain that it would hold up legally as an investment in Bendix in order to effect the ten-day hold. On Friday, September 17, Agee met with another possible white knight, chief of the Allied Corporation, Edward Hennessey, Jr.

I was finishing my breakfast when Hennessey walked in. Agee introduced us. "Would you like me to leave?" I asked. "No," Agee said. "I'm a friend of your boss, Phil Beekman," Hennessey said. We exchanged a few pleasantries and then Hennessey and Bill started talking strategy. What Agee wanted was to have Allied buy enough Bendix stock to delay Martin Marietta's offensive, but not enough to control Bendix.

What Agee didn't know at the time was that Hennessey was not much different from Harry Gray in that he was hungrier for more than just a piece of Bendix. Allied had been eying Bendix as a possible takeover target for several years. With Bendix vulnerable now, Hennessey was hoping to capture his target, and at a good price. But neither Agee nor I were aware of that at the time. Hennessey seemed only too eager to help.

What did strike me during the conversation was Hennessey's obvious antipathy toward Harry Gray. Every time Gray's name came up, Hennessey winced. Apparently Gray had once been Hennessey's boss at United Technologies and the two men were not exactly the best of friends. Hennessey's mention of secret files they had each compiled on the other told us just how deep their distrust was. I thought to myself, Is this how American businessmen exert their power? Secret files? It was as though they were playing out their own corporate form of the global balance of power. First the ballistic missile. Next the antiballistic missile. Then the anti-antiballistic missile. I felt more comfortable believing the relatively tame explanation that Hennessey felt eclipsed by Gray's high profile and resented not receiving more public credit for what he felt he had accomplished. Agee and I assumed this was only added incentive for Hennessey's stepping in to help Bendix out. If Allied could walk away with a piece of Bendix and a piece of Martin Marietta, and out-smart Gray in the process, what a coup for Hennessey. Agee and Hennessey agreed to meet again.

On Saturday when I woke up, I found that I couldn't move. The hotel doctor diagnosed it as acute muscle spasms and severe stress. He asked me if anything was upsetting me. I guess you might say that. It was odd how every autumn since the famous September 24 employees' meeting at Bendix—that memorable day—something always went wrong with my health. Last year it was my back, this year my neck. The doctor's prescription: plenty of R&R. Rest and Relaxation. Sure.

Efforts to reach Pownall intensified as each day passed. "I've got to speak to Pownall," Agee told Wasserstein. "This is ridiculous. Why won't he just talk to me?" Through an intermediary, word was sent to Pownall about just how badly Agee wanted to talk. On Sunday night we were told that Pownall had finally agreed. He would meet Agee at 11 A.M. at the offices of Dewey Ballantine, Bushby Palmer & Wood, his New York law firm.

Not since the whole episode had begun had the two adversaries actually met face to face. And yet, in some curious way, they were already on intimate terms. For weeks now they had lived with each other in thought and deed, each anticipating the other's every move. The two men shook hands and then asked their attorneys to leave the room. "I want you to know I bear no malice toward you personally, Bill," Pownall said. "I know that, Tom," Agee replied. "But the situation has gotten a little out of hand. Why haven't you been willing to see me up until now?" Pownall didn't respond. "I just want you to understand, Tom, that the last thing I want is to see both our companies crippled, and I'm sure you agree." "I do," said Pownall. "If this doomsday scenario goes on," Agee continued, "that's what's going to happen to both of us." "I know," Pownall said. "Then what's holding this up? What's causing the problem?" "The problem is that we have now committed ourselves to buying Bendix, no matter what happens. We signed a commitment to that extent and now we can't go back on it." "But you forced that problem on yourself," Agee said. "And it isn't as binding as you might think. My attorneys assure me there are several legitimate ways out of that commitment, and if you're worried about being sued, the Bendix board has authorized me to tell you we'll indemnify every one of your directors. That's how certain we are your commitment is not ironclad." "I'm not sure it's as easy as that," Pownall said.

After some further discussion, the lawyers were hauled in to see if they could work something out. At the same time, Agee urged Pownall to let him fly down to Bethesda and talk to his board. "Let me at least explain to them just what I've told you," he said. Pownall didn't sound enthusiastic. "Well," he said, "I can't promise that the board will talk to you, but if you want to try, you can."

"Are you sincere in really wanting to work this out?" Agee asked. "I am." "All right, then, don't lean on a legal technicality to prevent us from working this out. You know you should never have removed the conditions in the first place, Tom. But you also know, as well as I do, there are a few conditions still there." The two men agreed to talk again the next day. "I just want you to know, Tom," Agee said just before he left, "I believe that you didn't intend for all of this to turn out as ugly as it has." "Thank you, Bill," Pownall said. "I know that you didn't either."

Agee called me at work that morning. "Either he's lying to me or he's getting some bad advice. But he did seem willing to talk, even relieved that we'd finally met." "Well, that's good," I said. "Then your visit may be worth a try."

But Agee wasn't leaving any stone unturned. Just in case Pownall wasn't serious, Agee had scheduled another meeting at the urging of Allied chairman Ed Hennessey. He wanted to make sure he had a partial white knight in the wings. Hennessey and Agee worked out the basic terms of their deal. Hennessey agreed to purchase enough of Bendix to stall Marietta. They shook hands on it and Hennessey reassured Agee of his solid track record on delivering his board's vote. The deal seemed as good as done. "I'll call you after I inform the board," Hennessey said.

Later that afternoon, Agee went to get approval from his board. He told the directors about using Allied as an "extender" and filled them in on the events of the last few days. The board gave Agee its full support. Now all that remained was to hear again from Hennessey. He'd promised to call Agee by five. At five-thirty, I came back from Seagram's to find a nervous Agee waiting by the phone. At 6 P.M., no call. Six-thirty. Still no call. Finally, at 7 P.M., someone called to tell him the news. "Allied's board turned down the deal." Agee was stunned and noticeably shaken. He couldn't believe Hennessey had deceived him like that, leading him to believe approval was virtually certain. When he finally got hold of Hennessey, he asked, "Is it true you're backing out of the deal?" "I'm afraid so, Bill," Hennessey replied. "I ran into a little buzzsaw." "Why didn't you call me when you said you would?" "Look," Hennessey said, "a controlling interest isn't what they're interested in." The picture was now becoming clear. Allied wasn't coming after a piece of Bendix. Hennessey wanted the whole thing. "When's a deal a deal, Ed? I thought we had something worked out." But Hennessey didn't respond. There was only silence on the other end.

What Agee hadn't known, of course, was that same afternoon one of Hennessey's directors, Paul Thayer (then Chairman of LTV and later Deputy Secretary of Defense) had decided to take some action of his own. According to a later SEC charge, he apparently felt confident enough that the Bendix price would soon soar that he fed inside information to colleagues. After all, any target company's stock price always surges just before it is taken over. And Bendix was clearly a target.

Time was running out. And Agee still hadn't found an extender. Let down by Hennessey, he tried his next best bet, Donald Trump. Trump was supportive and anxious to help but still wasn't sure he could come up with the funds. And Agee didn't have the time to wait. September 23 was the day Marietta could go ahead and buy Bendix and it was only forty-eight hours away. Agee started concentrating now on his only remaining option: to talk some sense into Pownall's board.

\* \* \*

It was a fitful night we had. Neither Bill nor I could sleep. "Mary?" he said to me during one of his more anxious moments. "I'm going to take Wasserstein, Fleischer and a few of the others down to Maryland with me tomorrow. Do you think you can take the day off?" I knew he might want me there. It wasn't that he really needed me with so much high-priced talent around. But my presence did seem to offer a calming influence. When I did sit in on meetings with his staff, it wasn't as a strategist that he valued me most. I functioned mainly as his sounding board. We knew the way each other thought, and often it was easier for me to understand Bill's ideas than it was for anyone else. Sometimes I knew his feelings better than I knew my own. In addition, I was no longer merely his assistant. It didn't bother me, as it certainly would have when I was working for him, to answer the phone or get him a cup of tea. I was his wife. I wanted to comfort him. Sometimes the greatest service I performed was telling him a joke, buying him some flowers, or insisting that we go outside and take a walk around the block. Did I alter the nature of the decisions he made? I doubt it. If anything, I just gave him the opportunity to air his thoughts. And in the midst of that nervous, fast-talking crowd, that was often what he needed most.

"I think I'll be able to go," I told him. "I'll check with my office in the morning."

The next morning, I told Adrianne I'd be taking two or three days of "vacation"—although I knew from the way things were going that the next three days would hardly be full of fun and relaxation.

Tuesday morning, Agee tried to firm things up with Pownall. "Tom, my primary reason for coming is to meet with your board," Agee said. "I need your word that there's a reasonable chance that I can see them. Time is precious right now, as I'm sure you know." Pownall said he understood, although he couldn't "promise" Agee the board would meet with him—"not before one or two anyway," he said. But he encouraged Bill to put his proposal in writing. "That way for certain I can discuss it with the board and it will increase the chances that they'll meet with you." Agee agreed. Pownall said a lawyer would meet us at the airport to pick up the letter as soon as we arrived.

The plane ride down was almost exhilarating. The five of us—Wasserstein, Fleischer, one of Fleischer's associates Steve Frayidin, Agee and I (McDonald stayed in New York to see if he could work things out with Trump)—invested all our hopes in this meeting with Pownall. Finally, maybe, Agee would get them to back down. After all, what did they have to lose? A friendly merger with Bendix was surely better than the "unthinkable," in which both companies bit the dust. Our spirits were so high there was bound to be a crash. But we didn't sense it then. All we did was get busy writing the letter to the Martin Marietta board. We needed to put the indemnification proposal in writing. "It must be nice to have a wife who does more than cook," Wasserstein said as he had on several occasions when he'd seen me pitch in—Bruce Wasserstein's late awakening to feminism. To these men, the fact that I did more than straighten Agee's ties seemed like cause for celebration.

We landed at Washington's National Airport at noon. Jamie, the head driver for the Bendix Aerospace Division, and a man whose loyalty had won him Agee's trust, drove us to a Marriott Hotel in nearby Bethesda, a few miles from Martin Marietta headquarters. The first thing we did was rent two typewriters and have a secretary type up the letter to Pownall. Just before Agee signed it I noticed the letter had a terrible typo. "Any decision by your directors must clearly balance the benefits of our proposal against the enormous risk of *not* working together." Except that the "not" was left out so that it read "...the enormous risk of working together." In battles such as these, lesser errors are known to have set off World War III. A lawyer from Martin Marietta was dispatched to pick up the corrected letter.

In the meantime, we sat and watched the clock. Time moved slowly. The ice melted as we sipped our watery Cokes. Every time the phone rang, all of us jumped. We hoped it would be Pownall, but twice we were disappointed. "This is room service. Can we bring you more ice?" the first caller said. Or, "This is to let you know there's flamenco dancing tonight in the Moonraker Lounge upstairs."

Finally, at 1:45 P.M., the phone rang; it was an aide to Pownall. "Mr. Agee? This is Mr. Pownall's corporate secretary. Mr. Pownall asked me to tell you the board is still deliberating and it will be a while." More idle time. At 2:15 P.M. the phone rang again. "I'm sorry, Mr. Agee, but the jury is still out," the secretary said. "Well, could you tell the jury their star witness is eager to testify?" "I'll relay the message, sir." A little after 2:30 P.M. Pownall got on the line. "Bill, I'm sorry it took me so long," he said. "Is the board still in session?" Agee asked. "No, I'm afraid they've adjourned." "Adjourned? But I need to speak to them." "I'm sorry. They decided 'unconditional' is 'unconditional,' and they don't feel we can afford to back off now." "Tom, I can't believe you're doing this," Agee said. "You know that our lawyers can work something out." "Well, if you want, you can come down anyway. I'll talk with you here."

Agee was alarmed. Time was running out. Fleischer was geared up to explain several ways around the "unconditional" problem. He was upset. We all were. But we had come this far and weren't going to give up yet. The five of us got in the car and were driven to headquarters.

Pownall was especially gracious when we arrived. We didn't know it at the time but his board, at the urging of his advisers, had previously refused to let him meet with Agee. He must have felt sheepish for having us come this far, so he was especially solicitous. "It's nice to see you again, Mary," he said, shaking my hand and giving me a pat on the shoulder. He shook Agee's hand. "Why don't you folks use this office," Pownall said, ushering Wasserstein, Fleischer and me into a conference room, "and Bill and I will talk in here." I went off to the ladies room, but when I returned, I saw a disquieting thing. There was Wasserstein, our investment banker, laughing it up with Marty Siegel, the key architect of the Martin Marietta counteroffensive. The two of them looked like schoolboys chortling over a bad joke. I would have preferred it if they didn't seem to be enjoying themselves so much. There wasn't much for the rest of us to do while Pownall and Agee negotiated. We drank Cokes. We looked out the window. We tried to remain calm. I had the sinking feeling we were wasting our time. By midnight tomorrow, Martin Marietta would be able to buy Bendix stock, and that would be it. The "unthinkable" would have happened.

I looked at Wasserstein. "Bruce. Is this meeting for real?" I was hoping for reassurance. "Maybe we should get Agee out. At least in New York, he could be working on finding another extender," I said. "You never know,"

Wasserstein said, looking sheepish. "Maybe he'll be able to work a miracle." It didn't seem like it. At 4:30 P.M., Agee called Fleischer in. Several times in the next hour, Fleischer went back and forth. "Anything going on in there?" I asked. "I don't think so," Fleischer said. He looked tired. At five, after a brief discussion, Wasserstein and I finally suggested that Fleischer go and get Agee out of there if nothing was happening. Fleischer said he'd take a reading. At 5:30 P.M., he persuaded Agee to leave. Agee and Pownall had spoken politely to each other but nothing of substance had been done. We said our good-byes and piled back into the car.

All the way to the airport, Wasserstein and Fleischer kept stating how "absurd," how "irrational" the situation was. Agee asked to stop the car. "I can't believe this," he said. "There must be something we can do to stop this mess. Driver, is there a place where we can use a phone?" The Martin Marietta driver pulled up beside a gas station. The five of us got out. We walked up a grassy hill and conferred. "I think we should go back," Agee said to Fleischer. He continued, "If they're really serious that it's just that 'unconditional' provision that's holding them back, then we should be able to convince them that we can take care of that. Let's go back." But then he posed the question, "What if they're only using that as an excuse?" Fleischer replied, "It's our only chance." What did we have to lose? Besides, I remembered what Wasserstein had said. Agee had been known to work miracles.

Back into the car. Back down the expressway. Back to Martin Marietta headquarters. Agee had phoned Pownall to let him know we were returning. Wasserstein, Fleischer, Frayidin and I filed back into our waiting room. Agee and Pownall went into Pownall's office. Hours passed. We were hungry. No one had eaten since noon. Time was running out and Agee still didn't have a great extender. Someone brought in some sandwiches and potato chips. At 10:15 P.M., a weary-looking Agee emerged. Thumbs down. No miracles here. But the door wasn't closed yet. The two men had decided to prolong their agony. A phone talk was scheduled for 11 A.M. the next morning. I started to really wonder if Pownall was just toying with Agee.

It was after midnight when we arrived back in New York. The mood was grim. As exhilarated as we'd been on the plane ride down, that's how depressed we felt now. No one said anything. We all just went our separate ways and went to bed.

The next morning McDonald told Agee that Hennessey had been trying to reach him all day. Now it was feeding time, and the sharks, smelling blood, moved in for the kill. Still red-eyed and exhausted from the night before, I was drinking coffee when Hennessey walked in. "Your boss mind you taking time off like this?" he teasingly asked. It was after ten. "I've taken a few days off as vacation time," I said. "Some vacation," he said. Well, at least we agreed on that point. Agee came in and the two men started to talk. Agee was in trouble now and Hennessey knew it. At midnight tonight Martin Marietta was going to go ahead and purchase the Bendix stock. That meant the "unthinkable" would take place. The two companies would own each other and, at great expense, the courts would figure out who owed what to whom. Pownall was scheduled to call at eleven but Agee no longer had much hope there. Besides, it was already 11:15 A.M. And no other extenders had come through. There was only one way out, and that was the solution he'd been pondering for the last few days—to sell Bendix.

How devastating it seemed, to give up the company in which he had invested eleven years of his career and an immeasurable part of his soul. And yet now it was his only rational choice. If any good was going to come out of any of this, it would have to be by following this route. At least this way, the shareholders would benefit.

"I'll buy your aerospace group," Hennessey said. But selling off Bendix's "crown jewels" wasn't in line with Agee's thought. "No," Agee replied. "In case you've already forgotten, I'm not about to sit back and see Bendix dismembered." They continued to talk, but after a few minutes, Agee asked Hennessey if he'd excuse him for a moment. "I'd like to talk to Mary and Al in the other room." Wasserstein and Fleischer looked up. No one was certain what would happen next.

McDonald and I followed Agee into the other room. "We're down to two undesirable alternatives," Agee began. "Either Marietta buys us and the two companies are crippled, with horns locked in legal battles for the foreseeable future, or we agree to de-escalate this war and sell Bendix. No one else seems able to do anything to forestall the former. I believe it's up to us. At least the company will remain intact and the stockholders will make a profit. But the company won't be under our management. Of course you know what this means?" he said, looking at Al. "Both our jobs will be in jeopardy." Al nodded. "And the strategy that we've worked on so hard—" and here he nodded at me—"won't be in our hands." "I know," I said. He was trying to console us, although I knew the person who felt most hurt was he. I wanted to tell him, "You don't have to be so strong,

Bill. You're allowed to give in to your feelings," but I saw that he had already allowed himself the luxury. All three of us had tears in our eyes. McDonald grabbed Agee's arm and then Agee grabbed mine. There was a moment of silence we all understood. "All right," he said and we followed him out of the room.

"Okay," Agee said to Hennessey. "Let's talk." For the next forty minutes they wrangled over prices. Hennessey tried to bring his bid down to $65 or $70 for the remaining shares of Bendix, but Agee moved him up to $80. Hennessey also assured Agee he'd be the number two man in the new, combined company. Agee seemed less than convinced on this latter point because of the way Hennessey had handled their earlier so-called "deal." The two men shook on the present deal pending the approval of their boards—at which point Agee interjected, "Is this really a deal or are you presenting it to your board like you did the last time?" "No, this is for real," Hennessey replied. "And are you serious about wanting me as Allied's president or is this just a formality to complete the deal?" "No, I'm absolutely serious," Hennessey said. "I've watched you work and I recognize that you have incredible talent, the kind we need. Bendix is one of the best-managed companies in the country and we intend to capitalize on your expertise. It'll be a huge asset for Allied to have you on its side." "And you're certain that Bendix will be kept intact, that the company won't be dismembered?" "I have no plans to dismember Bendix." "Okay," Agee said, and the two men shook hands again. Agee stiffly walked Hennessey to the door.

The assumption was that Allied would buy up both Bendix and Martin Marietta and in that way call off the war. "What do you think of the price?" Agee asked me after Hennessey left. "It's fair," I said. I knew Agee had gotten top dollar for Bendix stock. "Do you think he meant what he said about not breaking up the company?" he asked me. "I don't know about that," I answered. "How about making me number two?" Agee asked. "You know he is an *ex*-seminarian." "When someone says that," I said, winking at Bill, "I start reaching for my wallet."

There was still a slim chance that Agee and Pownall could work something out, but Agee doubted it. It was 11:45 when Hennessey left, and still no word from Pownall. I couldn't stand to watch my husband wait like that any more. At 12:15 Pownall finally called, but he had little of substance to say. "All right, Tom," Agee said, his voice determined. "I've decided to go ahead with other options now."

Now it was time to sell the board on the Allied deal. Agee knew this wasn't going to be easy. The last time he'd met with the board, two days earlier, he'd talked about Allied as "a great extender," someone who was going to buy a piece of Bendix in order to forestall the Marietta deal. Now he had to sell them on the idea of *selling* all of Bendix. "We have a proposition from Allied to buy our entire company," he began. "At this time I believe it's the best we can do. This is clearly not the alternative I had in mind, but I think at this point it's the most intelligent move we can make."

The board was clearly stunned. None of them had lived through the nightmarish ups and downs of the last forty-eight hours. They didn't know that Hennessey had welshed on the first Allied deal or that Pownall and his board had probably been stalling for time. The last time they saw Agee he was rushing down to Maryland, full of confidence he could win over the hearts and minds of the Marietta board. Now they had to get used to the idea that there weren't any options left. Except to sell all of Bendix. "What the hell is going on?" Tavoulareas wanted to know. Tavoulareas was famous for his hard-nosed approach. Agee had anticipated his unwillingness to adapt to the new circumstances. He had known that Mobil had lost two other acquisition attempts in the recent past. Both the Marathon Oil and the Conoco take-over attempts had been unsuccessful, and Tavoulareas wasn't about to be party to a third. "Why are you giving up?" Tavoulareas demanded. "Why the change of heart?" Rumsfeld joined in.

In his usual patient and candid manner, Agee enumerated on the events of the previous two days, explaining why the Allied deal was the only choice left. "My God," Hugo Uyterhoeven said. "I was just getting used to the idea of having Allied buy a piece of us, and now we're losing the whole company?" "Why not just let Marietta go ahead and buy us," one of the directors suggested. "Let them drag us into court. Who cares? We'll fight to the end." Now they were talking like the military men. "What would be the point?" Agee said. "It would only hurt both companies worse. This way, at least the Bendix shareholders will do extremely well and the employees will benefit from their company's remaining intact."

"But how will it look to everyone? People will think we lost," Rumsfeld said. The Washington contingent was always concerned about image. "I'm not sure we have the luxury of worrying about that," Agee said. And Hugo. Dear Hugo. A professor at heart, he was hoping for more time. Perhaps a study or two to lay things out. "We don't have any more time," Agee said. "We don't even have another few hours, let alone a few weeks. Marietta's going to buy at midnight, and unless we sell to Allied, both companies will be locked into a losing battle." There was more heated discussion. But it was hard for the board to adjust. They hadn't spent the past few days living the nightmare as Agee had. And they hadn't had time to get used to the idea—not that Agee really had either. "I think we'd like to meet alone," Rumsfeld said to Agee. "All right," Agee said. "Why don't the outside directors go into the other room." Tavoulareas, Rumsfeld, Uyterhoeven, Scott, Stafford, Jack Fontaine and Wilbur Cohen went into the other room. The inside directors—Agee, McDonald, Bill Purple (head of the aerospace group), Hartz (head of Fram) and Searby (head of the industrial group)—stayed where they were. After fifteen minutes, the outside directors returned. "Okay," Agee said. "It's time to vote. We've got to be on the street with this by four P.M. or four-thirty P.M. The ayes?" Scott, Stafford, Fontaine, McDonald, Purple, Hartz and Searby raised their hands. "The nays?" Tavoulareas, Rumsfeld and Uyterhoeven. Cohen abstained. "All right," Agee said. "Let's get the release written up. McDonald, you call PR."

Agee went to get his note pad when Rumsfeld walked up to him. "Bill, a few of us would like to see you alone for a minute." Cohen, Uyterhoeven and Tavoulareas were behind him. "We just can't go along with what's happened. I think, in light of the outcome, we're going to resign." Great. Just when the game was getting toughest for Bill, part of the team walks away. "Well, if that's the decision you have to make, that's the decision. I'm sorry you feel that way. Is that it?" "That's it," Rumsfeld said. There wasn't even a handshake. The four directors left the room.

The rest of the afternoon was spent picking up the pieces. Wasserstein and Fleischer made their calls. People who understood all that had happened congratulated Bill. After all, in the midst of this, he'd managed to negotiate one of the best deals for Bendix shareholders in history and prevented the company from being carved up.

Bill arrived back in the hotel room about five-thirty. For the first time in weeks, it was just the two of us alone. Empty Coke bottles. Wads of paper. And all those empty chairs scattered around the room. "Maybe we ought to go upstairs and see how McDonald's doing," Agee said. "I know he's hurting." "I'll go up and talk to him," I said. I watched my husband try to carry on as usual. But I was starting to understand his ways. This was his method of coping. He would worry about Al so he wouldn't have to think about his own feelings. Cheer the team on so the leader doesn't collapse. I started to go up to see Al, but he came down to our suite first. We tried to talk for a while and then he went back to his room.

Bill sat in his chair, staring into space. "Well, look," he said. "I did the best I could. I ask myself 'Can I face myself in the morning?' and I think I can. What I did, I did for the right reasons even if the press tries to brand me as having lost. I made the only choice I could." I wanted to hug him but just at that moment Wasserstein and Fleischer came trooping into the room. There were a few business matters to attend to. And some phone calls to make. Someone offered to order up a bottle of champagne. The adrenalin had finally subsided. All I felt was exhaustion. And when it passed I knew the depression would set in.

It was a busy night at Martin Marietta headquarters. Tom Pownall entertained more than one visitor. Chairman

Hennessey had brought along one outside director in whom he had a special confidence, Paul Thayer, the chairman and chief executive of LTV. They had flown this mission together on LTV's corporate jet with the hopes of returning with Martin Marietta as part of the Allied empire. But well into the next morning, Hennessey and Pownall finally struck a deal whereby Allied would have to give Marietta its freedom in exchange for the Bendix shares. In effect, Allied would own Bendix but Marietta would go free.

That same morning Hennessey met Bill in his office. "Guess what," he said to Bill. "Martin Marietta went ahead and bought." "What?" Agee asked. "They went ahead and bought Bendix shares anyway last night." Agee's assumption had been that once Allied bought Bendix, Martin Marietta would drop its bid and Allied would make an attempt to buy both firms. But that was not the case. Marietta went ahead at midnight, just as planned, and bought a block of Bendix. After all, not to have gone ahead would have made their original argument sound flimsy.

Shortly after that meeting Al McDonald convinced Bill and me to return to Michigan and to join him and several guests for dinner with Jimmy Carter. It was such a pleasant evening that it felt out of context. I was struck by Carter's compassion about our most recent treatment by the press. After all he was the devoted husband of Rosalynn Carter, who had been criticized for being "assertive" during Carter's tenure in the White House. The press had made more than a few caustic comments like "Wonder who wears the pants in that house," etcetera. A certain element just didn't seem to like the combination of strong women and strong men.

As a curious epilogue to the whole event, a familiar name appeared in the newspapers the next day. On September 24, 1982 (September 24 seemed to be my lucky day), *The Wall Street Journal* carried a collection of letters from around the world about the Bendix-Martin Marietta affair. The article was illustrated with a picture of four sharks biting each other's tails. One of the letters was from a man named Robert W. Purcell, who described himself as a retired business consultant and former director of the Bendix Corporation. In the letter, Purcell wrote, "I think Martin Marietta has conducted itself well. They haven't dragged the Mary Cunningham business into it, and all of their actions have been taken in quiet dignity in defense of the corporation. I don't think anybody would want to be taken over by Bill Agee." Another statesmanlike message from Purcell.

But if Martin Marietta didn't drag my name into it, other people couldn't resist the temptation. *The Wall Street Journal* printed an article containing a headline "Mary Cunningham's Advice" and went on not only to have me in on the negotiations between Pownall and Agee, but actually cited me as one of the three reasons the deal blew up! *Time* and *Newsweek* and other magazines apparently bought that slant and ran with similar interpretations. In a major profile on Bill, the *Washington Post* went so far as to say, "Officials close to Martin Marietta reportedly resented Cunningham's involvement, and some of Agee's associates were embarrassed at Cunningham's presence then and her visibility in subsequent interviews."

To his credit, Pownall, who in fact, did not drag my name into the fray, issued a public release the next morning vehemently denying the *Post*'s assertion: "Most emphatically Miss Cunningham's presence was *not* an irritant to Martin Marietta, and her presence, alongside her husband, Mr. Agee, the Bendix chairman, did *not* contribute in any manner to the failure of Bendix and Martin Marietta to reach agreement. . . . Everyone present on both sides behaved professionally and with total propriety and civility. . . . It was apparent that Mr. Agee took some comfort from his wife's presence but not then or later did any of us find that to be either irritating or curious. . . . It strikes us as most unfortunate, when so many substantive issues are at stake, that your readers with an interest in the case might be led to believe that personalities could affect the outcome. . . . Miss Cunningham's presence definitely was not an obstacle. Anyone who purports to speak for Martin Marietta and conveys any different impression is not in possession of the facts." Yet another insight into what the press refers to as its "freedom."

The publicity in the aftermath of the Martin Marietta affair was enormous, and most of it was bad. Reporters got on the bandwagon and were routinely critical of Bill. There were pictures of him on a fishhook and implications that it was his egomania that was at fault. Was it less egomaniacal of Pownall to fight to the finish? Was it less egomaniacal of Hennessey or Gray to jump in when they smelled blood? At least Bill was able to get his own ego out of the way long enough to do what was best for his shareholders. Would any of the other executives have been capable of giving up their chairmanship to keep their company intact?

But the crowning blow in all of this was the interview in *People* magazine to be featured on their "Couples" page. We'd spoken to a reporter there on the explicit condition that the interview not run until well after the delicate Allied-Bendix deal was voted on by shareholders, which was to take place the end of January. We were enraged to find out that the magazine intended to run the story before the year was out, and to add insult to injury they had decided to make us "The Most Intriguing Couple of the Year." A phone call to the editor to see if there was some misunderstanding on my agreement with their reporter only resulted in a barrage of accusations: "Don't you believe in freedom of the press? You're trying to manipulate the news." And so on. I'd fallen for it again.

The latest attacks on Bill only reinforced our understanding of each other's role as victims. His experience during the Martin Marietta episode was no less distressing than the one I'd gone through at Bendix two years before. In some grim way we were both paying our dues. But we were never quite sure what for. And yet, Bill had a natural resiliency. Both he and I were learning to take things more in stride. "I've been a golden boy for so long, I figured I was bound to take a beating one of these days." But the curious thing about all this grief was that it seemed to be having quite another effect: it was welding us together. Like tempered steel, we were a fortified unit. We had each lost—and gained—many allies in our various bouts with publicity and with life, but in the end, we had earned each other's trust and respect.

Now when reporters mentioned my name, Bill spoke out with pride. No longer did he try to skirt the issue or find a suitable phrase. In an interview in one newspaper, he spoke about my participation in the Martin Marietta affair in these terms: "During this situation, and during all the time that Mary and I have been together," he said, "she has been one of those people who is totally intellectually honest. She's always candid with me. She has great skills. Therefore I would be foolish not to have her be one of my key advisers." When hoping to find a new controversy one reporter asked if this statement contradicted mine about serving primarily as a spouse, Agee pointed out that spouse and adviser need not be mutually exclusive roles. And when asked about our future, he comfortably said, "Our long-term dream is to work together...."

It turned out that several of Hennessey's executives knew what they were saying when they warned that Allied's chairman would not tolerate a strong number two man—certainly not someone as strong as Agee. In February 1983, only two days after Bendix shareholders had voted in favor of the deal, Hennessey let Al McDonald go as Bendix president. Agee was next, only a day or two later. All the time he'd been reassuring Agee that he was intended for the number two job. And yet, even as they were mapping out plans for Agee as Allied's new president, Hennessey had an executive search underway to find someone to replace him. Once Bill learned the truth, he resigned on February 8, effective June 1.

For the first time in twenty years, Bill was on his own. He knew instinctively what he wanted to do. A company we had formed as a partnership to engage in venture capital and strategic consulting activities was the perfect opportunity. He was now ready to devote himself full time as chief executive officer to a private company whose politics were friendly and whose media profile was relatively low. We knew that in time I would join him. And, in fact, in October 1983, I did, after fulfilling my agreement to Seagram's to see implemented my worldwide wine strategy.

We incorporated our partnership as Semper Enterprises; *semper* means "always" in Latin. Chairman and

Chief Executive Officer, William Joseph Agee. President and Chief Operating Officer, Mary Elizabeth Cunningham. I told Bill if he didn't behave I'd make him my executive assistant for a while.

# CHAPTER TWELVE

*I* *can't tell you how* many times in the last three and a half years I've thought, If only I hadn't gone to work at Bendix, or, If only I hadn't stayed past June, none of this would have happened. Maybe I'd be at Morgan Stanley, working as an investment banker. Who knows? One thing is for certain, though, I'd have my privacy and I wouldn't have the terrible nightmares I still have whenever the 24th of September rolls around.

They say suffering makes you wiser, but I'm not so sure. How much more guarded I am now. There was a period—it lasted for at least two years—when I didn't trust anyone. And in some ways that even applied to Bill. I kept waiting for a second Bendix. Would he say he'd stand by me and then, at the last minute, not come through again? I kept testing him, scrutinizing his every act. I'm sure I wasn't the easiest person to live with throughout all those times.

And the bitterness. That is almost the worst part of it. It doesn't make life pleasant for you or those around you to walk around angry all the time. Angry at everyone. At the people who used me as a scapegoat. At the people who knew better but deserted me anyway. At the people who, not even knowing me, swallowed the media's point of view. And the press. How odd to have a personality and a history forced on you. People who have never even met me feel they know what I'm like. You spend hours explaining away a version of yourself that isn't true. And being blind-sided that badly shakes your confidence to the core. Jealously you cling to your privacy and act as if you are always on guard. A car slows down beside us in traffic and I ask Bill, "Is that a photographer?" Would I be this paranoid had Bendix not been a part of my life?

But I did go to work at Bendix and I did stay beyond the point where I should have, and although I consider it the worst ordeal of my life, there is some good that's come out of it. I may not be a happier person but I am a stronger one. I may not be as optimistic but I am more practical. I learned some valuable lessons from the experience. Perhaps, in some ways, they were the very lessons I needed most to learn.

I wasn't very savvy when I first went to work for Bendix. Oh, I was intelligent, and like most of my classmates at the Business School, ambitious, but I lacked any real know-how about how the corporate world operates. What I knew about the world and people I'd learned from reading Plato and Thomas Aquinas. A crash course in Machiavelli might have been more relevant.

Who was I when I walked into Bendix in June of 1979? I was a twenty-eight-year-old female, a Phi Beta Kappa graduate of Wellesley, with an MBA from Harvard. I was also young, attractive, Catholic and married to a black. All those things influenced the way people viewed me, and had I been more aware of any of them, I might have been more aware of the need to protect myself. But I was young and I was a woman, and for all my well-trained poise, I lacked confidence. So eager was I to prove to everyone else that I could do the job that I hardly stopped to consider that it was my very competence that threatened them. I'd walk into a meeting, notebook and pencil in hand, and in my very businesslike manner, start talking about market shares and P/E ratios. This didn't win me points. In retrospect I might have been better off had I tried to crack a few jokes.

In addition, I was extremely naive about my position as a woman. It never occurred to me that anyone would think that I would do anything as scandalous as sleep my way to the top. Mary Cunningham? Saint Mary of Hanover High? I was in awe of Agee. I never looked at him as a man. He was my boss!

The irony is that had I really been having an affair with Agee I probably would have been much more careful about covering my tracks. As it was, it never occurred to me not to ride in the same limousine with him, not to spend late nights at the office alone with him, not to check in at the same hotel with him. I was too busy thinking about my work, too immersed in solving the business matters at hand to pay much attention to appearances. And how could I pay attention to them when having an affair with Agee was one of the furthest things from my mind?

Another fatal error was that I answered only to Agee. As his executive assistant, I had one major priority, and that was to prove myself to Bill Agee. I was loyal to a fault. I thought only about helping the chairman. How many times did I go into a meeting with Bill, and because my job was to make the chairman look good, not raise my hand when I had a good idea? I'd wait until after the meeting and offer my suggestions to Bill. Then, at the next meeting, when he'd make them, everyone would say,

"Brilliant!" People would praise Bill and Bill would praise me. That's how it worked. The problem with such a system was that it didn't let other people at Bendix know just how much work I did. In the end, when I most needed outside support, I didn't have it.

In retrospect, that was part of the inherent problem of being mentored. My fortunes were inextricably tied to Bill's. If he fell, I went too. Conversely, his survival didn't necessarily insure mine. And part of the problem was that I didn't work at cultivating other friends, other allies, other people in positions of power. I figured allies would come in good time—naturally—and I assumed other women executives would automatically support each other. I wasn't prepared for the kind of rivalry the Queen Bee syndrome instills, or, for that matter, I didn't stop to think about the resentment or insecurity that an executive's wife can feel when her husband comes home raving about his savvy, younger female executive assistant. I think, as a woman, I was naive about this. I didn't understand the art of power politics, where the good guys don't always win. Instead, I viewed myself as a latter-day Joan of Arc, rather than someone who was shrewdly assessing her way to the top.

I made other errors, too. Probably my biggest error was ignoring all the warning signals in the name of duty or loyalty. Often I return in my mind to the scene of the crime and go over the clues. It should have been clear to me, from my very first interviews at Bendix, that Bill Agee did not have a loyal staff on his side. With four of the five men I interviewed obviously hostile to me from the start, what made me think I could survive in such an unfriendly environment? Worse yet, what made me think I could change it?

Oh, I had my doubts. I remember feeling ill in the corridor of Bendix that first day and wanting to go home. But somehow the desire to overcome the obstacles, to prove myself to Bill Agee, drove me on. I thought, as so many women in business do, that I could get people to like me. That was my mistake. It's power that wins in business, not friendly smiles, although they help.

But then what about the second unmistakable sign, the anonymous letters? It was early in the summer when Agee first told me about those. Why didn't I leave then? I knew that the atmosphere at Bendix was tense. And I knew that someone was going to get burned. Didn't I realize it might be me? I did, and then, too, I considered leaving. My mother urged me to, and even Father Bill agreed. But I declined. Bill Agee told me he needed me, and that was all I needed to hear. Everything I'd been taught as a Catholic and as a woman—to stick close when the chips are down, to help, to endure—convinced me not to leave. Would a man have made a similar decision? Would a man have been so grandiose and at the same time so naive?

It is interesting to me and, in retrospect, instructive, that when Bill Agee was in a similar situation, he did not stay. He was working for his mentor, Bob Hansberger, at Boise-Cascade. The company wasn't doing well and it was clear that another, more powerful executive was posturing for Hansberger's job. Bill observed the signals, saw what was coming and opted out. At first I thought this was disloyal, but when I thought about it further, it made perfect sense. "It wouldn't have done Hansberger any good if I'd stayed," Bill told me. "The only thing that would have happened had I stayed was that we'd both have gone down." And, in retrospect, my staying at Bendix certainly didn't do anyone much good. Part of the problem, I think, is the different ways in which Bill and I—in which men and women—view their careers. Bill was interested in helping Hansberger, no doubt, but up to a point. Always he kept an eye on his own career. I viewed serving Bill as an end in itself and mistakenly viewed this as the means to best further my career.

Women, for whatever reasons, biological or cultural, have learned to act as nurturers. The emphasis for us has been more on people. For men, the emphasis has been more on careers. I'm quite content being a nurturer and believing in so many of those human values commonly attributed to women. But applied in the corporate world, these same values can work against us—unless we are careful. And I wasn't careful enough.

Bo and I used to debate which was more difficult, being a woman in business or being a black? Both had their ups and downs. In a way it's easier being a woman; at least men have had the experience of having dealt with women, whereas it's unlikely that many top male executives even know many blacks. On the other hand, the black is free to cut his own mold; the woman has the problem of stereotypes.

I became one the minute I walked through the door of Bendix. The fact that I had achieved some credibility and was physically attractive played into people's worst insecurities and awakened their more suspicious instincts. Sometimes the easiest outlet for jealousy is the old stereotype, "Oh, she must be where she is because she's sleeping with the boss." But what if I hadn't been attractive? I doubt I would have fared much better. One smart comment out of my mouth, and I would have immediately slipped into another convenient category—the pushy

"Harvard Business School bitch." It's hard to win. There just aren't many positive stereotypes around for businesswomen, and certainly not for women who are both intelligent and attractive.

Part of the problem, I think, is that women aren't taught the things they need in the business world. We're taught about virtue, not about power; about goodness, not about strength. The role models we have growing up—saints and the heroines of nineteenth-century novels—are concerned almost exclusively with doing good. In the end they triumph, but usually in a spiritual or emotional sense. I'm not sure even the Blessed Mother would have gotten very far at Bendix.

Men seem intuitively to take a more practical approach. Many care about being "right," but they also want to get the job done. And they don't view defeat as anything glorious no matter how noble the cause. I'm not sure one would want to trade pragmatism for virtue, but a harmonious blend might do some good. Perhaps as more women enter and succeed at business, they will care more about practicality, and men will care more about doing good.

It would be easier to dismiss what happened to me if I didn't know it was happening to other women. Granted, their experiences haven't made national headlines. Yet they too are working late nights at the office. They too are trying to be "friends" in the old boys' network sense. And they too, when they are finally promoted to positions of real power, are being accused of sleeping their way to the top.

It's such a vicious accusation—at least it was to me—that it's almost impossible to answer. It's one of the most effective ways in which a professional woman can be, to use a familiar phrase, rendered ineffective. It's the ultimate weapon. Fortunately, one thing that helped me throughout all of this was that I never doubted either my ethics or my capability. I knew that I had been faithful to my value system and that I was plenty competent. And I had the credentials and track record to prove it. But what about women who don't have that backup? What about all those who find themselves similarly accused, and who panic and start to question their own self-worth? I know they exist. I've received letters from literally thousands of them. In almost every case it's the outline of the same story: "I had to leave my job because people made it impossible for me to function by suggesting that I was having an affair with my boss. It wasn't true, of course, but I lost so much credibility from the rumors that I just couldn't continue."

I shudder to think how many women like that there are. Their plight is especially dangerous now, during this transition period, in which the corporate environment is just starting to adjust to the shock of having professional women around. As the number grows and the promotions to greater power increase, the situation will have to improve. But in the meantime, caution will have to be the watchword.

And yet, the situation won't really improve until men and women are given the freedom to be friends in the same comfortable way that men are with men. Instead of there being an "old boys' network," what's so terribly wrong with an "old people's network"? Men and women can close deals on golf courses just as successfully as men and men can. In fact, it's critical that men and women be allowed to be friends in an utterly nonsexual way in order for women to contribute on an equal footing in the corporate world. Unless and until professional women are allowed to use all the same legitimate methods for influence and promotion as their male counterparts, they will be unable to rise to their proper status.

In time, the male-female executive team will no longer be such a rarity, and the mere fact of a man and woman working together or befriending each other won't be occasion for notice or alarm. People will become more sophisticated. Late nights at the office between members of the opposite sex won't be an invitation for gossip and scandal. In retrospect, the suspicions people had about Bill and me already seem a trifle anachronistic, but in 1980 they certainly didn't read that way at all.

The fact is that Bill and I eventually did fall in love, which, I think, is something else that will happen more frequently as more women move up the ranks. Men and women who work together *will* fall in love. And why should this surprise anyone? People who work together come to know each other in a way that is far more meaningful by most standards than meeting in a singles bar. To put these people off limits to one another is unrealistic. And to presume that such romances are "not worthy of truly ambitious women," as one popular magazine would suggest, is an affront to love based on mutual admiration and respect.

And when business colleagues do eventually marry, people still tend to view this situation with dismay. "How do you expect a husband and wife to work together without letting personal issues get in the way?" Or, on a more practical plane, "How can he talk to her about contracts when all morning they've argued about her burning the toast?" This is an unfortunate corollary to the medieval notion that as soon as two people start sleeping together, one or both suddenly lose their judgment. I'm not so sure this is true, which may be sad for romance, but helps considerably in business.

That problems can ensue within a corporation because of these romantic liaisons must be admitted. But those can be solved with a little creativity and ingenuity. And it is possible to balance both dimensions as long as a couple adopt certain considerate ways—such as no longer functioning as husband and wife the minute they walk through the corporate door. Bill and I have adopted this approach on our current projects, and, with few exceptions, it works well. And it actually allows us to devote more time to our jobs. If we weren't working on some of the same projects, I think one or the other of us would eventually start to resent the hours the other spends at work. Working together isn't for every couple any more than it has been for every father and son. But for those who work well together, it shouldn't be denied them on the grounds of nepotism.

There is another lesson I learned, but it doesn't relate specifically to the world of men and women at work. It has to do with the media, in particular the press, and the way its exercise of freedom can affect people's lives.

When you've been hurt, the tendency is to generalize. Since I was hurt by the press, my tendency, for a long time, was to view the press as one evil monolithic force. But the press is not The Press. Even calling it "the press" makes it too easy to generalize about its behavior. The press is an industry composed of individuals—many who are talented and some who are not, many who are humane and some who are not, many who are ethical—and some who decidedly are not. In this respect the press is hardly unique. Every industry and organization has its weak links.

But what is perhaps unique about the press, and therefore worthy of critical note, is that it is the only institution in this country today that is not held accountable by any other authoritative body. No one in government, business or even the clergy dares to criticize it for fear of the repercussions. Even as I write this book, I'm made aware of who will be writing the reviews. I'm reminded, "Who wants to get on the wrong side of a media giant?" As a strategic planner, I have to worry about any industry that has no mechanism for objectively monitoring and correcting abuses—except itself.

Of course, the wronged party always has the recourse of going to court. But if you're that wronged party, and you've already been maligned by the press, you're not likely to risk further exposure by asking for a trial. Not to mention the fact that defending one's honor in a courtroom can be a mighty expensive effort—one that is easily thwarted when matched against the net worth of America's leading media empires.

But it is still legally true that as a private citizen there are limits to what the press can print about you. Even if the laws are weighted more to protect the freedom of the press than your right to privacy, there are still laws. And yet, the Catch-22 is that although I was a private citizen when my whole ordeal began, my very presence in the press, day after day, turned me into a "public person" almost overnight—which meant I soon was considered fair game. Only most people don't understand just how *un*fair that game can be. For once you've been made into a public figure you can win a libel suit only if you are able to prove "actual malice" on the part of the publication. That means knowledge of falsity or reckless disregard to whether a statement is true or false. Mere inaccuracy isn't enough. So what if a newspaper says you're a slut on page one. The reporter "didn't mean any harm." And, after all, one of those mysterious "unnamed sources close to the situation" said so. Just as easy as that, the reporter is off the hook. He doesn't even have to divulge his unnamed source who has just undermined your career and reputation.

Who are these individual journalists? They purport to be my "protector" or "the defenders of my freedom of speech." But I never elected them. I never even hired them. The unflattering truth is that newspapers are made up of editors and reporters, and these professionals, like any other human beings, have personal prejudices, cultural hangups and plain old-fashioned blind spots. The difference, of course, is the weight of impact that their bias or error can have. In business I've found that a personal bias often shows up in red ink on the bottom line. But too often in the press, the same bias shows up as a promotion to the ambitious reporter for writing "good copy."

Perhaps I'd feel a little more comfortable if the press—especially the less responsible element in it—would just admit to being a business. I know that doesn't sit well with those in the profession who prefer to duck behind slogans about serving as the watchdog for First Amendment freedoms. But despite these noble objectives, they are still in business—with profit-and-loss statements—just like any other commercial concern. A more honest appraisal of their profession would show that they live and die by the same rules of business as everyone else. Bonuses and promotions are in the not-so-long run still tied to higher circulation and larger advertising revenues. If it's "true," that's nice, but if it "sells," that's even better.

So whose business is it anyway? The growth of the mass media at this time seems to have caused a certain blurring between people's public and private lives. In two minutes, 200 million people learned that Thomas Eagleton had seen a psychiatrist—a fact that overnight cost him the Democratic vice presidential nomination. Think of what would have happened to Abraham Lincoln had one of his letters to Ann Rutledge, in which he admitted being from time to time "depressed," been so publicized? The result is that too often the most banal, wooden, one-dimensional people are the ones who seem to survive the publicity campaign. And who are the people who, therefore, win elections today? Not necessarily the best and the brightest, but those who are well versed in handling the media: actors, professional politicians and astronauts. The statesman who may thoroughly understand the issues or who sticks strictly to the matter of running the country doesn't fare nearly so well. In the post-Woodstein era, increasingly the best and brightest are electing not to run. Why should they subject themselves or their families to trial by media?

I know other people have been burned by irresponsible members of the press worse than I, but my case was enough to give me reason to wonder. If I were a strategic planner for the National Association of Newspaper Editors, I'd want to protect the vast majority of well-intentioned reporters and journalists whose authority and future freedom are jeopardized every time a few neglect to exercise responsibility. I'd put my staff to work right away on a thorough internal cleanup campaign—before someone offered to do it for them.

* * *

it was no
in corporate A
the game. You go aft
piece of weaponry, any piece
get it. That I happened to be the mo
around was merely coincidental. The obje
people had in mind had little to do with me.

And what were those objectives? High-minded professional that I was, I merely assumed everyone else was as
concerned with P/E ratios and new strategic plans as I
was. I thought executives fought over strategies, business
plans, the bottom line. But that was only part of the turmoil at Bendix. There were other motivations, deeper
concerns fueling this fight. And surprisingly, most of them
had not very much to do with business. They had to do
with jealousy and pride, ego and power—all the things
that are rarely, if ever, mentioned in any Business School
text. And why should they be? Most people assume that
if you're a professional, you do your job and vent your
personal antipathies at home. But that wasn't what happened at Bendix. People acted on their personal feelings,
and played out their private vendettas in the corporate
sphere.

In Business School they taught us about cash flow, not
about corporate politics; about return on equity, not about
egos and pride. Oh, there were optional courses on
"Organizational Behavior" and "Managerial Skills," but
these were a little too bloodless to convey what I learned
on the job. And they were merely electives, whereas my
experience taught me they should have been every bit as
much a part of the core curriculum as Production, Marketing, and Finance.

has caused me to be more _____, and yet, I'm not sorry for what I've learned. On the personal front, I have gleaned some valuable insights.

There were times, so many times, when I thought I'd never feel completely healed. I wondered if I'd ever want to "go the distance" for anyone again, ever believe in anyone, ever trust as fully as I did before. And I do. I do feel almost healed and I do work hard and I do trust. But it will never be in quite the same way.

How was I to know that even the chairman of Bendix wasn't invincible? Other people were calling the shots, but I didn't know that then. All I could see at the time was that my good friend couldn't save my neck. And because I looked up to my mentor as all-powerful and all-wise, I was all the more shattered when he didn't come through. And yet he couldn't. I see that now. Oh, in retrospect, there are many better ways in which he might have handled the situation. He might have stood up before those employees and told them in much stronger language that there was nothing going on between him and me and they should get their minds out of the gutter. Or he might not have said anything at all. But would that have stopped the campaign against us? I don't know. I'm not sure it would have. And then with his board—how many hours did I spend wishing he'd marched into that board room and said, just like a hero, "If Mary goes, I go too." But what good would that have done? Plenty of people would have believed we were having an affair then, if they hadn't before. And I'm not sure even I would have wanted to see him leave and throw the whole strategy down the drain.

In order to act as he did at the time, he had to harden

himself against me, and he succeeded in doing just that for longer than I care to remember. His "advisers," that coldblooded coterie of brilliant men, were able to persuade him, for the time being, to cut himself off from me—to get rid of the PR risk. But in the end, he was the one who suffered most over what he had done. He wasn't proud to be turning his back on a friend in the name of corporate stability. He felt terrible; and I knew then that he, more than anyone, wished he could have acted differently. But the situation was new and confusing for him too. No one had ever gone through an experience quite like ours before, and there were no precedents, none that involved survivors anyway, that could have taught us how to act.

I think, even more than I myself, Bill has changed as a result of our ordeal. In his own way he has suffered too. He was hurt by what happened to him, particularly in the aftermath of the Martin Marietta takeover attempt. People who revered him, who stuck by his side because they believed Bill Agee was all-powerful, slowly moved away. He saw that some of his friends, and even family, liked him not because he was Bill Agee, but because he was at the top—a winner. As soon as he was in trouble and needed help, most of them fled.

And yet, I think his ordeal made a better person of him too. The gung ho businessman, the *Wunderkind* who devoted all of his life to the corporation, is no longer such a round-the-clock corporate man. Oh, he still loves his work and has energy that even I have to marvel at, but his priorities have shifted. His values have changed. I think, had he the chance to live his life over again, he'd take more time to emphasize the personal side. It's ironic, but in the end Bill was just as hurt by what happened to him in business as I was by what happened to me. We were both dealt painful blows on the corporate front.

And in many ways, had he not become less of a hero, less of a *Wunderkind* and more of a person, I don't know that I ever could have fallen in love with him. It was the whole process of shared pain and recovery that brought us close. I lost an idol but I gained a friend, a true friend, a person capable of weakness and therefore a person who could be loved. In this sense I'm not sorry for what happened, at least in terms of how it affected us.

So here we are now, recovered, stronger and happier, too, I think. Both of us have a full life, which is another thing we learned. Success, no matter how great, is a pretty hollow experience unless you have someone to share it with. And home and hearth, while it's comforting, is also not enough unless you have work that fulfills you. People need both—love and work—and Bill and I are fortunate in that we have both, finally.

In the coming years we hope to have children as well. Certainly, if my whole ordeal taught me anything, it was the importance of family, love and support. My brothers, my sister and sister-in-law, Father Bill, and most of all, my mom. What would I ever have done without her?

There's just one other aspect of the healing process I learned, and that's the importance of faith. There were so many times when I wanted to give in, when I wanted to walk away and give up the fight. Even worse, there were those awful moments when I doubted myself. In those moments, I thought I had lost everything that mattered most to me—my home, my work and my faith. A person doesn't have to be religious to know what it means to lose one's faith. And yet, without it, without some kind of support, it's hard to go on. And many people don't. I know. I've read their letters.

But I did manage to go on, and in retrospect I see why. I went on because it was suggested to me that some good might come of all this. That when I was through with it, there might be something in the experience that I could salvage. That's important, whether one hears it in a church or in a psychiatrist's office. You learn not to regret the past but to make something of it. You learn not to deny the pain but to grow from it. In that sense, telling my story was the core of my recovery. I looked at what happened to me, and then I shared it with someone else. In the end, that's how I have graduated from the experience. This book is my graduation from everything that happened to me at Bendix.

# EPILOGUE

*A few final observations in* the aftermath of the Bendix story:

· Michael Blumenthal married his former executive assistant, a woman half his age.

· The Burroughs Corporation has engaged as its investment banker Lehman Brothers, whose services it requested before Pete Peterson "resigned." Blumenthal and Peterson were last seen together at the 1983 U.S. Tennis Open in Forest Hills, where Peterson was Blumenthal's guest and sat in the Burroughs' box.

· Michael Blumenthal tried, but failed, to buy the former Bendix headquarters. In September 1983, his bid of less than half the fair market value was turned down as "unacceptable."

· Nancy Reynolds left Bendix in 1982 and is now working for a political public relations firm located in Washington, D.C.

• Contrary to Ed Hennessey's promise to Agee, Bendix and its people have not been kept intact.

• Of the original Bendix executive team—Joe Svec, Jerry Jacobson, Larry Hastie, Charlie Donnelly and Bill Panny—none is still with Allied-Bendix.

# ABOUT THE AUTHORS

A native of Hanover, New Hampshire, Ms. Cunningham was graduated magna cum laude from Wellesley College, where she majored in logic and philosophy and was elected to Phi Beta Kappa. She received a fellowship for graduate study at Trinity College, Dublin, Ireland, and was graduated from Harvard Business School with honors. After a business career that included positions of high executive responsibility with The Bendix Corporation and Joseph E. Seagram & Sons, she is now partner with her husband in Semper Enterprises, a venture capital and strategy consulting company they founded together.

Fran R. Schumer is a writer whose articles have appeared in *The New York Times*, *Barron's*, and *The Nation*.